S0-AIF-854

POETRY
A Pocket Anthology

PENGUIN ACADEMICS

POETRY
A Pocket Anthology

SECOND CANADIAN EDITION

Edited by R. S. GWYNN *Lamar University*

WANDA CAMPBELL *Acadia University*

PEARSON
Longman

Toronto

Library and Archives Canada Cataloguing in Publication

Poetry : a pocket anthology / edited by R. S. Gwynn, Wanda Campbell.—2nd Canadian ed.

(Penguin academics)
Also issued as part of *Literature : a pocket anthology*. 2nd Canadian ed.

Includes index.
ISBN 978-0-321-42799-1

    1. Poetry—Collections. I. Gwynn, R. S. II. Campbell, Wanda, 1963– III. Series.

PN6101.P625 2008   808.81   C2006-906969-7

Copyright © 2008, 2004 Pearson Education Canada, a division of Pearson Canada Inc., Toronto, Ontario.

Pearson Longman. All rights reserved. This publication is protected by copyright, and permission should be obtained from the publisher prior to any prohibited reproduction, storage in a retrieval system, or transmission in any form or by any means, electronic, mechanical, photocopying, recording, or likewise. For information regarding permission, write to the Permissions Department.

Original edition published by Pearson Longman, a division of Pearson Education, Inc., Upper Saddle River, NJ. Copyright © 2005 by Pearson Education, Inc. This edition is authorized for sale in Canada only.

ISBN-13: 978-0-321-42799-1
ISBN-10: 0-321-42799-8

Editor-in-Chief, Vice-President of Sales: Kelly Shaw
Acquisitions Editor: Chris Helsby
Marketing Manager: Leigh-Anne Graham
Developmental Editor: Charlotte Morrison-Reed
Production Editor: Richard di Santo
Copy Editor: Sharon Kirsch
Proofreaders: Barbara Czarnecki, Nancy Carroll
Production Coordinator: Sharlene Ross
Composition: Integra
Art Director: Julia Hall
Interior and Cover Design: Susanna Brusikiewicz
Cover Image: Getty Images / Mark Lewis

1 2 3 4 5   12 11 10 09 08

Printed and bound in Canada.

PENGUIN
ACADEMICS

PEARSON
Longman

Contents

Preface

When the *Pocket Anthology* series first appeared a decade ago, the chief aim was to offer a clear alternative to the anthologies of fiction, poetry, and drama that were available at the time. We are very pleased to offer new Canadian editions of the *Pocket Anthology* series, including this second Canadian edition of *Poetry: A Pocket Anthology*.

Poetry addresses the four wishes and concerns most commonly expressed by both instructors and students. First, of course, is the **variety** of selections it contains. Admittedly, a pocket anthology has to be very selective in its contents, so we are especially proud that the over 200 poems in this book include both established canonical writers from the 16th century to the present as well as many new voices which reflect the diversity of gender, ethnic background, and national origin that is essential to any study of contemporary literature. We are also pleased that nearly one half of the selections in *Poetry* are by women, and that Canadian, international, and minority writers are well represented. Students will find engaging works from a variety of periods and styles, works that can be studied in conjunction with works of art, and works by writers under the age of 35. More important, the contents of *Poetry* have been shaped by the advice of experienced instructors who have cited the poems that are most often taught and that possess proven appeal to students. The editors have also made a strong effort to include a number of works that reflect contemporary social questions and thus will easily stimulate classroom discussion and writing assignments. We strongly believe that the works in *Poetry* will provide a reading experience that is not only educational but thought-provoking and enjoyable as well.

Our second aim is **flexibility**—a book that can be used as either a primary or supplemental text in a variety of courses, ranging from introduction to poetry to advanced poetic analysis to creative writing.

When combined with one of its companion volumes, *Fiction* or *Drama*, or with novels, collections of short stories or poems by individual authors, or plays available from Penguin, *Poetry* may also be used in introductory literature courses. *Poetry* contains, in addition to its generous selection of poems, biographical headnotes for authors, an introduction that covers the techniques and terminology of the genre, and a concise section on writing about poetry and on research procedures. As an aid to student writing assignments, *Poetry* also contains an appendix that groups works from all three genres thematically and provides suggestions for the application of a range of critical approaches. A *Question Book* for the Canadian edition, available to instructors on request, offers ideas for discussion questions and writing topics, as well as some additional background information.

The third goal is **affordability.** The second Canadian edition of *Poetry* reflects the original claims of the *Pocket Anthology* series, that these books represent "a new standard of value." Because of its affordability, *Poetry* may be easily supplemented in individual courses with handbooks of grammar and usage, manuals of style, introductions to critical theory, textbooks on research methods, or instructional texts in creative writing.

Finally, we stress **portability.** Many instructors express concern for students who must carry large literature books, many of which now approach 2000 pages, across large campuses in backpacks already laden with books and materials for other courses. A semester is a short time, and few courses can cover more than a fraction of the material that many bulkier collections contain. Because most instructors focus on a single genre at a time, *Poetry* and its companion volumes, *Fiction* and *Drama*, remain compact yet self-contained editions that, if a snug fit in most pockets, we trust that instructors and their students will be grateful for a book that is a more manageable size.

In its second edition, the *Pocket Anthology* series offers increased Canadian content, an updated critical framework, and enhanced audio/visual pedagogy with the addition of **MyLiteratureLab** at no extra charge. This extensive website provides a number of resources that will be of interest to users of this new edition. It contains interactive readings and lectures on a variety of well-known works, biographical information about authors, a glossary of literary and critical terms, and many other useful multimedia resources for your course.

In closing, we would like to express our gratitude to the instructors who reviewed all or part of the Canadian *Pocket Anthology* series and offered invaluable recommendations for improvements:

Julia Denholm, Langara College
Cecily Devereux, University of Alberta
Fraser Easton, University of Waterloo
Thomas Ezzy, Dawson College
Melanie Fahlman Reid, Capilano College
Gordon Fulton, University of Victoria
James Gifford, University of Lethbridge
Christopher E. Gittings, University of Alberta
Kathleen Irwin, University of Regina
Tobi Kazakewich, University of Ottawa
Christine Kerr, Champlain Regional College
Ric Knowles, University of Guelph
Jean-François Leroux, University of Ottawa
Kathy McConnell, Dalhousie University
Ninian Mellamphy, University of Western Ontario
Paul Milton, Okanagan University College
Paul Matthew St. Pierre, Simon Fraser University
Dawn Neill, University of Victoria
Catherine Nelson-McDermott, University of British Columbia
Miriam Pirbhai, Wilfred Laurier University
Nicole C. Rosevere, University of Winnipeg
Mary Silcox, McMaster University
Anna Smol, Mt. St. Vincent University
Cheryl Suzack, University of Alberta
Eleanor Ty, Wilfred Laurier University
Paul Tyndall, University of British Columbia
Lynn Wells, University of Regina
Patricia Whiting, University of Ottawa
Lorraine York, McMaster University

R. S. Gwynn
Lamar University

Wanda Campbell
Acadia University

Wanda Campbell has edited several other books, including *The Poetry of John Strachan* and *Hidden Rooms: Early Canadian Women Poets*. She has authored two collections of poetry, *Sky Fishing* and *Haw [Thorn]* and has published academic articles, fiction, and poetry in journals across Canada. She teaches Literature and Creative Writing at Acadia University in Wolfville, Nova Scotia.

R. S. Gwynn has edited several other books, including *Literature: A Pocket Anthology*, *Drama: A Pocket Anthology*, *Fiction: A Pocket Anthology*, *The Longman Anthology of Short Fiction* (with Dana Gioia), and *Contemporary American Poetry: A Pocket Anthology* (with April Lindner). He has also authored five collections of poetry, including *No Word of Farewell: Selected Poems, 1970–2000*. In 2004 he was awarded the Michael Braude Award for verse from the American Academy of Arts and Letters.

Professor Gwynn teaches at Lamar University in Beaumont, Texas.

Introduction

An Anecdote: Where Poetry Starts

Poetry readings are popular because they lift a curtain to give a behind-the-scenes glimpse of the poetic process. The poet probably will not look as we expect a poet to look. Surprisingly, he or she may not even begin with a poem. This time, a man in a chambray shirt adjusts his glasses and, in a relaxed voice, tells an anecdote about his younger daughter and an overdue science project. When he moves from the background story into reading the poem itself, there is little change in his volume level, and his tone remains conversational. The students find that the poem, which they had discussed in class only a couple of days before, takes on new meaning when its origins are explained by the poet himself. They find themselves listening attentively to his words, even laughing out loud several times. The hour goes by quickly, and at its end their applause, like that of the rest of the audience, is long and sincere.

At the next class meeting, the instructor asks for reactions to the reading. Although some of the class members are slightly critical, faulting the speaker for his informal manner and his failure to maintain eye contact with the room, most of the remarks are positive. The comments that surface most often have to do with how much more meaningful the poems in the textbook become when the poet explains how he came to write them. They now know that one poem is actually spoken in the voice of the poet's dead father and that another is addressed to a friend who was paralyzed in an automobile accident. Although these things could perhaps be inferred from the poems alone, the students are unanimous in their opinion that knowing the details beforehand adds a great deal to the first impression a poem makes. As one student puts it, "It's just that a poem makes a lot more sense when you know who's talking and when and where it's supposed to be taking place."

"It always helps to know where poetry starts," adds one of her classmates.

Speaker, Listener, and Context

The situation described above is hardly unique. Instructors have long been encouraging their students to attend events like the one described, and the poetry reading has become, for many, the closest encounter students will have with this complex and often perplexing art form. But what students often find at such readings, sometimes to their amazement, is that poetry need not be intimidating or obscure. Poems that are *performed* provide a gentle reminder that the roots of poetry, like those of all literature, have their origins in the **oral tradition.** In ancient societies, stories and poems were passed down from generation to generation and recited for all members of the tribe, from the wizened elders to the youngest children. For most of its long history, poetry has been a popular art form aimed at *audiences* (remember that the word audience means "hearers"). It is only recently, in the last three or four decades, that its most visible signs of life are to be found on campuses. Still, it is perhaps worth noting that we are exposed daily to a great deal of poetry in oral form, primarily through the medium of recorded song lyrics. The unique qualities of poetry throughout the ages—its ability to tell stories or summarize complicated emotions in a few well-chosen words—are demonstrated whenever we memorize the lines of a popular song and sing them to ourselves.

Of course, poetry written primarily for the page may be more demanding than song lyrics. Writers of popular songs aim at a wide commercial audience, and this simple fact of economics, added to the fact that the lyrics are not intended primarily for publication but for being recorded as a song with all the resources of studio technology, can make song lyrics appear simple and repetitive in print. There are, of course, exceptions like Leonard Cohen, whose work has received acclaim from both literary critics and the music industry. A poem will exist primarily as a printed text, although its effect may be enhanced greatly through a skillful oral performance in which the poet can also explain the background of the poem, its setting and speaker, and the circumstances under which it was written. In general, these details, so crucial to understanding a poem yet so often only implied when the poem appears in print, are called the **dramatic situation** of a poem. Situation can be summed up in a question: *Who is speaking to whom under what circumstances?* If the poet fails to provide us with clues or if we are careless in picking up the information that is provided, then we may begin reading with no sense of reference and, thus, may go far astray. Even such words as "on," "upon," or "to" in titles can be crucial to our understanding of dramatic situation, telling us something about an event or object that provided the stimulus for the poem or about the identity of the "you" addressed in the poem.

An illustration may be helpful. Suppose we look at what is arguably the most widely known poem ever written by a Canadian: John McCrae's "In Flanders Fields." It is a poem that many Canadians can recite because of its use on Remembrance Day. As Margaret Atwood said of this poem, "as a Canadian born in 1939, I had 'In Flanders Fields' hammered into my head at an early age, and will doubtless never be able to shake the notion that what one properly does with torches is to hold them high: otherwise you get haunted." Despite the controversy of the closing call to arms, it is still a powerful evocation of the sacrifices of the Great War, an event that many believe marked Canada's coming of age.

In Flanders Fields

In Flanders fields the poppies blow
Between the crosses, row on row
That mark our place; and in the sky
The larks, still bravely singing, fly
Scarce heard amid the guns below.

We are the Dead. Short days ago
We lived, felt dawn, saw sunset glow,
Loved and were loved, and now we lie
In Flanders fields.

Take up our quarrel with the foe:
To you from failing hands we throw

The torch; be yours to hold it high.
If ye break faith with us who die
We shall not sleep, though poppies grow
In Flanders fields.

The poem is an example of **occasional verse,** a poem that is written about or for an important event (or occasion), sometimes private but usually of some public significance. Although poems of this type are not often printed on the front pages of newspapers as they once were, they are still being written. The author of "In Flanders Fields," John McCrae (1872–1918), was a medical doctor who wrote poetry as an avocation. Yet like many men and women who are not professional writers, McCrae was so deeply moved by an event that he witnessed that occasional poetry was the only medium through which he could express his feelings.

Now let's go back to our question about dramatic situation, taking it one part at a time: *Who is speaking?* A technical word that is often used to designate the speaker of a poem is **persona** (plural: **personae**), a word that meant "mask" in ancient Greek. In this case, it is not the poet, who is still alive at the time of the writing of the poem, but rather his fallen comrades in arms, "the Dead," who are speaking. According to some accounts, the poem was inspired by the death of McCrae's friend Lieutenant Alexis Helmer, who was killed by an enemy shell on May 2, 1915. The voice-from-the-grave device, used by Hardy and others for ironic purposes, was here used to evoke emotion. The unusual perspective gained extra poignancy when on January 28, 1918, McCrae himself died of pneumonia and meningitis at the front, worn down from having treated the wounded from some of the war's most horrific battles, Ypres, Somme, and Vimy Ridge. He was buried at Wimereux, France, and within the year the war that claimed the life of eight and a half million soldiers was over.

It is important to look at poems carefully to see if they give any evidence that the speaker is someone other than the poet. Poems like "The Death of the Ball Turret Gunner" by Randall Jarrell or "The River-Merchant's Wife: A Letter" by Ezra Pound have titles that identify personae who are, respectively, a soldier who has died and a young bride. In neither case is the persona to be identified with the poet. Other poems may be somewhat more problematical. Edgar Allan Poe's "The Raven," like many of Poe's short stories, is spoken by a persona who is not to be identified with the author, even though he shares many of the same morbid preoccupations of Poe's other characters. Even in the work of Sylvia Plath, a poet usually associated with an extremely candid form of autobiographical poetry known as **confessional poetry,** it is a mistake to assume that there is no invention in the creation of characters. Sometimes poems have more than one persona, which is the case with Dudley Randall's "Ballad of Birmingham," a poem that opens with a dialogue between mother and daughter. In other poems, for instance in many ballads, the voice may simply be a third-person **narrator** such as we might find in a short story or novel. Thus, although it is perhaps true that many poems (including the majority of those included here) are in fact spoken by the poet out of his or her most private feelings, it is not a good idea to leap too quickly to the assumption that the persona of a poem is identical to the poet and shares his or her views. Conclusions about the degree to which a poem is autobiographical can be verified only by research and familiarity with a poet's other works.

To return to our question: Who is speaking *to whom?* Another useful term is **auditor,** the person or persons spoken to in a poem. Some poems identify no auditor; others clearly do specify an auditor or auditors, in most cases identified by name or by the second-person pronoun "you" (or "thee/thou" in older poetry). Again, the title may give clues: Poe's "To Helen" is addressed to the famous beauty of Homeric legend; as we discover in the final stanza of the villanelle by Dylan Thomas, "Do Not Go Gentle into That Good Night" is a plea from son to father. (The figure of speech **apostrophe**—discussed later in this introduction—is used when a non-human, inanimate, or abstract thing is directly addressed.) Relatively few poems are addressed directly to the reader, so when we read the opening of William Shakespeare's Sonnet 18 ("Shall I compare thee to a summer's day?") we should keep in mind that he is addressing not us but another individual, in this case a young male friend who is referred to in many of the sonnets.

Now the final part of the question: Who is speaking to whom *under what circumstances?* First, we might ask if there is a relationship, either implied or stated, between persona and auditor. Obviously many love poems take the form of verbal transactions between two parties and, because relationships have their ups and downs, these shifts of mood are reflected in the poetry. A "courtship ritual" poem such as Andrew Marvell's "To His Coy Mistress" is a witty argument in favour of the couple's engaging in sexual relations. An example from poetry about marital love is Matthew Arnold's "Dover Beach," which ends with the plea "Ah, love, let us be true / To one another" as the only hope for stability the persona can find in a world filled with uncertainty and fear. Other questions relating to circumstances of the dramatic situation might concern the poem's physical setting (if any), time (of day, year, historical era), even such matters as weather. Pauline Johnson's "The Idlers" provides a good example of a poem in which the setting, a canoe drifting through the languorous heat of a Canadian July, symbolically reinforces the erotic tension between the idlers. The shift in setting from the springtime idyll to the "cold hillside" in John Keats's "La Belle Dame sans Merci" cannot be overlooked in discussing the persona's disillusionment. Of course, many poems are explicitly occasional, like Dionne Brand's "Blues Spiritual for Mammy Prater," and may even contain an **epigraph** (a brief explanatory statement or quotation) or a **dedication**, which explains the setting. Sometimes footnotes or even outside research may be necessary. Joy Kogawa's poem "When I Was a Little Girl" will make little sense to readers if they do not know that Kogawa and her family, along with many other Japanese Canadians, were separated from their homes and possessions after the 1941 attack on Pearl Harbor.

To return, then, one final time to "In Flanders Fields," let us apply our question to the poem. We have already determined that the "we" in the poem refers to the soldiers who are dead. Who is the "you" mentioned in the final stanza? It seems that "you" would refer in part to the soldiers who were still alive to carry on, including McCrae himself. Though well aware of the grim realities of battle, McCrae wrote, "I am going because I think every bachelor, especially if he has experience of war, ought to go. I am really rather afraid, but more afraid to stay at home with my conscience." But the poem was also addressed to potential soldiers and supporters on the home front. In fact, Victory Loan Bonds, which used lines from the final stanza of McCrae's poem in their advertisements, raised $400 million for the war effort. Why would McCrae, who wrote, "It was HELL all the time. We really expected to die in our tracks," encourage others to join the fray? There is clearly a shift from the elegiac tone of the first stanzas to a call to arms that contrasts strongly with Wilfred Owen's assertion that dying for one's country is never sweet. Few people have argued that "In Flanders Fields" is a great poem. Still, it is an effective piece of verse that reveals one aspect of a formative event in Canadian history. As Paul Fussell writes in *The Great War and Modern Memory*, "it is an interesting poem because it manages to accumulate the maximum number of well-known motifs and images" before disintegrating into a "vicious and stupid" propaganda argument against peace. There may be ways to redeem the poem by suggesting that the foe in McCrae's poem is not the kaiser's army, but rather war itself. Language, often layered and ambiguous, becomes particularly so in times of propaganda. As George Elliott Clarke has argued in "Casualties," his poem about the 1991 Gulf conflict, "the first casualty of war is language."

Lyric, Narrative, Dramatic

The starting point for all literary criticism in Western civilization is Aristotle's *Poetics*, a work dating from the fourth century B.C. Although Aristotle's remarks on drama, and tragedy in particular, are more complete than his analysis of other types of literature, he does mention three main types of poetry: lyric, epic, and dithyrambic. In doing so, Aristotle outlines for the first time a theory of literature based on **genres,** or separate categories delineated by distinct style, form, and content. This three-fold division remains useful today, although in two cases different terminology is employed. The first genre, **lyric poetry,** originally comprised brief poems that were meant to be sung or chanted to the accompaniment of a lyre. Today we still use the word "lyrics" in a specialized sense when referring to the words of a song, but lyric poetry has become such a large category that it includes virtually all poems that are primarily *about* a subject and contain little narrative content. The subject of a lyric poem may be the poet's emotions, an abstract idea, a satirical insight, or a description of a person or place. The persona in a lyric is usually closely identified with the poet himself or herself. Because we tend to identify the essence of poetry with personal, subjective expression of feelings or ideas, lyric poetry remains the largest genre, with a number of subtypes. Among them are the **epigram,** a short, satirical lyric usually aimed at a specific person; the **elegy,** a lyric on the occasion of a death; and the **ode,** a long lyric in elevated language on a serious theme.

Aristotle's second genre, the **epic,** has been expanded to include all types of **narrative poetry,** that is, poetry whose main function is to tell a story. Like prose fiction, narrative poems have plots, characters, setting, and point of view and may be discussed in the same terms as, say, a short story. The epic is a long narrative poem about the exploits of a hero. **Folk epics** like the *Iliad* or *Beowulf* were originally intended for public recitation and existed in oral form for a long time before they were transcribed. Little or nothing is known about the authors of folk epics; even Homer, the purported author of the *Iliad* and the *Odyssey*, is primarily a legendary character. **Literary epics,** like Dante's *Inferno* or Milton's *Paradise Lost*, differ in that they are the products of known authors who *wrote* their poems for publication. **Ballads** generally are shorter narratives with song-like qualities that often include rhyme and repeated refrains. **Folk ballads,** like folk epics, come from the oral tradition and are usually published anonymously; "Sir Patrick Spens" is a typical example. **Art** or **literary ballads** are conscious imitations of the ballad style by later poets and are generally somewhat more sophisticated than folk ballads in their techniques. Examples of this popular genre include Keats's "La Belle Dame sans Merci," and ballads continue to be written and sung to this day. There are also other types of narrative poetry that have been popular through the centuries. **Metrical romances,** verse tales of the exploits of knights, were a popular genre during the Middle Ages and the Renaissance; Edmund Spenser's *The Faerie Queene* is one of the most ambitious examples of the type. At the opposite extreme are **mock-heroic narratives** like Lord Byron's *Don Juan*, which spoof the conventions of epic poetry for comic or satirical effect. **Realistic narratives** of medium length (under one thousand lines) have been popular since the early nineteenth century and are sometimes discussed as "poetic novels" or "short stories in verse."

There is no exact contemporary analogue for Aristotle's third category, **dithyrambic** poetry. This type of poem, composed to be chanted at religious rituals by a chorus, was the forerunner of tragedy. Today this third type is usually called **dramatic poetry,** because it has perhaps as much in common with the separate genre of drama as with lyric and narrative poetry. In general, the persona in a dramatic poem is an invented character not to be identified with the poet. The poem is presented as a speech or dialogue that might be acted out like a soliloquy or scene from a play. The **dramatic monologue** is a speech for a single character, usually delivered to a silent auditor. Browning's "My Last Duchess" is a famous example. A dramatic monologue sometimes implies, in the words of its persona, a distinct setting and interplay between persona and auditor. Tom Wayman's poem "Did I Miss Anything?" in which an instructor provides various answers to this question frequently asked by students after missing a class, is a witty twist on this convention. Dramatic poetry can also take the form of **dialogue poetry,** in which two personae speak alternately as in Dudley Randall's "Ballad of Birmingham." A popular type of dialogue poem that originated in the Middle Ages was the ***débat,*** or mock-debate, in which two characters, usually personified abstractions like the Soul and the Body, argued their respective merits.

Although it is easy enough to find examples of "pure" lyrics, narratives, and dramatic monologues, sometimes the distinctions among the three major types may become blurred, even in the same poem. "In Flanders Fields," for example, contains elements of all three genres. The opening stanza, with its vivid re-creation of the battlefields and cemeteries of Flanders, is closest to lyric poetry. The second stanza, describing the fate of the soldiers, is primarily narrative, and the final stanza, with its call for participation on the part of the listeners, is dramatic. Still, the three-fold division is useful in discussing a single author's various ways of dealing with subjects or in comparing examples of one type by separate authors.

The Language of Poetry

One of the most persistent myths about poetry is that its language is artificial, "flowery," and essentially different from the language that people speak every day. Although these beliefs may be true of some poetry, one can easily find numerous examples that demonstrate poetic diction of an entirely different sort. It is impossible to characterize poetic language narrowly, for poetry, which is after all the art of language, covers the widest possible range of linguistic possibilities. For example, here are several passages from different poets, all describing birds:

> Hail to thee, blithe Spirit!
>   Bird thou never wert—
> That from Heaven, or near it,
>   Pourest thy full heart
> In profuse strains of unpremeditated art.

> Higher still and higher
>   From the earth thou springest

Like a cloud of fire;
  The blue deep thou wingest,
And singing still dost soar, and soaring ever singest.
                                 Percy Bysshe Shelley, "To a Skylark"

I caught this morning morning's minion, king-
dom of daylight's dauphin, dapple-dawn-drawn Falcon, in his riding
Of the rolling level underneath him steady air, and striding
High there, how he rung upon the rein of a wimpling wing
In his ecstasy!
                            Gerard Manley Hopkins, "The Windhover"

On the stiff twig up there
Hunches a wet black rook
Arranging and rearranging its feathers in the rain.
                         Sylvia Plath, "Black Rook in Rainy Weather"

Lower down, Merlins slice the air with wings that say crisp crisp,
precise as sushi chefs, while Sharp-shins alternately glide and flap,
hunting as they go, each line break poised, ready to pivot like a
point guard. . . .
                                          Don McKay, "Icarus"

Of these quotes, only Shelley's from the early nineteenth century
possesses the stereotypical characteristics of what we mean when we
use the term "poetic" in a negative sense. Poetry, like any other art
form, follows fashions that change over the years; by Shelley's day, the
use of "thee" and "thou" and their related verb forms ("wert" and
"wingest") had come full circle from their original use as a familiar
form of the second person, employed to address intimates and ser-
vants, to an artificially heightened grammatical form reserved for
prayers and poetry. Hopkins's language, from a poem of the 1870s, is
artificial in an entirely different way; here the poet's **idiom,** the personal use of words that marks his poetry, is highly idiosyncratic;
indeed, it would be hard to mistake a poem by Hopkins, with its
muscular monosyllables and rich texture of sound patterns, with one
by any other poet. When we move to the contemporary period, we can

find little difference between the language of many poems and conversational speech, as Plath's lines indicate. McKay's comparison of falcons and hawks to sushi chefs and basketball players strikes us as especially contemporary.

Still, in reading a poem, particularly one from the past, we should be aware of certain problems that may impede our understanding. **Diction** refers to the individual words in a poem and may be classified in several ways. A poem's **level of diction** can range from slang at one extreme to formal usage at the other. Now, when most poems use a level of diction that stays in the middle of the scale, these distinctions are useful only when a poet is being self-consciously formal (perhaps for ironic effect) or going to the opposite extreme to imitate the language of the streets. In past eras the term **poetic diction** was used to indicate a level of speech somehow refined above ordinary usage and, thus, somehow superior to it. Today the same term would most likely be used as a way of criticizing a poet's language. We should keep in mind that the slang of one era may become the standard usage of another, as is the case with "OK," which has become a universal expression. A good dictionary is useful in many ways, particularly in dealing with **archaisms** (words that are no longer in common use) and other words that may not be familiar to the reader. Take, for example, the opening lines of Edgar Allan Poe's "To Helen":

Helen, thy beauty is to me
Like those Nicean barks of yore,
That gently, o'er a perfumed sea,
The weary, way-worn wanderer bore
To his own native shore.

Several words here may give trouble to the average contemporary reader. First, "o'er," like "ne'er" or similar words like "falt'ring" and "glimm'ring," is simply a contraction; this dropping of a letter, called **syncope,** is done for the sake of maintaining the poem's metre. "Barks of yore" will probably send most of us to the dictionary, for our sense of "bark" as either the outer surface of a tree or the noise that a dog makes does not fit here; likewise, "yore" is unfamiliar, possibly archaic. Looking up the literal sense of a word in a dictionary discloses its **denotation,** or literal meaning. Thus, we find that "barks" are small sailing ships and that "yore" refers to the distant past. Of course, Poe could have said "ships of the past" or a similar phrase, but his word choice was perhaps dictated by **connotation,** the implied meaning or feel that some words have acquired; it may be that even in Poe's day "barks of yore" had a remote quality that somehow evoked ancient Greece in a way that, say, "ancient ships" would not. But what are we to make of "Nicean," a proper adjective that sounds geographical but does not appear in either the dictionary or gazetteer? In this case we have encountered an example of a **coinage,** or **neologism,** a word made up by the poet. Speculation on the source of "Nicean" has ranged from Nice, in the south of France, to Phoenician, but it is likely that Poe simply coined the word for its exotic sound. Similarly, we might note that the phrase "weary, way-worn wanderer" contains words that seem to have been chosen primarily for their alliterated sounds.

When we put a poem into our own words, we **paraphrase** it, a practice that is often useful when passages are hard to understand. Other than diction, **syntax,** the order of words in a sentence, may also give readers problems. Syntax in poetry, particularly in poems that use rhyme, is likely to be different from that of both speech and prose; if a poet decides to rhyme in a certain pattern, then word order may be modified to fit the formal design, and this can present difficulties to readers in understanding the grammar of a passage. The passage from Poe's poem presents few difficulties of this order but does contain one example of **inversion,** words that fall out of their expected order (a related syntactical problem lies in **ellipsis,** words that are consciously omitted by the poet). If we do not allow for this, we are likely to be confused by "the weary, way-worn wanderer bore / To his own native shore." The wanderer bore *what?* A quick mental sentence diagram shows that "wanderer" is the direct object of "bore," not its subject. A good paraphrase should simplify both diction and syntax: "Helen, to me your beauty is like those Nicean (?) ships of the ancient past that carried the weary, travel-worn wanderer gently over a perfumed sea to his own native land." In paraphrasing, only the potentially troublesome words and phrases should be substituted, leaving the original language as intact as possible. Paraphrasing is a useful first step toward unfolding a poem's literal sense, but it obviously takes few of a poet's specific nuances of language into account; words like "thin," "slender," and "skinny" may denote the same thing, but each has its own connotation, and poets are particularly attuned to such nuances. "Poetry," Robert Frost famously remarked, "is what is lost in translation."

Several other matters relevant to poetic language are worth mentioning. **Etymology,** the study of the sources of words, is a particularly rewarding topic in English because our language has such an unusually rich history—just compare an unabridged French dictionary with its English counterpart. Old English (or Anglo-Saxon), the ancient language of the British Isles, was part of the Germanic family of languages. When the Norman French successfully invaded Britain in 1066 they brought with them their own language, part of the Romance language family (all originally derived from Latin). By the time of Chaucer's death in 1400 these two linguistic traditions had merged into a single language, Middle English, that can be read today, despite its differences in spelling, pronunciation, and vocabulary. We can still, however, distinguish the words that show their Germanic heritage from those of Latinate origin, and despite the fact that English is rich in synonyms, the Germanic and Latinate words often have different connotations. "Smart" (from the Old English *smeart*) is not quite the same as "intelligent" (from the Latin *intellegent*). A "map-maker" is subtly different from a "cartographer"—ask yourself which would have ink on his fingers. Although a poet's preference for words of a certain origin is not always immediately clear, we can readily distinguish the wide gulf that separates a statement like "I live in a house with my folks" from "I abide in a residence with my parents."

A final tension exists in poems between their use of **concrete diction** and **abstract diction.** Concrete words denote that which can be perceived by the senses, and the vividness of a poem's language resides primarily in the way it uses **imagery,** sensory details denoting specific physical experiences. Because sight is the most important of the five senses, **visual imagery** ("a dim light"; "a dirty rag"; "a golden daffodil") predominates in poems, but we should also be alert for striking examples of the other types of imagery: **auditory** ("a pounding surf"), **tactile** ("a scratchy beard"), **olfactory** ("the scent of apple blossoms"), and **gustatory** ("the bitter tang of gin"). The use of specific imagery has always been crucial for poetry. In the early twentieth century, a group of poets led by Americans Ezra Pound and H. D. (Hilda Doolittle) pioneered a poetic movement called **imagism,** in which concrete details predominate in short descriptive poems (see Ezra Pound's "In a Station of the Metro"). "Go in fear of abstractions," commanded Pound, and his friend William Carlos Williams modified the remark to become a poetic credo: "No ideas but in things."

Still, for some poets abstract words remain important because they carry the burden of a poem's overall meaning or theme. More often than not, one can expect to encounter the largest number of abstract words near the conclusion of poems. Probably the most famous abstract statement in English poetry, John Keats's "'Beauty is truth, truth beauty,' —that is all / Ye know on earth, and all ye need to know" appears in the last two lines of "Ode on a Grecian Urn," a fifty-line poem that is filled with lush, sensory details of description. Two other devices sometimes govern a poet's choice of words. **Onomatopoeia** refers to individual words like "buzz" or "thud" whose meanings are closely related to their sounds. Auditory imagery in a poem can often be enhanced by the use of onomatopoeic words. In some cases, however, a whole line can be called onomatopoeic, even if it contains no single word that illustrates the device. Archibald Lampman uses these lines to describe the "City of the End of Things": "The beat, the thunder and the hiss / Cease not, and change not, night nor day." Here the repetition of similar sounds helps to imitate the grim, noisy routine of a city dominated by machines. A second device is the **pun,** the use of one word to imply the additional meaning of a similar-sounding word (the formal term is **paranomasia**). Thus, when Anne Bradstreet compares her first book to an illegitimate child, she addresses the book in this manner: "If for thy father asked, say thou hadst none; / And for thy mother, she alas is poor, / Which caused her thus to send thee out of door." The closeness of the interjection "alas" to the article and noun "a lass" is hardly coincidental. Poets in Bradstreet's day considered the pun a staple of their repertoire, even in serious poetry, but contemporary poets are more likely to use it primarily for comic effect.

Figurative Language

We use figurative language in everyday speech without thinking of the poetic functions of the same devices. We can always relate experience in a purely literal fashion: "His table manners were deplorable. Mother scolded him severely, and Dad said some angry words to him. He left the table embarrassed and with his feelings hurt." But a more vivid way of saying the same thing might employ language used not in the literal but in the figurative sense. Thus, another version might run, "He made an absolute pig of himself. Mother jumped on his back about it, and Dad scorched his ears. You should have seen him slink off like a scolded puppy." At least four comparisons are made here in an attempt to describe one character's table manners, his mother's scolding, his father's words, and the manner in which the character retreated from the table. In every case, the thing being described, what is called the **tenor** of the figure of speech, is linked with a concrete image, or **vehicle.** By making comparisons we apply what we know to what is new to us, inevitably enhancing our understanding of both.

Traditionally, figurative language was divided into two categories: rhetorical figures in which the order or pattern of words changes and tropes (turns) in which the meaning of the words changes, often involving some kind of comparison, either explicit or implied. Thus, two of the figures in the above example specifically compare aspects of the character's behaviour to animal behaviour. The other two imply parental words that were delivered with strong physical force or extreme anger. Both rhetorical figures and tropes are now generally referred to as figures of speech. Some of the most common are:

Metaphor: a direct comparison between two unlike things. Metaphors may take several forms.

> His words were sharp knives.
> The sharp knife of his words cut through the silence.
> He spoke sharp, cutting words.
> His words knifed through the still air.
> "I will speak daggers to her . . ." *(William Shakespeare)*

Simile: a comparison using "like," "as," or "than" as a connective device.

> Because she was old and useless,
> Like a paddle broken and warped . . . *(D. C. Scott)*

Conceit: an extended or far-fetched metaphor, in most cases comparing things that apparently have almost nothing in common. A **Petrarchan conceit,** named after the first great master of the sonnet, is a clichéd comparison usually relating to a woman's beauty (Shakespeare's Sonnet 130 parodies this type of trope). The **metaphysical conceit** refers to the extended comparisons favoured by such so-called metaphysical poets as John Donne and George Herbert. The conceit in Donne's "Holy Sonnet 14" compares the heart to a town under enemy control.

I, like an usurped town, to another due *(John Donne)*

Hyperbole: an overstatement, a comparison using conscious exaggeration.

And I will luve thee still, my dear,
Till a' the seas gang dry. *(Robert Burns)*

Allusion: a metaphor making a direct comparison to a historical or literary event or character, a myth, a biblical reference, and so forth.

Order streamed from Noah in blue triangles . . . *(Anne Carson)*

Metonymy: use of a related object to stand for the thing actually being talked about.

And O ye high-flown quills that soar the skies,
And ever with your prey still catch your praise. *(Anne Bradstreet)*

Here, Bradstreet speaks of critics who may be hostile to her work. She identifies them as "quills," referring to their quill pens.

Synecdoche: use of a part for the whole, or vice versa.

Friends, Romans, countrymen: lend me your ears.
(William Shakespeare)

Personification: giving human characteristics to non-human things or to abstractions.

Thou still unravished bride of quietness . . . *(John Keats)*

Apostrophe: a variety of personification in which a non-human thing, abstraction, or person not physically present is directly addressed as if it could respond.

> Acadie, my too beautiful desecrated love . . .
> *(Herménégilde Chiasson)*

Paradox: an apparent contradiction or illogical statement.

> This is the beauty
> of strength broken by strength
> and still strong. *(A. J. M. Smith)*

Oxymoron: a short paradox, usually consisting of an adjective and noun with conflicting meanings.

> Yet from those flames / No light, but rather darkness visible . . .
> *(John Milton)*

Synesthesia: a conscious mixing of two different types of sensory experience.

> With Blue—uncertain stumbling Buzz— *(Emily Dickinson)*

Symbolism

Related to the figurative devices are the various types of symbolism that may occur in poems. Symbolism is important in fiction, but its use in poetry is perhaps even more complex. In many cases, a poem may seem so simple on the surface that we feel impelled to read deeper meanings into it. Robert Frost's "Stopping by Woods on a Snowy Evening" is a classic case in point. There is nothing wrong with searching for larger significance in a poem, but the reader should perhaps be wary of leaping to conclusions about symbolic meanings before fully exhausting the literal sense of a poem. Whatever the case, both symbolism and allegory share the demand that the reader supply abstract or general meanings to the specific concrete details of the poem.

The simplest form that this substitution takes occurs in **allegory,** which appears in poetry as well as prose. An allegory is usually a narrative that exists on at least two levels simultaneously, a concrete, literal level and a second level of abstract meaning; throughout an allegory a consistent sequence of parallels exists between the literal and the abstract. Christina Rossetti's "Goblin Market," for example, has been interpreted on feminist, economic, creative, and religious levels.

Many poems contain symbolic elements that are somewhat more elusive in meaning than the simple one-for-one equivalences presented by allegory. A **symbol,** then, is any concrete thing or action in a poem that implies a meaning beyond its literal sense. Many of these things or actions are called **traditional symbols,** that is, symbols that hold roughly the same meanings for members of a given society. Certain flowers, colours, natural objects, and religious emblems possess meanings that we can generally agree on, though these can change from culture to culture. In the West the colour associated with mourning is black, whereas in the Chinese tradition, white is associated with death—a difference that Margaret Avison explores in her poem "Snow." Other types of symbols can be identified in poems that are otherwise not allegorical. A **private symbol** is one that has acquired certain meanings from a single poet's repeated use of it. William Butler Yeats's use of "gyres" is explained in some of his prose writings as a symbol for the turning of historical cycles, and his use of the word in his poems obviously goes beyond the literal level. Some visionary poets like Yeats and William Blake devised complicated private symbolic systems, a sort of alternative mythology, and understanding the full import of these symbols becomes primarily the task of critics who have specialized in these poets. Other poets may employ **incidental symbols,** things that are not usually considered symbolic but may be in a particular poem, or symbolic acts, situations or responses that seem of greater than literal import. As noted earlier, one of the most famous poems using these two devices is Robert Frost's "Stopping by Woods on a Snowy Evening." In this poem some readers see the "lovely, dark and deep" woods as both inviting and threatening, and want to view the persona's rejection of their allure ("But I have promises to keep / And miles to go before I sleep") as some sort of life-affirming act. Frost himself was not particularly helpful in guiding his readers, often scoffing at those who had read too much metaphysical portent into such a simple lyric, although in other poems he presents objects such as a rock wall between neighbouring farms or an abandoned woodpile in a manner that leads the reader to feel that these objects obviously possess some larger significance. Many modern poems remain so enigmatic that readers have consistently returned to them seeking new interpretations. Poems like these were to a degree influenced by the symbolists, a group of French poets of the late nineteenth century, who deliberately wrote poems filled with vague nuances subject to multiple interpretations. Such American attempts at symbolist experiments as Wallace Stevens's "Thirteen Ways of Looking at a Blackbird" continue to perplex and fascinate readers, particularly those who are versed in recent schools of interpretation that focus on the indeterminacy of a poetic text.

Tone of Voice

Even the simplest statement is subject to multiple interpretations if it is delivered in several different tones of voice. Consider the shift in emphasis between saying "*I* gave you the money," "I *gave* you the money," and "I gave *you* the money." Even a seemingly innocent compliment like "You look lovely this morning" takes on a different meaning if it is delivered by a woman to her obviously hung-over husband. Still, these variations in **tone,** the speaker's implied attitude toward the words he or she says, depend primarily on vocal inflection. Because a poet only rarely gets the opportunity to elucidate his or her tones in a public performance, it is possible that readers may have difficulties in grasping the tone of a poem printed on the page, though the lineation (division into lines) gives some clues about where to place the emphasis, as in William Carlos Williams's poem "To a Poor Old Woman." Still, many poems establish their tone quite clearly from the outset. The opening of George Elliott Clarke's "Casualties" ("Snow annihilates all beauty / this merciless January") establishes a harsh tone of criticism toward the disguises we find for the cruelties we perpetrate. Keats's initial apostrophe in "Ode on a Grecian Urn" ("Thou still unravished bride of quietness, / Thou foster-child of silence and slow time . . .") strikes the reader as both passionate and reverent in the poet's response to an undamaged artifact of the ancient past. Thus, in many cases we can relate the tone of voice in poems to the emotions we employ in our own speech, and we would have to violate quite a few rules of common sense to argue that Clarke is being flippant or that Keats is speaking sarcastically.

Irony is the element of tone by which a poet may imply an attitude that is in fact contrary to what his or her words appear to say. Of course, the simplest form of irony is **sarcasm,** the wounding tone of voice we use to imply exactly the opposite of what we say: "That's really a *great* excuse!" or "What a *wonderful* performance!" For obvious reasons, sarcasm is appropriate primarily to spoken language. It has become almost universal to follow a bit of gentle sarcasm in an e-mail message with a symbolic :) to indicate that the remark is not to be taken "straight." **Verbal irony** is the conscious manipulation of tone by which the poet's actual attitude is the opposite of what he says. Verbal irony is also a conspicuous feature of **verse satire,** poetry that exists primarily to mock or ridicule, although often with serious intent. One famous example, in the form of a short satirical piece, or **epigram,** is Sarah N. Cleghorn's "The Golf Links," a poem written before the advent of child labour laws:

> The golf links lie so near the mill
> That almost every day
> The laboring children can look out
> And see the men at play.

Here the weight of the verbal irony falls on two words, "labouring" and "play," and the way each is incongruously applied to the wrong group of people.

"The Golf Links," taken as a whole, also represents a second form of irony, **situational irony,** in which the setting of the poem (labouring children watching playing adults) contains a built-in incongruity. **Dramatic irony,** the third type of irony, occurs when the persona of a poem is less aware of the full import of his or her words than is the reader.

Repetition: Sounds and Schemes

Because poetry uses language at its most intense level, we are aware of the weight of individual words and phrases to a degree that is usually lacking when we read prose. Poets have long known that the meanings that they attempt to convey often depend as much on the sound of the words as their meanings. We have already mentioned one sound device, onomatopoeia. Consider how much richer the experience of "the murmuring of innumerable bees" is than a synonymous phrase, "the low sound of a lot of bees." It has often been said that all art aspires to the condition of music in the way that it affects an audience on some unconscious, visceral level. By carefully exploiting the repetition of sound devices, a poet may attempt to produce some of the same effects that the musical composer does.

Of course, much of this sonic level of poetry is subjective; what strikes one listener as pleasant may overwhelm the ear of another. Still, it is useful to distinguish between a poet's use of **euphony,** a series of pleasant sounds, and **cacophony,** sounds that are deliberately unpleasant. Note the following passages from Alexander Pope's "An Essay on Criticism," a didactic poem that attempts to illustrate many of the devices poets use:

> Soft is the strain when Zephyr gently blows,
> And the smooth stream in smoother numbers flows . . .

The repetition of the initial consonant sounds is called **alliteration,** and here Pope concentrates on the *s* sound. The vowel sounds are generally long: str*ai*n, bl*ow*s, sm*oo*th, and fl*ow*s. Here the description of the gentle west wind is assisted by the generally pleasing sense of euphony. But Pope, to illustrate the opposite quality, follows this couplet with a second:

> But when loud surges lash the sounding shore,
> The hoarse, rough verse should like the torrent roar.

Now the wind is anything but gentle, and the repetition of the *r* sounds in su*r*ges, sho*r*e, hoa*r*se, *r*ough, ve*r*se, to*r*rent, and *r*oar forces the reader to speak from the back of the throat, making sounds that are anything but euphonious.

Repetition of sounds has no inherent meaning value (although some linguists may argue that certain sounds do stimulate particular emotions), but this repetition does call attention to itself and can be particularly effective when a poet wishes to emphasize a certain passage. We have already mentioned alliteration. Other sound patterns are **assonance,** the repetition of similar vowel sounds (st*ee*p, *e*v*e*n, rec*ei*ve, v*ea*l), and **consonance,** the repetition of similar consonant sounds (du*ck*, tor*que*, stri*ke*, tric*k*le). It should go without saying that spelling has little to do with any sound pattern; an initial *f* will alliterate with an initial *ph*.

Rhyme is the most important sound device, and our pleasure in deftly executed rhymes goes beyond mere sound to include the pleasure we take when an unexpected word is magically made to fit with another. There are several types of rhyme. **Masculine rhyme** occurs between single stressed syllables: *fleece*, re*lease*, sur*cease*, *niece*, and so on. **Feminine rhyme**, also called **double rhyme**, matches two syllables, the first stressed and the second usually unstressed: *stinging*, *upbringing*, *flinging*. **Triple rhyme** goes further: *slithering*, *withering*. **Slant rhyme** (also called **near rhyme** and **off rhyme**) contains hints of sound repetition (sometimes related to assonance and consonance): *chill*, *dull*, and *sale* are possibilities, although poets often grant themselves considerable leeway in counting as rhyming words pairs that often have only the slightest similarity. When rhymes fall in a pattern in a poem and are **end rhymes**, occurring at the ends of lines, it is then convenient to assign letters to the sounds and speak of a **rhyme scheme.** Thus, a stanza of four lines ending with *heaven, hell, bell, eleven* would be said to have a rhyme scheme of *abba*. Rhymes may also occasionally be found in the interior of lines, which is called **internal rhyme.** Note how both end and internal rhymes work in the complex stanza which Poe uses in "The Raven."

More complicated patterns of repetition involve more than mere sounds but whole phrases and grammatical units. Ancient rhetoricians, teaching the art of public speaking, identified several of these, and they are also found in poetry. **Parallel structure** is simply the repetition of grammatically similar phrases or clauses: Tennyson's "To strive, to seek, to find, and not to yield." **Anaphora** and **epistrophe** are repeated words or phrases at, respectively, the beginning and end of lines. This passage from Lorna Crozier's "Packing for the Future: Instructions" illustrates anaphora:

There may be water.
There may be stones.
There may be high places . . .

Antithesis is the matching of parallel units that contain contrasting meanings, such as "Man proposes, God disposes." Although such rhetorical schemes are perhaps more native to the orator, the poet can still make occasional effective use of them.

Metre and Rhythm

The subject of poetic metre and rhythm can be a difficult one, ⌐⌐ ⌐⌐⌐ ⌐⌐⌐ least, and it is doubtless true that such phrases as *trochaic octameter* or *spondaic substitution* have an intimidating quality. Still, discussions of metre need not be limited to experts, and even beginning readers should be able to apply a few of the metrical principles that are commonly found in poetry written in English.

First, let us distinguish between two terms that are often used syn-onymously: **poetry** and **verse.** Poetry refers to a whole genre of litera-ture and thus stands with fiction and drama as one of the three major types of writing, whereas verse refers to a mode of writing in lines of a certain length; thus, many poets still retain the old practice of capitaliz-ing the first word of each line to indicate its integrity as a unit of compo-sition. Virtually any piece of writing can be versified (and sometimes rhymed as well). Especially useful are bits of **mnemonic verse,** in which information like the number of days in the months (thirty days has September . . .) or simple spelling rules ("I before E / Except after C . . .") is cast in a form that is easy to remember. Although it is not strictly accurate to do so, many writers use verse to denote metrical writing that somehow does not quite measure up to the level of true poetry; phrases like **light verse** or **occasional verse** (lines written for a specific occasion, like a birthday or anniversary) are often used in this manner.

If a writer is unconcerned about the length of individual lines and is governed only by the width of the paper being used, then he or she is writing not verse but **prose.** All verse is metrical writing; prose is not. However, there is a body of writing called **prose poetry,** writing that uses language in a poetic manner but avoids any type of metre; Carolyn Forché's "The Colonel" is one example. Perhaps the simplest way to think of **metre** in verse is to think of its synonym, **measure** (think of the use of metre in words like "kilometre"). Thus, metre refers to the method by which a poet determines line length.

When we talk about metre in poetry we ordinarily mean that the poet is employing some kind of consistent **prosody,** or system of measure-ment. There are many possible prosodies, depending on what the poet decides to count as the unit of measurement in the line, but only three of these systems are common in English poetry. Perhaps the simplest is

syllabic verse. In verse of this type, the length of the line is determined by counting the total number of syllables the line contains (Sylvia Plath's "Metaphors," for one example, uses lines of nine syllables, a witty metaphor for the poem's subject, pregnancy). Much French poetry of the past was written in twelve-syllable lines, or **Alexandrines,** and in English **octosyllabic** denotes a line of eight syllables. Because English is a language of strong stresses, most of our poets have favoured other prosodic systems, but syllabic poetry has been attempted by many poets, among them Marianne Moore and Dylan Thomas. Moore, in particular, often wrote in **quantitative syllabics,** that is, stanzas containing the same number of lines with identical numbers of syllables in the corresponding lines of different stanzas. Moore's "The Fish" uses stanzas made of lines of one, three, nine, six, and nine syllables, respectively.

More natural to the English language is **accentual** verse, a prosodic system in which only accented or strongly stressed syllables are counted in a line, which can also contain a varying number of unaccented syllables. Much folk poetry, perhaps intended to be recited to the beat of a percussion instrument, retains this stress-based pattern, and the oldest verse in the British tradition, Anglo-Saxon poetry like *Beowulf,* is composed in four-stress lines that were recited to musical accompaniment. Many of the verses we recall from nursery rhymes, children's chanting games ("Red rover, red rover, / Send [any name from one to four syllables can be substituted here] right over"), and sports cheers ("Two, four, six, eight. Who do we appreciate?") retain the strong sense of rhythmical pulse that characterizes much accentual verse, a fact we recognize when we clap our hands and move rhythmically to the sound of the words. Indeed, the lyrics to much current rap music are actually composed to a four-stress accentual line, and the stresses, or "beats," can be heard plainly when we listen or dance. Gerard Manley Hopkins, attempting to recapture some of the flavour of Anglo-Saxon verse, pioneered a type of accentual prosody that he called **sprung rhythm,** in which he counted only the strong stresses in his lines. Accentual metres still supply possibilities for contemporary poets; indeed, what often appears to be free verse is revealed, on closer inspection, to be a poem written in accentual metre. Richard Wilbur's "The Writer," for example, is written in a stanza containing lines of three, five, and three strong stresses, respectively, but the stresses do not overwhelm the reader insistently.

Accentual-syllabic verse is the most important proso
English, dominating our poetry for the five centuries fro
time down to the early years of the twentieth century. Even though free
verse has become the prevailing style in which poetry is now written,
accentual-syllabic verse still has many able practitioners. An accentual-
syllabic prosody is somewhat more complicated than the two systems
we have mentioned, because it requires that the poet count both the
strongly stressed syllables and the total number of syllables in the line.
Because stressed and unstressed syllables alternate fairly regularly in
this system, four **metrical feet,** representing the most common patterns, designate the subdivisions of rhythm that make up the line (think
of a yardstick divided into three feet). These feet are the **iamb** (or
iambic foot), one unstressed and one stressed syllable; the **trochee**
(or **trochaic foot**), one stressed and one unstressed syllable; the
anapest (or **anapestic foot**), two unstressed syllables and one stressed
syllable; and the **dactyl** (or **dactylic foot**), one stressed and two
unstressed syllables. The first two of these, iambic and trochaic, are
called **double metres;** the second two, **triple metres.** Iambic and
anapestic metres are sometimes called **rising metres** because they
"rise" toward the stressed syllable; trochaic and dactylic metres are
called **falling metres** for the opposite reason. Simple repetition of
words or phrases can give us the sense of how these lines sound in a
purely schematic sense. The **breve** (∪) and **ictus** (/) are used to denote
unstressed and stressed syllables, respectively,

Iambic:

release / release / release

to fall / into / despair

Marie / discov / ers candy

Trochaic:

melting / melting / melting / melting

Peter / disa / greed en / tirely

clever / writing / filled the / page

Anapestic:

to the top / to the top

a retriev / er appeared

and a ter / ri ble thunder

Dactylic:

shivering / shivering / shivering / shivering / shivering

terribly / ill with the / symptoms of / viral pneu / monia

note how the / minister / whispered at / Emily's / grave

Because each of these lines contains a certain number of feet, a second specialized term is used to denote how many times a pattern is repeated in a line:

one foot	monometer
two feet	dimeter
three feet	trimeter
four feet	tetrameter
five feet	pentameter
six feet	hexameter
seven feet	heptameter
eight feet	octameter

Thus, in the examples above, the first set of lines is iambic trimeter; the second, trochaic tetrameter; the third, anapestic dimeter; and the fourth, dactylic pentameter. The third lines in the iambic and anapestic examples are **hypermetrical;** that is, they contain an extra unstressed syllable, or **feminine ending.** Conversely, the third lines in the trochaic and dactylic examples are missing one and two unstressed final syllables, respectively, a common practice called **catalexis.** Although over thirty combinations of foot type and number per line theoretically are possible, relatively few are ordinarily encountered in poetry. The iambic foot is most common in English, followed by the anapest and the trochee; the dactylic foot is relatively rare. Line lengths tend to be from

three to five feet, with anything shorter or longer used on
Still, there are famous exceptions like Poe's "The Raven," w
posed in trochaic octameter.

Metre denotes regularity, the "blueprint" for a line from which the
poet works. Because iambic pentameter is the most common metre used
in English poetry, our subsequent discussion will focus on poems written in it. Most poets quickly learn that a metronomic regularity, five
iambic feet marching in lockstep line after line, is not a virtue and
quickly becomes predictable. Thus, there are several ways by which
poets can add variety to their lines so that the actual **rhythm** of the line,
what is actually heard, plays a subtle counterpoint against the regular-
ity of the metre. One way is to vary the placement of the **caesura** (||), or
pause, within a line (usually indicated by a mark of punctuation).
Another is by mixing **end-stopped lines,** which clearly pause at their
conclusion, with **enjambed** lines (or *enjambment*), which run on into
the next line with no pause.

Another technique of varying regularity is **metrical substitution,**
where feet of a different type are substituted for what the metre calls for.
In iambic metre, trochaic feet are often encountered at the beginnings of
lines, or after a caesura. Two other feet, the **pyrrhic** ($\cup$ $\cup$), consisting of
two unstressed syllables, and the **spondee** ($\prime$ $\prime$), consisting of two
stressed syllables, are also commonly substituted. The poem "Metrical
Feet," which Samuel Taylor Coleridge wrote for his sons, illustrates some
of these variations.

How far can a poet depart from the pattern without losing contact
with the original metre? That question is impossible to answer in general terms. The following scansion will probably strike us at first as a far
departure from regular iambic pentameter:

$$\prime \ || \ \prime \ / \ \cup \ || \ \prime \ / \ \cup \ \cup \ || \ / \ \prime \ \cup \ / \ \cup \ \prime$$

Yet it is actually the opening line of one of Shakespeare's most
often quoted passages, Mark Antony's funeral oration from *Julius
Caesar:*

$$\acute{F}riends, \ || \ R\acute{o} \ / \ m\breve{a}ns, \ || \ c\acute{o}un \ / \ tr\breve{y}m\breve{e}n, \ || \ / \ l\acute{e}nd \ m\breve{e} \ / \ your \ \acute{e}ars$$

Poets who have learned to use the full resources of metre do not consider it a restraint; instead, they are able to stretch the pattern to its limits without breaking it. A good analogy might be made between poetry and dance. Beginning dancers watch their feet and count the steps while making them; after considerable practice, the movements become second nature, and a skillful pair of partners can add dips and passes without losing the basic step of the music.

Free Verse and Open Form

Nothing has been so exhaustively debated in poetry as the exact nature of **free verse.** The simplest definition may be the best: Free verse is verse with no consistent metrical pattern. As Ezra Pound put it, "some poems may have form as a tree has form, some as water poured into a vase." Fixed forms serve as the vase that holds the subject matter in a predetermined shape, whereas free verse grows organically, branching out according to the demands of the material. In free verse, line length is a subjective decision made by the poet, and length may be determined by grammatical phrases, the poet's own sense of individual "breath-units," or even by the visual arrangement of lines on the page. Clearly, it is easier to speak of what free verse is not than to explain what it is. Even its practitioners do not seem very happy with the term free verse, which is derived from the French *vers libre* movement established by French poets of the late nineteenth century such as Rimbaud and Laforgue, who were rebelling against the strictness of established French verse patterns. The extensive use of free verse is a fairly recent phenomenon in the history of poetry. Even though there are many examples of free verse from the past (including the Psalms, Ecclesiastes, and the Song of Solomon from the King James Bible), the modern history of free verse begins in 1855 with the publication of Walt Whitman's *Leaves of Grass*, and subsequent poets who have used free verse have written lines that vary widely in syllable count. As this anthology reveals, contemporary poetry has been enriched by a variety of influences from around the world. International and indigenous voices have contributed their own rhythms both in English and in translation. Good free verse, as T. S. Eliot remarked, still contains some kind of "ghost of meter," and its rhythms can be terse and clipped or lushly sensuous. The poet who

claims that free verse is somehow easier to write than m
would find many arguments to the contrary. As Eliot said,
free for the poet who wants to do a good job."

All poems have form, the arrangement of the poem on the page
that differentiates it from prose. Sometimes this arrangement indicates that the poet is following a preconceived plan—a metrical
pattern, a rhyme scheme, a purely visual design like that of **concrete**
or **spatial poetry,** or a scheme like that of **acrostic verse,** in which
the first letters of the lines spell a message. An analysis of poetic form
notes how the lines are arranged, how long they are, and how they are
grouped into blocks, or **stanzas.** Further analysis might reveal the
existence of types of repetition, rhyme, or the use of a **refrain,** or a
repeated line or groups of lines. A large number of the poems composed in the twentieth and twenty-first centuries have been written in
open form, which simply means that there is no strict pattern of regularity in the elements mentioned above; that is, there is no consistent
metre and no rhyme scheme. Still, even a famous poem in open
form like William Carlos Williams's "The Red Wheelbarrow" can be
described in formal terms:

> so much depends
> upon
>
> a red wheel
> barrow
>
> glazed with rain
> water
>
> beside the white
> chickens.

Here we observe that the eight-line poem is divided into **uniform
stanzas** of two lines each (or couplets). Line length varies between four
and two syllables per line. The odd-numbered lines each contain three
words; the even, one. Although there is no apparent use of rhyme or
repetition here, many poems in open form contain some rhyme and
metrical regularity. A type of free verse called **dispersed,** or "open,"

verse isolates words across the page in fragmented lines, but even among the discontinuous and seemingly scattered lines, one can often discern a pattern of multiple margins or other strategies of emphasis.

Unlike open form, **closed form** denotes the existence of some kind of regular pattern of metre, stanza, rhyme, or repetition. **Stanza forms** are consistent patterns in the individual units of the poem (stanza means "room" in Italian); **fixed forms** are patterns that encompass a complete poem, for example, a sonnet or a villanelle. **Traditional forms** are patterns that have been used for long periods of time and thus may be associated with certain subjects, themes, or types of poems; the sonnet is one example, for it has been used primarily (but by no means exclusively) for lyric poetry. Sometimes poems that are in traditional fixed forms in the original language, like Émile Nelligan's sonnet "Les Angéliques" ("Evening Bells"), are translated into free verse. **Nonce forms** are patterns that originate in an individual poem and have not been widely used by other poets. Of course, it goes without saying that every traditional form was at first a nonce form; the Italian poet (now lost to memory) who first wrote a lyric consisting of fourteen rhymed eleven-syllable lines could not have foreseen that in subsequent centuries poets the world over would produce literally millions of sonnets that are all variations on the original model. Some of the most common stanza and fixed forms are briefly discussed herein.

Stanza Forms

Blank verse is not, strictly speaking, a stanza form because it consists of individual lines of iambic pentameter that do not rhyme. However, long poems in blank verse may be arranged into verse **paragraphs,** or stanzas with a varying number of lines. Blank verse originally appeared in English with the Earl of Surrey's translation of the *Aeneid* in the fifteenth century; it has been used extensively for narrative and dramatic purposes since then, particularly in epics like Milton's *Paradise Lost* and in Shakespeare's plays. Also written in stanzas of varying lengths is the **irregular ode,** a poem that employs lines of varying lengths (although usually of a regular rhythm that is iambic or matches one of the other feet) and an irregular rhyme scheme.

Paired rhyming lines (*aabbcc . . .*) are called **couplets,** although they are only rarely printed as separate stanzas. **Short couplets** have a metre of iambic tetrameter (and are sometimes called **octosyllabic couplets**). If their rhymes are predominantly feminine and seem chosen for comic effect, they may be called **Hudibrastic couplets** after Samuel Butler's satirical poem *Hudibras* of the late 1600s. **Heroic couplets** have a metre of iambic pentameter and take their name from John Dryden's translation of the *Aeneid* (1697) and Alexander Pope's hugely successful translation of Homer's *Iliad* and *Odyssey* (1720–1726); all three of these are "heroic" or epic poems. Heroic couplets have also been used effectively in satirical poems like Alexander Pope's "mock epic" *The Dunciad* and even in dramatic monologues like Robert Browning's "My Last Duchess," where the rhymes are so effectively buried by enjambment that the poem approximates speech. Two other couplet forms, both rare, are **poulter's measure,** rhyming pairs of alternating lines of iambic hexameter and iambic heptameter, and **fourteeners,** pairs of iambic heptameter (fourteen-syllable) lines which, because a natural caesura usually falls after the fourth foot, closely resemble common metre (see below). A three-line stanza is called a **tercet.** If it rhymes in an *aaa bbb . . .* pattern, it is a **triplet;** sometimes triplets appear in poems written in heroic couplets, especially at the end of sections or where special emphasis is desired. Iambic pentameter tercets rhyming *aba bcb cdc . . .* form **terza rima,** a pattern invented by Dante for *The Divine Comedy.*

A four-line stanza is known as a **quatrain.** Alternating lines of tetrameter and trimeter in any foot, rhyming *abcb* or *abab*, make up a **ballad stanza;** if the feet are strictly iambic, then the quatrain is called **common metre,** the form of many popular hymns like "Amazing Grace." **Long metre,** also widely used in hymns, consists of iambic tetrameter lines rhyming *abcb* or *abab*; **short metre** has a similar rhyme scheme but contains first, second, and fourth lines of iambic trimeter and a third line of iambic tetrameter. The *In Memoriam* **stanza,** named after Tennyson's long poetic sequence, is iambic tetrameter rhyming *abba.* The *Rubaiyat* **stanza,** an import from Persia, consists of lines of either iambic tetrameter or pentameter, rhyming *aaba bbcb . . .;* Edward FitzGerald's translation *The Rubaiyat of Omar Khayyam* employs this form. Four lines of iambic pentameter rhyming *abab* are known as an **English quatrain,** also known as the **elegiac stanza** (after Thomas Gray's "Elegy Written in a Country Churchyard"). Lines of the same metre rhyming *abba* make up an **Italian quatrain.** One other unusual quatrain stanza is an import from ancient Greece, the **Sapphic stanza,** named after the poet Sappho. The Sapphic stanza consists of three **hendecasyllabic** (eleven-syllable) lines of this pattern:

/ ᴗ / / ᴗ / / ᴗ ᴗ / / ᴗ / / ᴗ

and a fourth line called an **Adonic,** which is five syllables long and consists of one dactylic foot and one trochaic foot. The Sapphic stanza is usually unrhymed. The quatrain stanza is also used in another import, the **pantoum,** a poem in which the second and fourth lines of the first stanza become the first and third of the second, and the second and fourth of the second become the first and third of the fourth, and so on. Pantoums may be written in any metre and may or may not employ rhyme.

A five-line stanza is known as a **quintet** and is relatively rare in English poetry. The **sestet,** or six-line stanza, can be found with a number of different metres and rhyme schemes. A seven-line stanza is called a **septet;** one septet stanza form is **rime royal,** seven lines of iambic pentameter rhyming *ababbcc.* An eight-line stanza is called an **octave;** one widely used stanza of this length is **ottava rima,** iambic pentameter lines rhyming *abababcc.* Another octave form is the **Monk's Tale stanza,** named after one of Chaucer's tales. It is iambic pentameter and rhymes *ababbcbc.* The addition of a ninth line, rhyming *c* and having a metre of iambic hexameter, makes a **Spenserian stanza,** named after Edmund Spenser, the poet who invented it for *The Faerie Queene,* a long metrical romance.

Fixed Forms

Fixed forms are combinations of metre, rhyme scheme, and repetition that constitute complete poems. One familiar three-line fixed form is the **haiku,** a Japanese import consisting of lines of five, seven, and five syllables, respectively. Related to the haiku is the **tanka,** which adds two additional seven-syllable lines.

Two five-line fixed forms are the **limerick** and the **cinquain.** The limerick consists of anapestic trimeter in lines one, two, and five, and anapestic dimeter in lines three and four. The rhymes, *aabba,* are usually double rhymes used for comic effect.

A cinquain, the invention of American poet Adelaide Crapsey (1878–1914), consists of five unrhymed lines of two, four, six, eight, and two syllables, respectively. The most important of the fixed forms is the **sonnet,** which consists of fourteen lines of rhymed iambic pentameter. The original form of the sonnet is called the **Italian sonnet,** or the **Petrarchan sonnet,** after the fourteenth-century poet who popularized it. An Italian sonnet is usually cast in two stanzas, an octave rhyming *abbaabba* and a sestet with a variable rhyme scheme; *cdcdcd, cdecde,* and *cddcee* are some of the possible patterns. A **volta,** or "turn," usually a conjunction or conjunctive adverb like "but" or "then," may appear at the beginning of the sestet, signifying a slight change of direction in thought. Many Italian sonnets have a strong logical connection between octave and sestet problem/solution, cause/effect, question/answer and the volta helps to clarify the transition. The **English sonnet,** also known as the **Shakespearean sonnet** after its prime exemplar, was developed in the sixteenth century after the sonnet was imported to England and employs a different rhyme scheme that takes into consideration the relative scarcity of rhymes in English (compared with Italian). The English sonnet has a rhyme scheme of *ababcdcdefefgg* and is usually printed as a single stanza. The pattern of three English quatrains plus a heroic couplet often forces a slightly different organizational scheme on the poet, although many of Shakespeare's sonnets still employ a strong volta at the beginning of the ninth line. Other English sonnets may withhold the turn until the beginning of the closing couplet. A third sonnet type, relatively rare, is the **Spenserian sonnet,** named after Edmund Spenser, author of *Amoretti,* one of the earliest sonnet sequences in English. The Spenserian sonnet rhymes *ababbcbccdcdee.* Many other sonnets have been written over the years that have other rhyme schemes, often hybrids of the Italian and English types. These are usually termed **nonce sonnets;** Shelley's "Ozymandias," with its unusual rhyme scheme of *ababacdcedefef,* is one notable example. A fourteen-line stanza rhyming *aba bcb cdc ded ee* has been called a **terza rima sonnet.**

Several other fixed forms, all French imports, have appeared frequently in English poetry. The **rondeau** has fifteen lines of iambic tetrameter or pentameter arranged in three stanzas: *aabba aabR aabbaR;* the *R* here stands for the unrhymed refrain, which repeats the first few words of the poem's first line. A maddeningly complex variation is the thirty-one line **rondeau redoublé,** through which Wendy Cope wittily manoeuvres in her poem of the same name. The **villanelle** is a nineteen-line poem, usually written in iambic pentameter, employing two refrain lines, A_1 and A_2, in a pattern of five tercets and a final quatrain: A_1bA_2 abA_1 abA_2 abA_1 abA_2 abA_1A_2. "Do Not Go Gentle into That Good Night" by Dylan Thomas is a famous example. A related form, also nineteen lines long, is the **terzanelle,** which uses several more repeating lines (capitalized here): A_1BA_2 bCB cDC dED eFE f A_1FA_2. The **ballade** is twenty-eight lines of iambic tetrameter employing a refrain that appears at the end of its three octaves and final quatrain, or **envoy:** *ababbcbC ababbcbC ababbcbC bcbC.* Obviously the rhyming demands of the villanelle, the terzanelle, and the ballade pose serious challenges to English-language poets. A final fixed form is the thirty-nine-line **sestina,** which may be either metred or in free verse and uses a complicated sequence repeating, in different order, the six words that end the lines of the initial stanza. The sequence for the first six sestets is *123456 615243 364125 532614 451362 246531.* A final tercet uses three words in the interior of the lines and three at the ends in the pattern *(2)5(4)3(6)1.* Many sestinas hinge on the poet's choice of six end words that have multiple meanings and can serve as more than one part of speech. There are many other less familiar types of stanza forms and fixed forms. Lewis Turco's *The Book of Forms* and Miller Williams's *Patterns of Poetry* are two reference sources that are useful in identifying them.

Literary History and Poetic Conventions

What a poet attempts to do in any given poem is always governed by the tension that exists between originality and convention, or between the poet's desire, in Ezra Pound's famous phrase, to "make it new," and the various stylistic devices that other poets and readers are familiar with through their understanding of the poetic tradition which has become increasingly international and diverse. Examples of diversity from this anthology include Canadian poet P. K. Page's building a poem around lines from a poem by Chilean poet Pablo Neruda, along with Québécois and Acadian poets in translation, First Nations voices from Canada, the United States, and Australia, and international poets who combine a number of traditions within their work. If we look at some of the most obscure passages of Pound's *Cantos* (a single page may contain passages in several foreign languages), we may think that the poet has departed about as far from conventional modes of expression as possible, leaving his audience far behind him. Yet it is important to keep two facts in mind. First, this style was not arrived at overnight; Pound's early poetry is relatively traditional and should present little difficulty to most readers. He arrived at the style of the *Cantos* after a twenty-year apprenticeship to the styles of writers as different as Li-Po, Robert Browning, and William Butler Yeats. Second, by the time Pound was writing his mature poetry the modernist movement was in full flower, forcing the public not only to read poems but also to look at paintings and sculpture and to listen to music in ways that would have been unimaginable only a decade or two earlier. When we talk about the stylistic conventions of any given literary period, we should keep in mind that poets are rarely willing to go much beyond what they have educated their audiences to understand. This mutual sense of agreement is the essence of poetic convention.

One should be wary of making sweeping generalizations about "schools" of poetry or the shared conventions of literary periods. In any era, there is always a significant amount of diversity among nations and even among individual poets. Further, an anthology of this limited scope, which by its very nature must exclude most long poems, is likely to contribute to a misleading view of literary history and the development of poetry. When we read Shakespeare's or Milton's sonnets, we should not forget that the major reputations of these authors rest on poetry of a very different sort. The neoclassical era in English poetry, stretching from the late seventeenth century until almost the end of the eighteenth, is poorly represented in this anthology because the satires of John Dryden and Alexander Pope do not readily lend themselves to being excerpted. Edgar Allan Poe once claimed that a long poem is "simply a contradiction in terms," but the continued high reputations of *The Faerie Queene, Paradise Lost,* and *Don Juan* demonstrate that Poe's was far from the last word on the subject. bp Nichol, represented in this anthology by two very brief concrete poems, also wrote *The Martyrology,* a poem that extends over nine volumes.

The earliest poems in this volume, all anonymous, represent poetry's links to the oral folk tradition, from the songs and orature of the First Nations of North America to popular English ballads. The poets of the Tudor (1485–1558) and Elizabethan (1558–1603) eras excelled at lyric poetry; Sir Thomas Wyatt and Henry Howard, Earl of Surrey, had imported the sonnet form from Italy, and the form was perfected during this period. Much of the love poetry of the age is characterized by conventional imagery, so-called Petrarchan conceits, which Shakespeare satirizes brilliantly in his Sonnet 130 ("My mistress' eyes are nothing like the sun").

The poetry of the first half of the seventeenth century has several major schools: a smooth lyricism influenced by dramatist Ben Jonson; a serious body of devotional poetry by John Donne, George Herbert, and John Milton; and the metaphysical style, which uses complex extended metaphors or metaphysical conceits—Donne and Herbert are its chief exemplars, followed by early American poets such as Anne Bradstreet. Shortly after the English Restoration in 1660, a profound period of conservatism began in the arts, and the neoclassical era, lasting through most of the eighteenth century, drew heavily on Greek and Roman models. Poetry written during this period—the age of Jonathan Swift and Alexander Pope—was dominated by one form, the heroic couplet; the genres of epic and satire; and an emphasis on human reason as the poet's chief guide. Never has the private voice been so subordinated to the public as in this period when, as Pope put it, a poet's highest aspiration should be to utter "What oft was thought, but ne'er so well expressed."

The first inklings of the romantic era coincide with the American and French revolutions, and poets of the latter half of the eighteenth century like William Blake exhibit some of its characteristics. But it was not until the publication of *Lyrical Ballads,* a 1798 book containing the best early work of William Wordsworth and Samuel Taylor Coleridge, that the romantic era can be said to have truly flowered. Wordsworth's famous formulation of a poem as "the spontaneous overflow of powerful feeling recollected in tranquillity" remains one of romanticism's key definitions, with its emphasis on emotion and immediacy and reflection; Wordsworth's own poetry, with its focus on the natural world, was tremendously influential. Most of the English and North American poets of the first half of the nineteenth century had ties to romanticism in its various guises, and even a poet as late as Walt Whitman (b. 1819) inherited many of its liberal, democratic attitudes. Poets of the Victorian era (1837–1901), such as Alfred, Lord Tennyson and Elizabeth Barrett Browning, continued to explore many of the same themes and genres as their romantic forebears, but certainly much of the optimism of the early years of the century had dissipated by the time poets like Matthew Arnold, Thomas Hardy, and William Butler Yeats, with their omnipresent irony and pessimism, arrived on the scene in the century's last decades.

The twentieth century and the beginning of the twenty-first have been ruled by the upheavals that modernism caused in every art form. If anything characterized the first half of the twentieth century, it was its tireless experimentation with the forms of poetry. There is a continuum in poetry from early beginnings through to the present day, but Ezra Pound, H. D., and T. S. Eliot, to mention only three chief modernists, published poetry that would have totally mystified readers of their grandparents' day, just as Picasso and Matisse produced paintings that represented radical breaks with the visual forms of the past. Although many of the experiments of movements like imagism and surrealism seem not much more than historical curiosities today, they parallel the unusual directions that most of the other arts took during the same period.

For the sake of convenience more than anything else, it has been useful to refer to the era following the end of World War II as the post-modern era. Certainly many of the hard-won modernist gains—open form and increased candour in language and subject matter—have been taken for granted by poets writing in the contemporary period. The confessional poem, a frankly autobiographical narrative that reveals what poets in earlier ages might have striven desperately to conceal, surfaced in the late 1950s in the works of Robert Lowell, Sylvia Plath, and Anne Sexton, and remains one of the chief contemporary genres. Postmodernism incorporates an eclectic mix of styles while denying the supremacy of any one mode of expression. Often abandoning or playing with conventional formal structures and questioning the stability of meaning, postmodern works draw attention to their own status as constructs. As the selections here will attest, there is considerable variety to be found in the contemporary scene both in North America and around the world, and it will perhaps be many years before critics have the necessary historical distance to assess the unique characteristics of the present period.

Writing About Poetry

Writing assignments vary widely and your teacher's instructions may range from general ("Discuss any two poems in your text that contain an effective use of imagery.") to very specific ("Write an explication, in not less than 1000 words, of Margaret Avison's sonnet 'Snow,' focusing on how form relates to content."). Such processes as choosing, limiting, and developing a topic; "brainstorming" by taking notes on random ideas and refining those ideas further through group discussion or conferences with your instructor; using the library and the Internet to locate supporting secondary sources; and revising a first draft in light of critical remarks are undoubtedly techniques you have practised in other composition classes. Basic types of organizational schemes learned in "theme-writing" courses can also be applied to writing about poetry. Formal assignments of these types should avoid contractions and jargon and should be written in a clear, straightforward style. Most literary essays are not of the personal experience type, and you should follow common sense in avoiding the first person and slang. It goes without saying that you should carefully proofread your rough and final drafts to eliminate errors in spelling, punctuation, usage, and grammar.

Writing assignments on poetry usually fall into two categories: explication (or close reading) of single poems and analysis of poetic techniques in one or more poems. Because explication involves the careful "unfolding" of individual poems on a line-by-line basis, an assignment of this type will usually focus on a single short poem or a passage from a longer one. Some poems yield most of their meaning on a single reading; others, however, may contain complexities and nuances that deserve close inspection of how the poet utilizes the elements discussed in this introduction. A typical explication might examine both form and content. Because assignments in analysis usually involve many of the same techniques as explication, we will look at explication more closely. The following is a checklist of questions that you might ask yourself before explicating a poem; the sample passages of analysis apply to a poem from this book, William Shakespeare's "Sonnet 73."

Form

1. How many lines does the poem contain? How are they arranged into stanzas? Is either the whole poem or the stanza an example of a traditional poetic form?

> Shakespeare's "Sonnet 73" contains fourteen lines, printed as one stanza but grammatically divided into three quatrains of four lines each, followed by a concluding couplet that is characteristic of an English sonnet, in contrast to the octave and sestet division of an Italian sonnet.

2. Is there anything striking in the visual arrangement of the poem—indentation, spacing, etc.? Are capitalization and punctuation unusual?

> Capitalization and punctuation are standard in the poem, and Shakespeare follows the traditional practice of capitalizing the first word of each line.

3. In what metre, if any, is the poem written? Does the poet use any notable examples of substitution in the metre? Are the lines primarily end-stopped or enjambed?

> The metre is fairly regular iambic pentameter ("That time / of year / thou mayst / in me / behold") with occasional substitution of trochees, particularly to emphasize the opening word of a line (Bare ru / ined choirs, ‖ / where late / the sweet / birds sang.")

Enjambment occurs at the ends of lines one, two, and five. This has the effect of masking the regular metre and rhymes and enforcing a quiet conversational tone, an effect that is assisted by the caesurae in lines two, four, eight, and thirteen. The caesura in this penultimate line emphasizes the direct involvement of the listener who must now apply the lesson that nothing lasts forever directly to strengthening the relationship with the persona. The couplet at the end of an English sonnet is often a commentary on the preceding quatrains that brings the poem to an epigrammatic close.

4. What is the rhyme scheme, if any, of the poem? What types of rhyme are used?

The rhyme scheme of this poem is ababcdcdefefgg. Shakespeare uses exact masculine rhyme, though it could be argued that, in addition to the rhyming of "strong" and "long," the last words of lines thirteen and fourteen, "love more" and "leave ere," are slant or near rhymes.

5. Are significant sound patterns evident? Is there any repetition of whole lines, phrases, or words?

Alliteration is present in "by and by black night" in line seven and "second self that seals" in line eight, and there are also instances of assonance ("shake against"; "take away") and consonance ("youth doth"; "that which it"). However, these sound patterns do not call excessive attention to themselves and depart from the poem's quiet reflective tone. "Sonnet 73" contains repetition in the three different metaphors used to explore the aging process, and the emphasis on the listener's evolving perception, "in me behold," "in me thou see'st" (twice), and "this thou perceiv'st." An instance of parallel phrasing occurs in line two "or none, or few."

Content

1. To what genre (lyric, narrative, dramatic) does the poem belong? Does it contain elements of more than one genre?

    The sonnet form has traditionally been used for
    lyric poetry, and this is a lyric poem, but it also
    contains narrative elements in the aging of the persona,
    and dramatic elements in that the persona is directly
    addressing a listener who is encouraged to love deeply
    because time is passing.

2. Who is the persona of the poem? Is there an auditor? If so, who? What is the relationship between persona and auditor? Does the poem have a specific setting? If so, where and when is it taking place? Is there any action that has taken place before the poem opens? What actions take place during the poem?

    The persona here is the speaker who is describing
    his own aging process through a variety of metaphors to
    inspire his younger friend to love well against the
    inevitable end of the relationship. Considerable research
    and speculation have been directed toward the mystery of
    the unnamed auditor in Shakespeare's sonnets. Sonnets 1
    to 126 appear to be directed toward a handsome young
    aristocrat whose identity has never been firmly
    established. Subsequent sonnets seem directed toward a
    "Dark Lady," and others toward a rival poet. The sonnets
    were probably written over a number of years, many before
    1598, but some perhaps right up to the date of first
    publication in 1609, when Shakespeare was fifty-five. The
    setting is not explicitly stated, though the "bare ruined
    choirs" are a reminder of specific events in English
    history. In 1534, the Act of Supremacy declared that King
    Henry VIII was the Supreme Head of the Church of England.
    Roman Catholic monasteries throughout England were
    dissolved and their vast lands and goods were turned over
    to the king. Some confiscated church buildings were
    destroyed or vandalized, and left in ruins. Choirs are the
    areas of the church where the choirs once sang, and here

the persona is comparing them to the empty branches of a
winter tree after the birds have flown south, and to the
bare, shaking arms of an old man.

3. Does the poem contain any difficulties with grammar or syntax?
What individual words or phrases are striking because of their
denotation or connotation?

    The syntax of "Sonnet 73" is relatively
straightforward, though it contains several inversions
in which the words do not appear in the expected order.
A paraphrase of the opening line might be "you see in me
that time of year . . ." The three quatrains and the one
couplet are each distinct grammatical units containing a
single sentence. The only exception to the commas dividing
the clauses is the semi-colon in line six, a punctuation
mark now generally used only where one could use a period
instead. The poem's vocabulary is not unusual, though
Shakespeare uses "thou" instead of "you" and "ere" instead
of "before." Night is described as "Death's second self"
because it brings darkness and sleep which, although
temporary, resemble the permanent sleep of death. One
other element to note is Shakespeare's use of syncope, or
the use of an apostrophe in place of an absent letter, so
that a word like "perceivest," which would ordinarily be
three syllables, becomes the two-syllable "perceiv'st" for
the sake of preserving the metre.

4. Does the poem use any figures of speech? If so, how do they add to
the overall meaning? Is the action of the poem to be taken literally,
symbolically, or both ways?

    "Sonnet 73" makes marvellously complex use of
metaphor, comparing growing old to autumn, twilight, and
the dying of a fire. The image of autumn is developed
through the loss of leaves, which symbolically indicates
the loss of youthful vitality, but might also, on the
literal level, be analogous to balding. The shivering
caused by wind and cold suggests the shaking of hands and
voice that sometimes accompany aging. Even though the

metaphors are largely visual, Shakespeare also employs
the tactile and the auditory to more fully evoke the
experience he is describing. "Black night" is personified
as a thief who steals the twilight, and is further
described as "Death's second self." In Greek mythology,
the personification of night is Nyx, who gives birth to
Thanatos (death) and his twin brother Hypnos (sleep).

In the third quatrain the persona compares himself
to glowing embers in the ashes, all that remain of the
bright fire of youth amidst the greying (both symbolic and
literal) of age. Paradoxically, the wood is turned to ash
by the very flame it feeds. The time frame becomes
increasingly urgent in each successive quatrain, from the
dying of the year, to the dying of the day, to the dying
of the fire. This last event may take only moments as the
final spark flickers out. Similarly, the setting becomes
increasingly intimate, moving from outdoors to indoors,
and bringing the poem full circle as the bare boughs of
the opening stanza may well become the logs that have now
turned to ash.

5. Is the title of the poem appropriate? What are its subject, tone of voice, and theme? Is the theme stated or implied?

Generally, titles of poems provide vitally important
clues about significance and meaning but, as far as we
know, Shakespeare did not title his sonnets. The numbers
we use have been added for the sake of identification, and
do not necessarily represent Shakespeare's intentions for
the ordering of his sonnet sequence. In the absence of a
title by the author, poems are often referred to by the
first line of the poem inside square brackets to indicate
that this is not original to the author.

Shakespeare's subject matter, the necessity of
caring intensely for those we will not always have with
us, is powerfully evoked through comparisons between human
beings and the familiar processes of nature. Critics have
noted that the theme of separation haunts many of
Shakespeare's sonnets, and this one is no exception, but
the obsession with the passing of time is tempered by the
ways that such knowledge inspires us to live and love more

fully. An awareness of mortality should result not in
despair but in a re-evaluation of priorities, for example,
those prompted by such questions as "What would you do if
you knew you only had a month to live?" The poet's
metaphors, though sobering, contain a ray of hope in that
winter gives way to spring, night gives way to dawn, and
fires can be rekindled. Though friends and lovers may be
parted by distance or death, love itself endures.

Your instructor may ask you to employ specific strategies in your
explication and may require a certain type of organization for the paper.
It is important not just to identify formal elements and figures of speech
but to consider how these contribute to our understanding of the poem.
Any written text represents a series of choices on the part of the author.
You should assume that the poet has made particular choices for
particular reasons, and seek to explain what those reasons might be,
using evidence from the poem to support your arguments in a coherent
and careful way. In writing the body of the explication, you will
probably proceed through the poem from beginning to end,
summarizing and paraphrasing some lines and quoting others fully
when you feel an explanation is required. It should be stressed that
there are many ways, in theory, to approach a poem and that no two
explications of the same poem will agree in every detail. Some
instructors may favour an explication that links the poem to events in
the author's life, to the socio-historical context in which it was written,
or to some other critical approach.

An assignment in analysis, which looks closely at the way a single
element—dramatic situation, metre, form, imagery, one or more figures
of speech, theme—functions in poetry, would probably require that you
write on two or more poems; in such cases a comparison-contrast or
definition-illustration paper may be called for. An assignment of this
type might examine two related poems by the same poet, or it might
inspect the way that several poets have used a poetic device or theme.
Comparison-contrast essays look for both similarities and differences in
two poems. Definition-illustration papers usually begin with a general
discussion of the topic, say, a popular theme like the *carpe diem* motif,
and then go on to illustrate how this motif may be found in several
different poems. Assignments in analysis often lead to longer papers

that may require the use of secondary sources. Appendix 1 lists some groups of poems that have elements in common.

You may be required to use secondary sources from the library or Internet in writing your paper. A subject search through your library's books is a good starting place, especially for material on older poets who have attracted extensive critical attention. Reference books like *Twentieth Century Authors*, *Contemporary Authors*, *Critical Survey of Poetry*, the *Dictionary of Literary Biography*, *Oxford Companion to Canadian Literature*, and the *Encyclopedia of Literature in Canada* provide compact overviews of poets' careers. *Canadian Writers and Their Works* is a helpful multi-volume reference work that covers both poets and writers of fiction. *Contemporary Literary Criticism* and *Poetry Criticism* contain excerpts from critical pieces on poets' works, and the *MLA Index* will direct you to articles on poets and poems in scholarly journals. A number of journals deal specifically with Canadian literature, including *Essays on Canadian Writing*, *Canadian Poetry*, and *Studies in Canadian Literature*. There are several popular indexes of book reviews; one of these, the annual *Book Review Digest*, reprints brief passages from the most representative reviews. In recent years, the Internet has facilitated the chores of research, and many online databases, reference works, and periodicals may be quickly located using search engines like Google (www.google.com). The Internet also holds a wealth of information in the form of individual Web sites devoted to authors, most of which are run by universities or organizations. Information on Canadian poets can be found at the League of Canadian Poets Web site (www.poets.ca) and the University of Toronto Library Canadian Poetry Web site (www.library. utoronto.ca/canpoetry). Navigating the Internet can be a forbidding task, and a book like Lester Faigley's *The Longman Guide to the Web* is an invaluable traveller's companion. Students should be aware, however, that Web sites vary widely in quality. Some are legitimate academic sources displaying sound scholarship; others are little more than "fan pages" that may contain erroneous or misleading information.

Careful documentation of your sources is essential; if you use any material other than what is termed "common knowledge," you must cite it in your paper. Common knowledge includes biographical information, an author's publications, prizes and awards received, and other information that can be found in more than one reference book. Anything else—direct quotes or material you have put in your own words by paraphrasing—requires both a parenthetical citation in the body of your paper and an entry on your works cited pages. Doing less than this is to commit an act of plagiarism, for which the penalties are usually severe. Internet materials, which are so easily cut and pasted into a manuscript, provide an easy temptation but are immediately noticeable. Nothing is easier to spot in a paper than an uncited "lift" from a source; in most cases, the vocabulary and sentence structure will be radically different from the rest of the paper.

The fifth edition of the *MLA Handbook for Writers of Research Papers*, which can be found in the reference section of almost any library and which, if you plan to write papers for other English courses, is a good addition to your personal library, contains formats for bibliographies and manuscripts that most instructors consider standard; indeed, most of the handbooks of grammar and usage commonly used in English courses follow MLA style and may be sufficient for your needs. The MLA Web site at (www.mla.org) covers some frequently asked questions. If you have doubts, ask your instructor about what format is preferred. The type of parenthetical citation used today to indicate the source of quotations is simple to learn and dispenses with such time-consuming and repetitive chores as footnotes and endnotes. In using parenthetical citations remember that your goal is to direct your reader from the quoted passage in the paper to its source in your bibliography, and from there, if necessary, to the book or periodical from which the quote is taken. A good parenthetical citation gives only the *minimal* information needed to accomplish this. Following are a few examples:

> In describing the season in which "yellow leaves, or none, or few, do hang / Upon those boughs" (1856), Shakespeare does not follow the expected progression from few leaves to no leaves, an inversion that merits consideration.

Here you should note a couple of conventions about writing about poetry. One is that the present tense is used in discussing the poem; in general, use the present tense throughout your critical writing except when you are giving biographical or historical information. Second, note how only parts of lines are quoted here to support the sentence and how the parts fit smoothly into the author's sentence structure. In general, brackets and ellipses [. . .] are not necessary at the beginning or end of these quotes because it is clear that they are quoted fragmentarily; they should, however, be used if something is omitted from the middle of a quote ("black night [. . .] Death's second self"). The virgule or slash (/) is used to indicate line breaks; a double slash (//) indicates a stanza break. Quotes of up to three lines should be treated in this manner. If a quote is longer than three lines, it should be indented ten spaces (with no quotation marks) and printed as it appears in the original poem:

> Shakespeare's use of seasonal imagery to convey mortality can be compared with lines from Canadian poet Margaret Avison's twentieth century sonnet "Snow:"

> But soft, there is snow's legend: colour of mourning
> Along the yellow Yangtze where the wheel
> Spins an indifferent stasis that's death's warning.
> Asters of tumbled quietness reveal
> Their petals. (17)

The parenthetical citation here lists only a page number because only one work by Avison appears in the Works Cited (note that the *MLA Handbook* suggests that you also include line numbers, a practice that is probably unnecessary in discussing a short poem). If several works by the poet had been listed among the works cited, the parenthetical citation would clarify which one was being referred to by adding the book's title in a complete or shortened form: (*Winter Sun*, 17). The reader finds the following entry among the sources:

> Avison, Margaret. <u>Winter Sun</u>. Toronto: U of Toronto P, 1960.

Similarly, quotes and paraphrases from secondary critical sources should follow the same rules of common sense.

Peter Hyland cautions against equating the persona
of Shakespeare's poems with the poet himself: "Even if
real events do lie behind the Sonnets, they have been
fictionalized into a complex artistic structure that has
a richer range of potential meanings than any
autobiographical reading could provide" (146).

In this case, the author of the quote is identified, so only the page
numbers are included in the parenthetical citation. The reader knows
where to look among the sources:

Hyland, Peter. An Introduction to Shakespeare's Poems.
New York: Palgrave Macmillan, 2003.

To simplify the whole matter of parenthetical citation, it is
recommended that quotes from secondary sources be introduced,
wherever possible, in a manner that identifies the author so that only
the page number of the quote is needed inside of the parentheses.

Of course, different types of sources—reference book entries, poems
in anthologies, articles in periodicals, and book reviews—require
different bibliographical information, so be sure to check the *MLA
Handbook* if you have questions. Here are a few more examples of the
most commonly used bibliographical formats:

A BOOK WITH AN AUTHOR AND AN EDITOR

Shakespeare, William. The Riverside Shakespeare. Ed. G.
Blakemore Evans. 2nd Edition. Boston: Houghton
Mifflin, 1997.

A CASEBOOK OR COLLECTION OF CRITICAL ESSAYS

Kent, David, ed. "Lighting Up the Terrain": The Poetry of
Margaret Avison. Toronto: ECW, 1987.

A POEM REPRINTED IN AN ANTHOLOGY OR TEXTBOOK

Shakespeare, William. "Sonnet 73." Poetry: A Pocket
Anthology.

AN ARTICLE IN A REFERENCE BOOK

"Margaret Avison." Encyclopedia of Literature in Canada.
Toronto: U of Toronto P, 2002. 53-55.

AN ARTICLE IN A SCHOLARLY JOURNAL

Calverly, Margaret. "'Service is Joy': Margaret Avison's
Sonnet Sequence in Winter Sun." Essays on Canadian
Writing. 50 (Fall 1993): 210-30.

A BOOK REVIEW IN A PERIODICAL

Babstock, Ken. "Awesome Avison." Rev. of Concrete and Wild
Carrot, by Margaret Avison. Globe and Mail. 21 June
2003: D13.

A WEB SITE

"Margaret Avison." 16 July 2003. <http://www.library.
utoronto.ca/canpoetry/avison/>.

AN ONLINE REFERENCE BOOK

"Shakespeare, William." Encyclopædia Britannica Online.
2003. 16 July 2003. <http://search.eb.com/eb/
article?eu=117520>.

Poetry

This traditional song is taken from a collection by John Robert Colombo, Poems of the Inuit *(1981), based on the work of Knud Rasmussen. According to Daniel David Moses and Terry Goldie, editors of* An Anthology of Canadian Native Literature in English *(1998), in which this song appears, it should be considered as a "sample of a recording process which comments on both cultures involved."*

Inuit Traditional Song

Magic Words/Aua

To Lighten Heavy Loads

I speak with the mouth of Qeqertuanaq, and say:
I will walk with leg muscles strong as the sinews on the shin of
   a little caribou calf.
I will walk with leg muscles strong as the sinews on the shin of
   a little hare.   5
I will take care not to walk toward the dark.
I will walk toward the day.

—Date Unknown

This selection from editor John Robert Colombo's Songs of the Indians *(1983) bears the heritage of both the Native oral tradition and the folklorists who have translated and recorded it.*

Southern First Nations
Traditional Orature

Fragment of a Song

There was a woman, long, long ago:
she came out of a hole.
In it dead people were buried.
She made her house in a tree;
She was dressed in leaves,   5

All long ago.
When she walked among the dry leaves
Her feet were so covered
The feet were invisible.
She walked through the woods,   10
Singing all the time,
'I want company; I'm lonesome!'
A wild man heard her:
From afar over the lakes and mountains
He came to her.   15
She saw him; she was afraid;
She tried to flee away,
For he was covered with the rainbow;
Colour and light were his garments.
She ran, and he pursued rapidly;   20
He chased her to the foot of a mountain.
He spoke in a strange language;
She could not understand him at first.
He would make her tell where she dwelt.
They married; they had two children.   25
One of them was a boy.
He was blind from his birth,
But he frightened his mother by his sight.
He could tell her what was coming,
What was coming from afar.   30
What was near he could not see.
He could see the bear and the moose
Far away beyond the mountains;
He could see through everything.

—*Date Unknown*

Some of the popular ballads and lyrics of England and Scotland, composed for the most part between 1300 and 1500, were first collected in their current forms by Thomas Percy, whose Reliques of Ancient English Poetry *(1765) helped to revive interest in folk poetry. Francis James Child (1825–1896), an American, gathered over a thousand variant versions of the three hundred–odd core of poems. The Romantic poets of the early nineteenth century showed their debt to the folk tradition by writing imitative "art ballads" (see Keats's "La Belle Dame sans Merci"), which incorporate many of their stylistic devices.*

Anonymous
Western Wind

Western wind, when will thou blow,
　　The small rain down can rain?
Christ, if my love were in my arms
　　And I in my bed again!

—1450?

Sir Patrick Spens

The king sits in Dumferling town,
　　Drinking the blude-reid° wine:
"O whar will I get guid sailor,
　　To sail this ship of mine?"

Up and spak an eldern knicht,°　　　　　　　　　　5
　　Sat at the king's richt° knee:
"Sir Patrick Spens is the best sailor
　　That sails upon the sea."

The king has written a braid° letter,
　　And signed it wi' his hand,　　　　　　　　　　10
And sent it to Sir Patrick Spens,
　　Was walking on the sand.

---

2 blude-reid blood-red　**5 eldern knicht** elderly knight　**6 richt** right　**9 braid** long

The first line that Sir Patrick read,
    A loud lauch° lauched he;
The next line that Sir Patrick read,   *15*
    The tear blinded his ee.°

"O wha is this has done this deed,
    This ill deed done to me,
To send me out this time o' the year,
    To sail upon the sea?   *20*

"Mak haste, mak haste, my mirry men all,
    Our guid ship sails the morn."
"O say na sae,° my master dear,
    For I fear a deadly storm.

"Late, late yestre'en° I saw the new moon,   *25*
    Wi' the auld moon in hir arm,
And I fear, I fear, my dear master,
    That we will come to harm."

O our Scots nobles wer richt laith°
    To weet° their cork-heeled shoon,°   *30*
But lang or a'° the play were played,
    Their hats they swam aboon.°

O lang, lang may their ladies sit,
    Wi' their fans into their hand,
Or ere they see Sir Patrick Spens   *35*
    Come sailing to the land.

O lang, lang may the ladies stand,
    Wi' their gold kems° in their hair,
Waiting for their ain dear lords,
    For they'll see them na mair.   *40*

Half o'er, half o'er to Aberdour
    It's fifty fadom deep,
And there lies guid Sir Patrick Spens
    Wi' the Scots lords at his feet.

—1500?

14 lauch laugh   **16 ee** eye   **23 na sae** not so   **25 yestre'en** last evening   **29 laith** loath   **30 weet**
wet   **shoon** shoes   **31 lang or a'** long before   **32 Their hats they swam aboon** their hats swam
above them   **38 kems** combs

Sir Thomas Wyatt (1503?–1542) served Henry VIII as a diplomat in Italy. Wyatt read the love poetry of Petrarch (1304–1374) and is generally credited with having imported both the fashions of these lyrics — hyperbolic "conceits" or metaphorical descriptions of the woman's beauty and the lover's suffering — and their form, the sonnet, to England. "They Flee from Me," an example of one of his original lyrics, displays Wyatt's unique grasp of the rhythms of speech.

Sir Thomas Wyatt

They Flee from Me

They flee from me, that sometime did me seek,
With naked foot stalking in my chamber.
I have seen them gentle, tame and meek,
That now are wild, and do not remember
That sometime they put themself in danger   5
To take bread at my hand; and now they range,
Busily seeking with a continual change.

Thanked be Fortune it hath been otherwise,
Twenty times better; but once in special,
In thin array, after a pleasant guise,°   10
When her loose gown from her shoulders did fall,
And she me caught in her arms long and small,
And therewith all sweetly did me kiss
And softly said, "Dear heart, how like you this?"

It was no dream, I lay broad waking.   15
But all is turned, thorough° my gentleness,
Into a strange fashion of forsaking;
And I have leave to go, of her goodness,
And she also to use newfangleness.
But since that I so kindely° am served,   20
I fain° would know what she hath deserved.

—*1557*

10 guise appearance **16 thorough** through **20 kindely** in this manner **21 fain** gladly

Queen Elizabeth I (1533–1603) was an amateur poet who drew praise from the members of her court, many of whom were also versifiers. A few of her lyrics survive, as do translations she made from the Roman writers Seneca and Horace. Her reign (1558–1603) established England as a world power and also nurtured the talents of Edmund Spenser, William Shakespeare, Christopher Marlowe, and Ben Jonson.

Queen Elizabeth I

When I Was Fair and Young

When I was fair and young, and favor gracèd me,
Of many was I sought, their mistress for to be;
But I did scorn them all, and answered them therefore,
    "Go, go, go seek some otherwhere!
        Importune me no more!"   5

How many weeping eyes I made to pine with woe,
How many sighing hearts, I have no skill to show;
Yet I the prouder grew, and answered them therefore,
    "Go, go, go seek some otherwhere!
        Importune me no more!"   10

Then spake fair Venus' son,° that proud victorious boy,
And said, "Fine dame, since that you be so coy,
I will so pluck your plumes that you shall say no more,
    'Go, go, go seek some otherwhere!
        Importune me no more!'"   15

When he had spake these words, such change grew in my breast
That neither night nor day since that, I could take any rest.
Then lo! I did repent that I had said before,
    "Go, go, go seek some otherwhere!
        Importune me no more!"   20

—*1585*

11 Venus' son Eros or Cupid, god of love

Edmund Spenser (1552–1599) was born in London, and spent most of his adult life in Ireland, where he held a variety of minor government posts. The Faerie Queene, *a long allegorical romance about Elizabethan England, was uncompleted at his death. The eighty-odd sonnets that make up the sequence called* Amoretti *are generally thought to detail his courtship of his second wife, Elizabeth Boyle, whom he married in 1594.*

Edmund Spenser

Amoretti: Sonnet 75

One day I wrote her name upon the strand,
But came the waves and washèd it away:
Agayne I wrote it with a second hand,°
But came the tyde, and made my paynes his pray.
"Vayne man," sayd she, "that doest in vaine assay,°   5
A mortall thing so to immortalize,
For I my selve shall lyke° to this decay
And eek° my name bee wypèd out lykewize."
"Not so," quod° I, "let baser things devize
To dy in dust, but you shall live by fame: 10
My verse your vertues rare shall eternize,
And in the hevens wryte your glorious name.
Where whenas death shall all the world subdew
Our love shall live, and later life renew."

—*1595*

3 second hand second time   **5 assay** attempt   **7 lyke** be similar to   **8 eek** also   **9 quod** said

William Shakespeare (1564–1616) *first printed his sonnets in 1609, during the last years of his active career as a playwright, but they had circulated privately a dozen years before. Given the lack of concrete details about Shakespeare's life outside the theatre, critics have found the sonnets fertile ground for biographical speculation, and the sequence of 154 poems does contain distinct characters —a handsome youth to whom most of the first 126 sonnets are addressed, a "Dark Lady" who figures strongly in the remaining poems, and the poet himself, whose name is the source of many puns in the poems. There is probably no definitive "key" to the sonnets, but there is also little doubt that their place is secure among the monuments of English lyric verse.*

William Shakespeare
Sonnet 18

Shall I compare thee to a summer's day?
Thou art more lovely and more temperate:
Rough winds do shake the darling buds of May,
And summer's lease hath all too short a date:
Sometimes too hot the eye of heaven shines,   5
And often is his gold complexion dimmed;
And every fair from fair° sometimes declines,
By chance or nature's changing course untrimmed;°
But thy eternal summer shall not fade,
Nor lose possession of that fair thou ow'st;°   10
Nor shall death brag thou wander'st in his shade,
When in eternal lines to time thou grow'st:
So long as men can breathe, or eyes can see,
So long lives this, and this gives life to thee.

—*1609*

---

7 fair from fair every fair thing from its fairness   **8 untrimmed** stripped   **10 ow'st** ownest

Sonnet 30

When to the sessions° of sweet silent thought
I summon up remembrance of things past,
I sigh the lack of many a thing I sought,
And with old woes new wail my dear time's waste:
Then can I drown an eye, unused to flow,   *5*
For precious friends hid in death's dateless° night,
And weep afresh love's long since canceled woe,
And moan the expense of many a vanished sight:
Then can I grieve at grievances foregone,
And heavily from woe to woe tell o'er   *10*
The sad account of fore-bemoanèd moan,
Which I new pay as if not paid before.
But if the while I think on thee, dear friend,
All losses are restored and sorrows end.

         —*1609*

Sonnet 73

That time of year thou mayst in me behold
When yellow leaves, or none, or few, do hang
Upon those boughs which shake against the cold,
Bare ruined choirs, where late the sweet birds sang.
In me thou see'st the twilight of such day   *5*
As after sunset fadeth in the west;
Which by and by black night doth take away,
Death's second self, that seals up all in rest.
In me thou see'st the glowing of such fire,
That on the ashes of his youth doth lie,   *10*
As the deathbed whereon it must expire,
Consumed with that which it was nourished by.
This thou perceiv'st, which makes thy love more strong,
To love that well which thou must leave ere long.

         —*1609*

1 sessions as in sessions of a court of law   **6 dateless** endless

Sonnet 130

My mistress' eyes are nothing like the sun;
Coral is far more red than her lips' red;
If snow be white, why then her breasts are dun;
If hairs be wires, black wires grow on her head.
I have seen roses damasked,° red and white,   5
But no such roses see I in her cheeks;
And in some perfumes is there more delight
Than in the breath that from my mistress reeks.
I love to hear her speak, yet well I know
That music hath a far more pleasing sound;   10
I grant I never saw a goddess go;
My mistress, when she walks, treads on the ground.
And yet, by heaven, I think my love as rare
As any she belied° with false compare.°

—1609

John Donne (1572–1631) *was trained in the law for a career in government service, but Donne became the greatest preacher of his day, ending his life as dean of St. Paul's Cathedral in London. Only two of Donne's poems and a handful of his sermons were printed during his life, but both circulated widely in manuscript and his literary reputation among his contemporaries was considerable. His poetry falls into two distinct periods: the witty love poetry of his youth and the sober religious meditations of his maturity. In both, however, Donne shows remarkable originality in rhythm, diction, and the use of metaphor and conceit, which marks him as the chief poet of what has become commonly known as the metaphysical style.*

John Donne
Song

Go and catch a falling star,
    Get with child a mandrake root,°

---

5 damasked multi-coloured   **14 belied** lied about   **compare** comparisons
2 mandrake root forked like the lower half of the human body and said to shriek when pulled from the ground

Tell me where all past years are,
  Or who cleft the Devil's foot,
Teach me to hear mermaids singing,   5
Or to keep off envy's stinging,
      And find
      What wind
Serves to advance an honest mind.

If thou beest born to strange sights,   10
  Things invisible to see,
Ride ten thousand days and nights,
  Till age snow white hairs on thee,
Thou, when thou return'st, wilt tell me,
All strange wonders that befell thee,   15
      And swear,
      No where
Lives a woman true, and fair.

If thou find'st one, let me know,
  Such a pilgrimage were sweet;   20
Yet do not, I would not go,
  Though at next door we might meet;
Though she were true, when you met her,
And last till you write your letter,
      Yet she   25
      Will be
False, ere I come, to two, or three.

                                        —1633

Holy Sonnet 14

Batter my heart, three-personed God; for You
As yet but knock, breathe, shine, and seek to mend;
That I may rise, and stand, o'erthrow me, and bend
Your force to break, blow, burn, and make me new.
I, like an usurped town, to another due,   5
Labor to admit You, but O, to no end;
Reason, Your viceroy in me, me should defend,
But is captived, and proves weak or untrue.
Yet dearly I love You, and would be lovèd fain,°
But am betrothed unto Your enemy.   10
Divorce me, untie or break that knot again;
Take me to You, imprison me, for I,
Except You enthrall me, never shall be free,
Nor ever chaste, except You ravish me.

—*1633*

Robert Hayman (1575–1629) was born in Devonshire, England, and came to Harbour Grace, Newfoundland, in 1621 as governor. Here he wrote Quodlibets *(1628), one of the earliest books of poetry about North America to be written in English. A quodlibet is a musical medley or a scholastic debate based on questions; both meanings apply to Hayman's efforts to celebrate Newfoundland and encourage settlement.*

Robert Hayman
The Four Elements in Newfoundland

To the worshipful Captain John Mason, who did
wisely and worthily govern there divers years.

The Air in Newfoundland is wholesome, good;
The Fire as sweet as any made of wood;

9 fain gladly

The Waters, very rich, both salt and fresh;
The Earth more rich, you know it no less.
Where all are good, Fire, Water, Earth, and Air,   5
What man made of these four would not live there?

—1628

Mary Wroth (1587?–1651) was the niece of Sir Philip Sidney and the cousin of Sir Walter Raleigh, both distinguished poets and courtiers. A friend of poet Ben Jonson, who dedicated The Alchemist *to her, she was prominent in the court of King James I. Her prose romance,* Urania *(1621), stirred controversy because of its similarities to actual people and events. Wroth may have fallen into disfavour at court after the publication of* Urania, *and few facts are known about her later life.*

Mary Wroth
[In this strange labyrinth how shall I turn?]

In this strange labyrinth how shall I turn?
    Ways° are on all sides, while the way I miss:
    If to the right hand, there in love I burn,
    Let me go forward, therein danger is.
If to the left, suspicion hinders bliss: 5
    Let me turn back, shame cries I ought return:
    Nor faint, though crosses° with my fortunes kiss.
    Stand still is harder, although sure to mourn.
Thus let me take the right, or left hand way,
    Go forward, or stand still, or back retire: 10
    I must these doubts endure without allay°
    Or help, but travail find for my best hire
Yet that which most my troubled sense doth move,
Is to leave all and take the thread of Love°

—1621

2 ways paths   **7 crosses** troubles   **11 allay** alleviation   **14 Love** an allusion to the myth of Theseus, who, with the help of Ariadne, unrolled a thread behind him as he entered the labyrinth of Crete

George Herbert (1593–1633) *was the great master of the English devotional lyric. Herbert was born into a distinguished family, which included his mother, the formidable literary patroness Lady Magdalen Herbert, and his brother, the poet and statesman Edward, Lord Herbert of Cherbury. Like John Donne, with whom he shares the metaphysical label, Herbert early aimed at a political career but turned to the clergy, spending several happy years as rector of Bemerton before his death at age forty.* The Temple, *which contains most of his poems, was published posthumously in 1633.*

George Herbert

Easter Wings

Lord, who createdst man in wealth and store,°
Though foolishly he lost the same,
Decaying more and more
Till he became
Most poor: *5*
With Thee
O let me rise
As larks, harmoniously,
And sing this day Thy victories:
Then shall the fall further the flight in me.   *10*

My tender age in sorrow did begin;
And still with sicknesses and shame
Thou didst so punish sin,
That I became
Most thin.   *15*
With Thee
Let me combine,
And feel this day thy victory;
For, if I imp my wing on thine,°
Affliction shall advance the flight in me.   *20*

—1633

---

1 store abundance   **19 imp my wing on thine** to graft feathers from a strong wing onto a weak one, a term from falconry

John Milton (1608–1674) is best known as the London-born author of Paradise Lost *(1667), the great epic poem that sought to "justify the ways of God to men" (Book 1.122) in twelve "books" of blank verse. Though he also wrote prose, lyric poetry, sonnets, and powerful elegies such as "Lycidas," Milton is principally remembered for his verse epics, which, because of the blindness of his later years, he composed in his head and dictated to assistants.*

John Milton

Paradise Lost, Book X: 720–770

"O miserable of happy! Is this the end   720
Of this new glorious world, and me so late
The glory of that glory? who now, become
Accursed of blessèd, hide me from the face
Of God, whom to behold was then my height
Of happiness! Yet well, if here would end   725
The misery; I deserved it, and would bear
My own deservings; but this will not serve.
All that I eat or drink, or shall beget,
Is propagated curse.° O voice, once heard
Delightfully, 'Increase and multiply,'   730
Now death to hear! for what can I increase
Or multiply but curses on my head?
Who, of all ages to succeed, but, feeling
The evil on him brought by me, will curse
My head: 'Ill fare our ancestor impure!   735
For this we may thank Adam!' but his thanks
Shall be the execration;° so besides
Mine own that bide upon me, all from me
Shall with a fierce reflux on me redound,
On me, as on their natural center, light   740
Heavy, though in their place. O fleeting joys

729 propagated curse multiplied curse   **737 execration** curses

Of Paradise, dear bought with lasting woes!
Did I request thee, Maker, from my clay
To mold me man? Did I solicit thee
From darkness to promote me, or here place   745
In this delicious garden? As my will
Concurred not to my being, it were but right
And equal to reduce me to my dust,
Desirous to resign and render back
All I received, unable to perform   750
Thy terms too hard, by which I was to hold
The good I sought not. To the loss of that,
Sufficient penalty, why hast thou added
The sense of endless woes? Inexplicable
Thy justice seems; yet to say truth, too late   755
I thus contèst; then should have been refused
Those terms whatever, when they were proposed.
Thou didst accept them; wilt thou enjoy the good,
Then cavil the conditions? And though God
Made thee without thy leave, what if thy son   760
Prove disobedient, and reproved, retort,
'Wherefore didst thou beget me? I sought it not.'
Wouldst thou admit for his contempt of thee
That proud excuse? Yet him not thy election,
But natural necessity begot.   765
God made thee of choice his own, and of his own
To serve him; thy reward was of his grace;
Thy punishment then justly is at his will.
Be it so, for I submit; his doom is fair,
That dust I am and shall to dust return.   770

—*1667*

Anne Bradstreet (1612–1672) was an American Puritan who was one of the first settlers of the Massachusetts Bay Colony, along with her husband, Simon, later governor of the colony. The Tenth Muse Lately Sprung Up in America, *published abroad by a relative without her knowledge, was the first American book of poetry published in England, and the circumstances of its appearance lie behind the witty tone of "The Author to Her Book."*

Anne Bradstreet

The Author to Her Book

Thou ill-formed offspring of my feeble brain,
Who after birth didst by my side remain,
Till snatched from thence by friends, less wise than true,
Who thee abroad, exposed to public view,
Made thee in rags, halting to th' press° to trudge,   5
Where errors were not lessened (all may judge).
At thy return my blushing was not small,
My rambling brat (in print) should mother call,
I cast thee by as one unfit for light,
Thy visage was so irksome in my sight;   10
Yet being mine own, at length affection would
Thy blemishes amend, if so I could:
I washed thy face, but more defects I saw,
And rubbing off a spot still made a flaw.
I stretched thy joints to make thee even feet,°   15
Yet still thou run'st more hobbling than is meet;
In better dress to trim thee was my mind,
But nought save homespun cloth i' th' house I find.
In this array 'mongst vulgars° may'st thou roam.
In critic's hands beware thou dost not come,   20
And take thy way where yet thou art not known;
If for thy father asked, say thou hadst none;
And for thy mother, she alas is poor,
Which caused her thus to send thee out of door.

—1678

---

5 press printing press; also a clothes closet or chest   **15 even feet** a pun on metrical feet
19 vulgars common people, i.e., average readers

Richard Lovelace (1618–1658) was a Cavalier lyricist who was a staunch supporter of Charles I, serving as a soldier in Scotland and France. He composed many of his poems in prison following the English Civil War.

Richard Lovelace

To Lucasta, Going to the Wars

Tell me not, sweet, I am unkind
That from the nunnery
Of thy chaste breast and quiet mind,
To war and arms I fly.

True, a new mistress now I chase,   5
The first foe in the field;
And with a stronger faith embrace
A sword, a horse, a shield.

Yet this inconstancy is such
As you too shall adore;   10
I could not love thee, dear, so much,
Loved I not honor more.

—1649

Andrew Marvell (1621–1678) was widely known for the playful sexual wit of this most famous example of the carpe diem *poem in English. Marvell was a learned Latin scholar who moved in high circles of government under both the Puritans and Charles II, serving as a member of parliament for two decades. Oddly, Marvell was almost completely forgotten as a lyric poet for almost two hundred years after his death, although today he is considered the last of the great exemplars of the metaphysical style.*

Andrew Marvell

To His Coy Mistress

Had we but world enough, and time,
This coyness,° lady, were no crime.
We would sit down, and think which way
To walk, and pass our long love's day.
Thou by the Indian Ganges' side   5
Shouldst rubies find; I by the tide
Of Humber° would complain. I would
Love you ten years before the flood,
And you should, if you please, refuse
Till the conversion of the Jews.°   10
My vegetable° love should grow
Vaster than empires, and more slow;
An hundred years should go to praise
Thine eyes, and on thy forehead gaze;
Two hundred to adore each breast,   15
But thirty thousand to the rest;
An age at least to every part,
And the last age should show your heart.
For, lady, you deserve this state,°
Nor would I love at lower rate.   20
     But at my back I always hear
Time's wingèd chariot hurrying near;
And yonder all before us lie
Deserts of vast eternity.

---

2 coyness here, artificial sexual reluctance   **7 Humber** an English river near Marvell's home
10 conversion of the Jews at the end of time   **11 vegetable** flourishing   **19 state** estate

Thy beauty shall no more be found;   *25*
Nor, in thy marble vault, shall sound
My echoing song; then worms shall try°
That long-preserved virginity,
And your quaint° honor turn to dust,
And into ashes all my lust: *30*
The grave's a fine and private place,
But none, I think, do there embrace.
    Now therefore, while the youthful hue
Sits on thy skin like morning glow,
And while thy willing soul transpires   *35*
At every pore with instant fires,
Now let us sport us while we may,
And now, like amorous birds of prey,
Rather at once our time devour
Than languish in his slow-chapped° power.   *40*
Let us roll all our strength and all
Our sweetness up into one ball,
And tear our pleasures with rough strife
Thorough the iron gates of life:
Thus, though we cannot make our sun   *45*
Stand still, yet we will make him run.

                                                        —*1681*

Margaret Cavendish *(1623?–1673)* Best known for Poems and Fancies: Written by the Right Honourable, the Lady Newcastle *(1653), this English noblewoman also wrote plays, fiction, biography, and essays on science, while battling objections to her writing career. In poems like "Nature's Cook," she offers a witty combination of domestic imagery and vivid personification.*

Margaret Cavendish

Nature's Cook

Death is the *Cook of Nature:* and we find
Meat dressed several ways to please her *Mind.*
Some *Meats she* roasts with *Fevers, burning hot,*
And some *she* boils with *Dropsies* in a *Pot.*
Some for *Jelly* consuming by degrees,   5
And some with *Ulcers,* Gravy out to squeeze.
Some *Flesh* as *Sage she* stuffs with *Gouts* and *Pains,*
Others for tender *Meat* hang up in *Chains.*
Some in the *Sea she pickles* up to keep,
Others, as *Brawn* is soused, those in *Winesteep.*   10
Some with the *Pox,* chops *Flesh,* and *Bones* so small,
Of which *She* makes a *French Fricasse* withall.
Some on *Gridirons* of *Calentures°* is broiled
And some is trodden on, and so quite spoiled.
But those are *baked,* when smothered they do die,   15
By *Hectic Fevers* some *Meat* She doth *fry.*
In *Sweat* sometimes *she stews* with *savoury smell,*
A *Hodge-Podge* of *Diseases* tasteth well.
Brains dressed with *Apoplexy* to *Nature's* wish,
Or swims with *Sauce* of *Megrimes°* in a *Dish.*   20
And *Tongues* she dries with *Smoke* with *Stomachs* ill,
Which as the second *Course* she sends up still.
Then *Death* cuts *Throats,* for *Blood-puddings* to make,
And puts them in the *Guts,* which *Colics* rack.

---

13 Calentures tropical fevers similar to sunstroke   **20 Megrimes** migraine headaches

Some hunted are by *Death*, for *Deer* that's red,   25
Or *Stall-fed Oxen*, knocked on the *Head*.
Some for *Bacon* by *Death* are *Singed*, or *scaled*,
Then powdered up with *Phlegm*, and *Rheum* that's salt.

—1653

John Dryden (1631–1700) excelled at long forms—verse dramas like All for
Love, *his version of Shakespeare's* Antony and Cleopatra, *his translation of*
Virgil's Aeneid, *political allegories like* Absalom and Achitophel, *and*
MacFlecknoe, *the first great English literary satire. Dryden's balance and formal conservatism introduced the neoclassical style to English poetry, a manner
that prevailed for a century after his death. He became poet laureate of England
in 1668.*

John Dryden

Epigram on Milton

Three poets, in three distant ages born,
Greece,° Italy,° and England did adorn.
The first in loftiness of thought surpassed,
The next in majesty, in both the last:
The force of Nature could no farther go;   5
To make a third, she joined the former two.

—1688

---

2 **Greece** i.e., Homer   **Italy** i.e., Virgil

Aphra Behn (1640–1689) Considered England's first professional woman writer, Behn is most remembered for eighteen plays, including The Rover *(1677), and for her novel* Oroonoko *(1688), set in Surinam, which she visited as a young woman. She may have been the daughter of Mary Wroth's illegitimate daughter, but many details of her life remain mysterious. Her surprising career did include international travel and a stint as a spy. In her poetry, she often treated "scandalous" topics such as impotence and adultery with great wit, but here in this song from her play* Abdelazer, or The Moor's Revenge *(1676), she looks at the darker side of love.*

Aphra Behn

Love Armed

Love in fantastic triumph sat
Whilst bleeding hearts around him flowed,
For whom fresh pains he did create
And strange tyrannic power he showed.

From thy bright eyes he took the fires   5
Which round about in sport he hurled,
But 'twas from mine he took desires
Enough t'undo the amorous world.

From me he took his sighs and tears,
From thee his pride and cruelty;   10
From me his languishments and fears.
And every killing dart° from thee.

Thus thou and I the God have armed
And set him up a deity;
But my poor heart alone is harmed,   15
Whilst thine the victor is, and free.

—1676

---

12 killing dart The Roman god of love, Cupid (from the Latin cupido meaning "desire"), was portrayed with a bow he used to shoot arrows into the hearts of his victims.

Anne Finch (1661–1720) From a prominent English family, the well-educated Finch served Mary of Modena, the second wife of James II. After his deposition, she retired to the countryside in Kent and continued to write poetry, some of which appeared in Miscellany Poems on Several Occasions *(1713). She was admired by Swift and Wordsworth for her nature lyrics and her wit. She also wrote poems about the role of women, like this one in which Adam is "posed" (puzzled and perplexed) by his new partner.*

Anne Finch
Adam Posed

Could our first father, at his toilsome plough,
Thorns in his path, and labor on his brow,
Clothed only in a rude, unpolished skin,
Could he a vain fantastic nymph have seen,
In all her airs, in all her antic graces,   5
Her various fashions, and more various faces;
How had it posed that skill, which late assigned
Just appellations° to each several kind,
A right idea of the sight to frame;
T'have guessed from what new element she came;   10
T'have hit the wavering form, or given this thing a name!

—1709

8 just appellations In Genesis 2:19–20, Adam chooses names for all the animals.

Jonathan Swift (1667–1745), *the author of* Gulliver's Travels, *stands unchallenged as the greatest English prose satirist, but his poetry too is remarkable in the unsparing realism of its best passages. Like many poets of the neoclassical era, Swift adds tension to his poetry by ironically emphasizing parallels between the heroic past and the familiar characters and scenes of contemporary London. A native of Dublin, Swift returned to Ireland in his maturity as dean of St. Patrick's Cathedral.*

Jonathan Swift

A Description of a City Shower

Careful observers may foretell the hour
(By sure prognostics)° when to dread a shower:
While rain depends,° the pensive cat gives o'er
Her frolics, and pursues her tail no more.
Returning home at night, you'll find the sink°   *5*
Strike your offended sense with double stink.
If you be wise, then go not far to dine;
You'll spend in coach hire more than save in wine.
A coming shower your shooting corns presage,
Old aches throb, your hollow tooth will rage.   *10*
Sauntering in coffeehouse is Dulman° seen;
He damns the climate and complains of spleen.°
   Meanwhile the South, rising with dabbled wings,
A sable cloud athwart the welkin° flings,
That swilled more liquor than it could contain,   *15*
And, like a drunkard, gives it up again.
Brisk Susan whips her linen from the rope,
While the first drizzling shower is borne aslope:
Such is that sprinkling which some careless quean°
Flirts on you from her mop, but not so clean: *20*
You fly, invoke the gods; then turning, stop
To rail; she singing, still whirls on her mop.

---

2 prognostics forecasts   **3 depends** is imminent   **5 sink** sewer   **11 Dulman** i.e., dull man
12 spleen mental depression   **14 welkin** sky   **19 quean** ill-mannered woman

Not yet the dust had shunned the unequal strife,
But, aided by the wind, fought still for life,
And wafted with its foe by violent gust,   25
'Twas doubtful which was rain and which was dust.
Ah! where must needy poet seek for aid,
When dust and rain at once his coat invade?
Sole coat, where dust cemented by the rain
Erects the nap, and leaves a mingled stain.   30
    Now in contiguous drops the flood comes down,
Threatening with deluge this devoted° town.
To shops in crowds the daggled° females fly,
Pretend to cheapen° goods, but nothing buy.
The Templar° spruce, while every spout's abroach,°   35
Stays till 'tis fair, yet seems to call a coach.
The tucked-up sempstress walks with hasty strides,
While streams run down her oiled umbrella's sides.
Here various kinds, by various fortunes led,
Commence acquaintance underneath a shed.   40
Triumphant Tories and desponding Whigs°
Forget their feuds, and join to save their wigs.
Boxed in a chair° the beau impatient sits,
While spouts run clattering o'er the roof by fits,
And ever and anon with frightful din   45
The leather sounds; he trembles from within.
So when Troy chairmen bore the wooden steed,
Pregnant with Greeks impatient to be freed
(Those bully Greeks, who, as the moderns do,
Instead of paying chairmen, run them through),   50
Laocoön° struck the outside with his spear,
And each imprisoned hero quaked for fear.
    Now from all parts the swelling kennels° flow,
And bear their trophies with them as they go:
Filth of all hues and odors seem to tell   55
What street they sailed from, by their sight and smell.

---

32 **devoted** doomed   33 **daggled** spattered   34 **cheapen** inspect prices of   **35 Templar** law
student   **abroach** pouring   41 **Tories . . . Whigs** rival political factions   43 **chair** sedan chair
51 Laocoön For his attempt to warn the Trojans, he was crushed by sea serpents sent by Poseidon.
53 kennels storm drains

They, as each torrent drives with rapid force,
From Smithfield° or St. Pulchre's shape their course,
And in huge confluence joined at Snow Hill ridge,
Fall from the conduit prone to Holborn Bridge.   *60*
Sweepings from butchers' stalls, dung, guts, and blood,
Drowned puppies, stinking sprats,° all drenched in mud,
Dead cats, and turnip tops, come tumbling down the flood.

—1710

Henry Kelsey (1667–1771) *Born in England, Kelsey joined the Hudson's Bay Company as a young man and spent much of his life in Canada. This is the poetic record of the voyage he took in 1690 from Churchill, Manitoba, on Hudson Bay deep into the interior. He and his Native guides travelled by canoe and on foot across the prairie, making him the first European to see what is now Saskatchewan. He makes particular note of elements of economic interest to the fur trade.*

Henry Kelsey

Now Reader Read . . .

FROM HENRY KELSEY HIS BOOK BEING THE GIFT OF JAMES HUBBUD
IN THE YEAR OF OUR LORD 1693

Now Reader Read for I am well assur'd
Thou dost not know the hardships I endur'd
In this same desert where Ever that I have been
Nor wilt thou me believe without that thou had seen
The Emynent Dangers that did often me attend   *5*
But still I lived in hopes that once it would amend
And makes me free from hunger & from Cold
Likewise many other things which I cannot here unfold
For many times I have often been oppresst
With fears & Cares that I could not take my rest   *10*
Because I was alone & no friend could find
And once that in my travels I was left behind

58 Smithfield site of London cattle exchange   **62 sprats** small fish

Which struck fear & terror into me
But still I was resolved this same Country for to see
Although through many dangers I did pass   15
Hoped still to undergo them at the Last
Now Considering that it was my dismal fate
for to repent I thought it now too late
Trusting still unto my masters Consideration
Hoping they will Except of this my small Relation   20
Which here I have pend & still will Justifie
Concerning of those Indians & their Country
If this wont do farewell to all as I may say
And for my living i'll seek some other way
In sixteen hundred & ninety'th year   25
I set forth as plainly may appear
Through Gods assistance for to understand
The natives language & to see their land
And for my masters interest I did soon
Sett from the house the twealth of June   30
Then up the River I with heavy heart
Did take my way & from all English part
To live amongst the Natives of this place
If god permits me for one two years space
The Inland Country of Good report hath been   35
By Indians but by English yet not seen
Therefore I on my Journey did not stay
But making all the hast I could upon our way
Gott on the borders of the stone Indian Country
I took possession on the tenth Instant July   40
And for my masters I speaking for them all
This neck of land I deerings point did call
Distance from hence by Judgement at the lest
From the house six hundred miles southwest
Through Rivers which run strong with falls   45
thirty three Carriages five lakes in all
The ground begins for to be dry with wood
Poplo & birch with ash thats very good
For the Natives of that place which knows
No use of Better than their wooden Bows   50

According to the use & custom of this place
In September I brought those Natives to a peace
But I had no sooner from those Natives turnd my back
Some of the home Indians° came upon their track
And for old grudges & their minds to fill   55
Came up with them Six tents of which they kill'd
This ill news kept secrett was from me
Nor none of those home Indians did I see
Untill that they their murder all had done
And the Chief acter was he thats called the Sun   60
So far I have spoken concerning of the spoil
And now will give account of that same Country soile
Which hither part is very thick of wood
Affords small nutts with little cherryes very good
Thus it continues till you leave the woods behind   65
And then you have beast of severall kind
The one is a black a Buffillo great
Another is an outgrown Bear which is good meat
His skin to gett I have used all the ways I can
He is mans food & he makes food of man   70
His hide they would not me it preserve
But said it was a god & they should Starve
This plain affords nothing but Beast & grass
And over it in three days time we past
getting unto the woods on the other side   75
It being about forty sixe miles wide
This wood is poplo ridges with small ponds of water
there is beavour in abundance but no Otter
with plains & ridges in the Country throughout
Their Enemies many whom they cannot rout   80
But now of late they hunt their Enemies
And with our English guns do make them flie
At deerings point after the frost
I set up their a Certain Cross
In token of my being there   85

---

54 home Indians Kelsey's term for the Natives already trading at the Hudson's Bay Company post at York Factory

Cut out on it the date of year
And Likewise for to veryfie the same
added to it my master sir Edward deerings name
So having no more to trouble you withall I am
Sir your most obedient & faithful Servant at Command   90

—*1693*

Alexander Pope (1688–1744) was a tiny man who was afflicted in childhood by a crippling disease. Pope was the dominant poet of eighteenth–century England, excelling as a master of mock-epic satire in "The Rape of the Lock" and "The Dunciad." Both his much-quoted "An Essay on Criticism" (1711) and "An Essay on Man" (1733–1734) are written in heroic couplets indicative of a neo-classical aesthetic.

Alexander Pope
from An Essay on Man

1. Know then thyself, presume not God to scan,
The proper study of mankind is Man.
Placed on this isthmus of a middle state,
A being darkly wise, and rudely great:
With too much knowledge for the skeptic side,   5
With too much weakness for the Stoic's pride,
He hangs between; in doubt to act, or rest;
In doubt to deem himself a god, or beast;
In doubt his mind or body to prefer,
Born but to die, and reasoning but to err;   10
Alike in ignorance, his reason such,
Whether he thinks too little, or too much:
Chaos of thought and passion, all confused;
Still by himself abused, or disabused;
Created half to rise, and half to fall;   15

Great lord of all things, yet a prey to all;
Sole judge of truth, in endless error hurled:
The glory, jest, and riddle of the world!

—*1733*

Christopher Smart (1722–1771) *was educated, like Thomas Gray, at Cambridge, but fell victim to religious mania and insanity yet continued to write throughout his life.* Jubilate Agno *("Rejoice in the Lamb") is a long meditation on the immanence of God, even in such insignificant forms as Smart's cat Jeoffry. The poem is one of the earliest examples of free verse in English.*

Christopher Smart
from Jubilate Agno

For I will consider my Cat Jeoffry.
For he is the servant of the Living God, duly and daily serving him.
For at the first glance of the glory of God in the East he worships in his way.
For is this done by wreathing his body seven times round with elegant quickness.
For then he leaps up to catch the musk,° which is the blessing of God upon his prayer.   5
For he rolls upon prank to work it in.
For having done duty and received blessing he begins to consider himself.
For this he performs in ten degrees.
For first he looks upon his forepaws to see if they are clean.
For secondly he kicks up behind to clear away there.   10
For thirdly he works it upon stretch with the forepaws extended.
For fourthly he sharpens his paws by wood.
For fifthly he washes himself.
For sixthly he rolls upon wash.

---

5 musk scented object or toy

For seventhly he fleas himself, that he may not be
    interrupted upon the beat.°   *15*
For eighthly he rubs himself against a post.
For ninthly he looks up for his instructions.
For tenthly he goes in quest of food.
For having considered God and himself he will consider his
    neighbor.
For if he meets another cat he will kiss her in kindness.   *20*
For when he takes his prey he plays with it to give it a chance.
For one mouse in seven escapes by his dallying.
For when his day's work is done his business more properly
    begins.
For he keeps the Lord's watch in the night against the
    adversary.°
For he counteracts the powers of darkness by his electrical
    skin and glaring eyes.   *25*
For he counteracts the Devil, who is death, by brisking about
    the life.
For in his morning orisons he loves the sun and the sun loves him.
For he is of the tribe of Tiger.
For the Cherub Cat is a term° of the Angel Tiger.
For he has the subtlety and hissing of a serpent, which in
    goodness he suppresses.   *30*
For he will not do destruction if he is well-fed, neither will he
    spit without provocation.
For he purrs in thankfulness when God tells him he's a good Cat.
For he is an instrument for the children to learn benevolence
    upon.
For every house is incomplete without him, and a blessing is
    lacking in the spirit.

                                                      —ca. 1760

---

15 beat accustomed path   **24 adversary** i.e., Satan   **29 term** immature version

Mary Leapor (1722–1746) A working-class upbringing in Marston St. Lawrence in England, and her work as a kitchen maid, put Leapor in a good position to comment on the role of women in her time. Her Poems upon Several Occasions *(1748) was published after she died of measles at the age of 24.*

Mary Leapor

An Essay on Woman

Woman, a pleasing but a short-lived flower,
Too soft for business and too weak for power:
A wife in bondage, or neglected maid;
Despised, if ugly; if she's fair, betrayed.
'Tis wealth alone inspires every grace,   *5*
And calls the raptures to her plenteous face.
What numbers for those charming features pine,
If blooming acres round her temples twine!
Her lip the strawberry, and her eyes more bright
Than sparkling Venus° in a frosty night;   *10*
Pale lilies fade and, when the fair appears,
Snow turns a negro and dissolves in tears,
And, where the charmer treads her magic toe,
On English ground Arabian odours grow;
Till mighty Hymen° lifts his sceptred rod,   *15*
And sinks her glories with a fatal nod,
Dissolves her triumphs, sweeps her charms away,
And turns the goddess to her native clay.
    But, Artemisia,° let your servant sing
What small advantage wealth and beauties bring.   *20*
Who would be wise, that knew Pamphilia's fate?
Or who be fair, and joined to Sylvia's mate?
Sylvia, whose cheeks are fresh as early day,
As evening mild, and sweet as spicy May:
And yet that face her partial husband tires,   *25*
And those bright eyes, that all the world admires.

10 **Venus** the Roman goddess of love   15 **Hymen** the Greek god of marriage   19 **Artemisia**, etc. women's names. Pamphilia, meaning "all-loving," may refer to Mary Wroth's sonnet sequence *Pamphilia to Amphilanthus.*

Pamphilia's wit who does not strive to shun,
Like death's infection or a dog-day's sun?
The damsels view her with malignant eyes,
The men are vexed to find a nymph so wise: 30
And wisdom only serves to make her know
The keen sensation of superior woe.
The secret whisper and the listening ear,
The scornful eyebrow and the hated sneer,
The giddy censures of her babbling kind, 35
With thousand ills that grate a gentle mind,
By her are tasted in the first degree,
Though overlooked by Simplicus and me.
Does thirst of gold a virgin's heart inspire,
Instilled by nature or a careful sire? 40
Then let her quit extravagance and play,
The brisk companion and expensive tea,
To feast with Cordia in her filthy sty
On stewed potatoes or on mouldy pie;
Whose eager eyes stare ghastly at the poor, 45
And fright the beggars from her hated door;
In greasy clouts she wraps her smoky chin,
And holds that pride's a never-pardoned sin.
    If this be wealth, no matter where it falls;
But save, ye Muses, save your Mira's° walls: 50
Still give me pleasing indolence and ease,
A fire to warm me and a friend to please.
    Since, whether sunk in avarice or pride,
A wanton virgin or a starving bride,
Or wondering crowds attend her charming tongue, 55
Or, deemed an idiot, ever speaks the wrong;
Though nature armed us for the growing ill
With fraudful cunning and a headstrong will;
Yet, with ten thousand follies to her charge,
Unhappy woman's but a slave at large. 60

—*1748*

50 **Mira** Leapor's pen name

Phillis Wheatley (1753–1784) *Purchased from a slave ship as a child by the man whose last name she adopted, Wheatley showed herself to be an avid student while working as Mrs. Wheatley's personal servant. Sometimes criticized for her admiration of Western culture and the Christian religion, she is praised by Alice Walker for "keeping the notion of song alive" against tremendous odds. Her* Poems on Various Subjects, Religious and Moral *was published in England in 1773 and in America in 1786.*

Phillis Wheatley
On Being Brought from Africa to America

'Twas mercy brought me from my pagan land,
Taught my benighted° soul to understand
That there's a God, that there's a Savior too:
Once I redemption neither sought nor knew.
Some view that sable race with scornful eye: 5
"Their color is a diabolic dye."
Remember, Christians, Negroes black as Cain°
May be refined and join the angelic strain.

—*1773*

---

2 benighted involved in intellectual or moral darkness   **7 Cain** Adam and Eve's son Cain, the first murderer, was marked and sent to wander the earth (Genesis 4:13–16). Some interpreted this story as the origin of the Blacks.

William Blake (1757–1827) was a poet, painter, engraver, and visionary. Blake does not fit easily into any single category, although his political sympathies link him to the later romantic poets. His first book, Poetical Sketches, attracted little attention, but his mature works, starting with Songs of Innocence and Songs of Experience, combine poetry with his own remarkable illustrations and are unique in English literature. Thought mad by many in his own day, Blake anticipated many future directions of both literature and modern psychology.

William Blake
The Tyger

Tyger! Tyger! burning bright
In the forests of the night,
What immortal hand or eye
Could frame thy fearful symmetry?

In what distant deeps or skies   5
Burnt the fire of thine eyes?
On what wings dare he aspire?
What the hand, dare seize the fire?

And what shoulder, & what art,
Could twist the sinews of thy heart?   10
And when thy heart began to beat,
What dread hand? & what dread feet?

What the hammer? what the chain?
In what furnace was thy brain?
What the anvil? what dread grasp   15
Dare its deadly terrors clasp?

When the stars threw down their spears,
And water'd heaven with their tears,
Did he smile his work to see?
Did he who made the Lamb make thee?   20

Tyger! Tyger! burning bright
In the forests of the night,
What immortal hand or eye,
Dare frame thy fearful symmetry?

—1794

The Sick Rose

O Rose, thou art sick.
The invisible worm
That flies in the night
In the howling storm

Has found out thy bed   5
Of crimson joy,
And his dark secret love
Does thy life destroy.

—1794

Robert Burns (1759–1796) *was a Scot known in his day as the "Ploughman Poet" and was one of the first English poets to put dialect to serious literary purpose. Chiefly known for his realistic depictions of peasant life, he was also an important lyric poet who prefigured many of the later concerns of the romantic era.*

Robert Burns

A Red, Red Rose

O my luve's like a red, red rose,
    That's newly sprung in June;
O my luve's like the melodie
    That's sweetly played in tune.

As fair art thou, my bonnie lass,   5
   So deep in luve am I;
And I will luve thee still, my dear,
   Till a' the seas gang° dry.

Till a' the seas gang dry, my dear,
   And the rocks melt wi' the sun;   10
O I will luve thee still, my dear,
   While the sands o' life shall run.

And fare thee weel, my only luve,
   And fare thee weel awhile!
And I will come again, my luve   15
   Though it were ten thousand mile.

—*1791*

William Wordsworth (1770–1850) is generally considered the first of the English romantics. Lyrical Ballads, *the 1798 volume that introduced both his poetry and Samuel Taylor Coleridge's to a wide readership, remains one of the most influential collections of poetry ever published. Wordsworth's preface to the revised edition of 1800 contains the famous romantic formulation of poetry as the "spontaneous overflow of powerful feelings," a theory exemplified in short lyrics like "I Wandered Lonely as a Cloud" and in longer meditative pieces like "Tintern Abbey." Wordsworth served as poet laureate from 1843 to his death.*

William Wordsworth
I Wandered Lonely as a Cloud

I wandered lonely as a cloud
That floats on high o'er vales and hills,
When all at once I saw a crowd,
A host, of golden daffodils;

8 gang go

Beside the lake, beneath the trees,   5
Fluttering and dancing in the breeze.

Continuous as the stars that shine
And twinkle on the milky way,
They stretched in never-ending line
Along the margin of a bay: 10
Ten thousand saw I at a glance,
Tossing their heads in sprightly dance.

The waves beside them danced, but they
Outdid the sparkling waves in glee;
A poet could not but be gay,   15
In such a jocund company;
I gazed—and gazed—but little thought
What wealth the show to me had brought:

For oft, when on my couch I lie
In vacant or in pensive mood,   20
They flash upon that inward eye
Which is the bliss of solitude;
And then my heart with pleasure fills,
And dances with the daffodils.

—1807

The World Is Too Much with Us

The world is too much with us; late and soon,
Getting and spending, we lay waste our powers;
Little we see in Nature that is ours;
We have given our hearts away, a sordid boon!°
This Sea that bares her bosom to the moon;   5

4 sordid boon corrupted gift

The winds that will be howling at all hours,
And are up-gathered now like sleeping flowers;
For this, for every thing, we are out of tune;
It moves us not.—Great God! I'd rather be
A Pagan suckled in a creed outworn;   *10*
So might I, standing on this pleasant lea,
Have glimpses that would make me less forlorn;
Have sight of Proteus° rising from the sea;
Or hear old Triton° blow his wreathèd horn.

—1807

---

*Samuel Taylor Coleridge (1772–1834), inspired but erratic, did his best work,
like Wordsworth, during the great first decade of their friendship, the period that produced* Lyrical Ballads. *Coleridge's later life is a tragic tale of financial and marital
problems, unfinished projects, and a ruinous addiction to opium. A brilliant critic,
Coleridge lectured on Shakespeare and other writers and wrote the* Biographia
Literaria, *perhaps the greatest literary autobiography ever written.*

Samuel Taylor Coleridge
Kubla Khan°

OR A VISION IN A DREAM,° A FRAGMENT

In Xanadu did Kubla Khan
A stately pleasure-dome decree:
Where Alph, the sacred river, ran
Through caverns measureless to man

---

13 Proteus old man of the sea capable of changing shape   **14 Triton** sea god who blows on a
conch shell
Kubla Khan ruler of China (1216–1294)   **vision in a dream** Coleridge's own account tells how he
took opium for an illness and slept for three hours, during which time he envisioned a complete poem
of some three hundred lines. When he awoke, he began to write down the details of his dream. "At
this moment he was unfortunately called out by a person on business from Porlock, and detained by
him above an hour, and on his return to the room found, to his no small surprise and mortification,
that though he still retained some vague and dim recollection of the general purport of the vision, yet,
with the exception of some eight or ten scattered lines and images, all the rest had passed away like
the images on the surface of a stream into which a stone has been cast . . ." [Coleridge's note].

Down to a sunless sea.   5
So twice five miles of fertile ground
With walls and towers were girdled round:
And there were gardens bright with sinuous rills,
Where blossomed many an incense-bearing tree;
And here were forests ancient as the hills,   10
Enfolding sunny spots of greenery.

But oh! that deep romantic chasm which slanted
Down the green hill athwart a cedarn cover!
A savage place! as holy and enchanted
As e'er beneath a waning moon was haunted   15
By woman wailing for her demon lover!
And from this chasm, with ceaseless turmoil seething,
As if this earth in fast thick pants were breathing,
A mighty fountain momently was forced:
Amid whose swift half-intermitted burst   20
Huge fragments vaulted like rebounding hail,
Or chaffy grain beneath the thresher's flail:
And 'mid these dancing rocks at once and ever
It flung up momently the sacred river.
Five miles meandering with a mazy motion   25
Through wood and dale the sacred river ran,
Then reached the caverns measureless to man,
And sank in tumult to a lifeless ocean:
And 'mid this tumult Kubla heard from far
Ancestral voices prophesying war!   30

    The shadow of the dome of pleasure
    Floated midway on the waves;
    Where was heard the mingled measure
    From the fountain and the caves.
It was a miracle of rare device,   35
A sunny pleasure-dome with caves of ice!

    A damsel with a dulcimer
    In a vision once I saw:
    It was an Abyssinian maid,
    And on her dulcimer she played,   40

Singing of Mount Abora.
Could I revive within me
Her symphony and song,
To such a deep delight 'twould win me,
That with music loud and long,   *45*
I would build that dome in air,
That sunny dome! those caves of ice!
And all who heard should see them there,
And all should cry, Beware! Beware!
His flashing eyes, his floating hair!   *50*
Weave a circle round him thrice,
And close your eyes with holy dread,
For he on honey-dew hath fed,
And drunk the milk of Paradise.

                                                    —*1797–98*

Metrical Feet

LESSON FOR A BOY

Trōchĕe trips frŏm lŏng tŏ shōrt;
From long to long in solemn sort
Slōw Spōndēe stālks; strŏng fōot! yet ill able
Ēvĕr tŏ cōme ŭp wĭth Dāctўl trĭsўllăblĕ.
Ĭ āmbĭcs mārch frŏm shōrt tŏ lōng—   *5*
Wĭth ă lēap ănd ă bōund thĕ swĭft Ănăpĕsts thrōng;
One syllable long, with one short at each side,
Ămphĭbrăchўs hāstes wĭth ă stātelў stride—
Fīrst ănd lāst bĕing lōng, mĭddlĕ shōrt, Amphĭmācer
Strīkes hĭs thūndĕrĭng hōofs līke ă prōud hĭgh-brĕd Rācer.   *10*
If Derwent° be innocent, steady, and wise,
And delight in the things of earth, water, and skies;
Tender warmth at his heart, with these meters to show it,

11 Derwent Coleridge's younger son

With sound sense in his brains, may make Derwent a poet—
May crown him with fame, and must win him the love   15
Of his father on earth and his Father above.
       My dear, dear child!
Could you stand upon Skiddaw,° you would not from its whole ridge
See a man who so loves you as your fond S. T. Coleridge.

                                        —1806

George Gordon, Lord Byron (1788–1824) attained flamboyant celebrity status, leading an unconventional lifestyle that contributed to his notoriety. Byron was the most widely read of all the English romantic poets, but his verse romances and mock-epic poems like Don Juan *have not proved as popular in this century. An English aristocrat who was committed to revolutionary ideals, Byron died while lending military assistance to the cause of Greek freedom.*

George Gordon, Lord Byron
When a Man Hath No Freedom to Fight for at Home

When a man hath no freedom to fight for at home,
    Let him combat for that of his neighbors;
Let him think of the glories of Greece and of Rome,
    And get knock'd on the head for his labors.

To do good to mankind is the chivalrous plan,   5
    And is always as nobly requited;
Then battle for freedom wherever you can,
    And, if not shot or hang'd, you'll get knighted.

                                         —1824

18 Skiddaw mountain in England's lake country

Percy Bysshe Shelley (1792–1822), like his friend Byron, has not found as much favour in recent eras as the other English romantics, although his political liberalism anticipates many currents of our own day. Perhaps his unbridled emotionalism is sometimes too intense for modern readers. His wife, Mary Wollstonecraft Shelley, will be remembered as the author of the classic horror novel Frankenstein.

Percy Bysshe Shelley
When the Lamp Is Shattered

When the lamp is shattered
The light in the dust lies dead—
When the cloud is scattered
The rainbow's glory is shed—
When the lute is broken   5
Sweet tones are remembered not—
When the lips have spoken
Loved accents are soon forgot.

As music and splendour
Survive not the lamp and the lute,   10
The heart's echoes render
No song when the spirit is mute—
No song—but sad dirges
Like the wind through a ruined cell,
Or the mournful surges   15
That ring the dead seaman's knell.

When hearts have once mingled
Love first leaves the well-built nest—
The weak one is singled
To endure what it once possest.   20
O Love! who bewailest
The frailty of all things here,
Why choose you the frailest
For your cradle, your home and your bier?

Its passions will rock thee 25
As the storms rock the ravens on high—
   Bright Reason will mock thee
Like the Sun from a wintry sky—
   From thy nest every rafter
Will rot, and thine eagle home 30
   Leave thee naked to laughter,
When leaves fall and cold winds come.

—1824

Ozymandias°

I met a traveler from an antique land
Who said: Two vast and trunkless legs of stone
Stand in the desert. . . . Near them, on the sand,
Half sunk, a shattered visage lies, whose frown,
And wrinkled lip, and sneer of cold command, 5
Tell that its sculptor well those passions read
Which yet survive, stamped on these lifeless things,
The hand that mocked them, and the heart that fed:
And on the pedestal these words appear:
"My name is Ozymandias, king of kings: 10
Look on my works, ye Mighty, and despair!"
Nothing beside remains. Round the decay
Of that colossal wreck, boundless and bare
The lone and level sands stretch far away.

—1818

Ozymandias Ramses II of Egypt (c. 1250 B.C.)

John Keats (1795–1821) *is now perhaps the most admired of all the major roman-tics. Certainly his tragic death from tuberculosis in his twenties gives poignancy to thoughts of the doomed young poet writing feverishly in a futile race against time; "Here lies one whose name was writ in water" are the words he chose for his own epitaph. Many of Keats's poems are concerned with glimpses of the eternal, whether a translation of an ancient epic poem or a pristine artifact of a vanished civilization.*

John Keats
La Belle Dame sans Merci°

O what can ail thee, Knight at arms,
    Alone and palely loitering?
The sedge has withered from the Lake
    And no birds sing!

O what can ail thee, Knight at arms,   *5*
    So haggard, and so woebegone?
The squirrel's granary is full
    And the harvest's done.

I see a lily on thy brow
    With anguish moist and fever dew,   *10*
And on thy cheeks a fading rose
    Fast withereth too.

"I met a Lady in the Meads,
    Full beautiful, a faery's child,
Her hair was long, her foot was light,   *15*
    And her eyes were wild.

"I made a Garland for her head,
    And bracelets too, and fragrant Zone;°
She looked at me as she did love
    And made sweet moan.   *20*

La Belle Dame sans Merci "the beautiful lady without pity"   **18 Zone** belt

"I set her on my pacing steed
    And nothing else saw all day long,
For sidelong would she bend and sing
    A faery's song.

"She found me roots of relish sweet,   25
    And honey wild, and manna dew,
And sure in language strange she said
    'I love thee true.'

"She took me to her elfin grot°
    And there she wept and sighed full sore,   30
And there I shut her wild wild eyes
    With kisses four.

"And there she lullèd me asleep,
    And there I dreamed, Ah Woe betide!
The latest dream I ever dreamt   35
    On the cold hill side.

"I saw pale Kings, and Princes too,
    Pale warriors, death-pale were they all;
They cried, 'La belle Dame sans merci
    Hath thee in thrall!'   40

"I saw their starved lips in the gloam
    With horrid warning gapèd wide,
And I awoke, and found me here
    On the cold hill's side.

"And this is why I sojourn here   45
    Alone and palely loitering;
Though the sedge is withered from the Lake,
    And no birds sing."

          —1819

29 grot cave

Ode on a Grecian Urn

1

Thou still unravished bride of quietness,
    Thou foster-child of silence and slow time,
Sylvan historian, who canst thus express
    A flowery tale more sweetly than our rhyme:
What leaf-fringed legend haunts about thy shape   *5*
    Of deities or mortals, or of both,
        In Tempe or the dales of Arcady?°
    What men or gods are these? What maidens loath?°
What mad pursuit? What struggle to escape?
        What pipes and timbrels?° What wild ecstasy?   *10*

2

Heard melodies are sweet, but those unheard
    Are sweeter; therefore, ye soft pipes, play on;
Not to the sensual ear, but, more endeared,
    Pipe to the spirit ditties of no tone:
Fair youth, beneath the trees, thou canst not leave   *15*
    Thy song, nor ever can those trees be bare;
        Bold Lover, never, never canst thou kiss,
Though winning near the goal—yet, do not grieve;
        She cannot fade, though thou hast not thy bliss,
    Forever wilt thou love, and she be fair!   *20*

3

Ah, happy, happy boughs! that cannot shed
    Your leaves, nor ever bid the Spring adieu;
And, happy melodist, unwearièd,
    Forever piping songs forever new;
More happy love! more happy, happy love!   *25*
    Forever warm and still to be enjoyed,
        Forever panting, and forever young;

---

7 Tempe or the dales of Arcady idealized Greek settings   **8 loath** reluctant   **10 timbrels** tambourines

All breathing human passion far above,
    That leaves a heart high-sorrowful and cloyed,
        A burning forehead, and a parching tongue.   *30*

    4

Who are these coming to the sacrifice?
    To what green altar, O mysterious priest,
Lead'st thou that heifer lowing at the skies,
    And all her silken flanks with garlands dressed?
What little town by river or sea shore,   *35*
    Or mountain-built with peaceful citadel,
        Is emptied of this folk, this pious morn?
And, little town, thy streets forevermore
    Will silent be; and not a soul to tell
        Why thou art desolate, can e'er return.   *40*

    5

O Attic° shape! Fair attitude! with brede°
    Of marble men and maidens overwrought,
With forest branches and the trodden weed;
    Thou, silent form, dost tease us out of thought
As doth eternity: Cold Pastoral!   *45*
    When old age shall this generation waste,
        Thou shalt remain, in midst of other woe
Than ours, a friend to man, to whom thou say'st,
"Beauty is truth, truth beauty,"—that is all
    Ye know on earth, and all ye need to know.   *50*

                          —1819

41 Attic Greek   **brede** ornamental pattern

Susanna Moodie (1803–1885) was born in Suffolk, England, and is best known for Roughing It in the Bush *(1852), her prose account of her arrival and settlement in Upper Canada in 1832, which later inspired Margaret Atwood's* Journals of Susanna Moodie *(1970). This poem first appeared in the* Literary Garland *in 1847, then in* Roughing It in the Bush *as an epigraph to Moodie's chapter on Brian, who practised a method of hunting that requires absolute stillness.*

Susanna Moodie

Brian, the Still-Hunter

O'er memory's glass I see his shadow flit,
Though he was gathered to the silent dust
Long years ago. A strange and wayward man,
That shunn'd companionship, and lived apart;
The leafy covert of the dark brown woods,   5
The gleamy lakes, hid in their gloomy depths,
Whose still, deep waters never knew the stroke
Of cleaving oar, or echoed to the sound
Of social life, contained for him the sum
Of human happiness. With dog and gun   10
Day after day he track'd the nimble deer
Through all the tangled mazes of the forest.

—1847

Elizabeth Barrett Browning (1806–1861) was already a famous poet when she met her husband-to-be, Robert Browning, who had been corresponding with her on literary matters. She originally published her famous sonnet sequence, written in the first years of her marriage, in the guise of a translation of Portuguese poems, perhaps to mask their personal revelations.

Elizabeth Barrett Browning
Sonnets from the Portuguese, 1

I thought once how Theocritus had sung
Of the sweet years, the dear and wish'd-for years,
Who each one in a gracious hand appears
To bear a gift for mortals, old or young:
And, as I mus'd it in his antique tongue,   5
I saw, in gradual vision through my tears,
The sweet, sad years, the melancholy years,
Those of my own life, who by turns had flung
A shadow across me. Straightway I was 'ware,
So weeping, how a mystic Shape did move   10
Behind me, and drew me backward by the hair;
And a voice said in mastery, while I strove,—
"Guess now who holds thee!"—"Death," I said. But, there,
The silver answer rang—"Not Death, but Love."

—*1812*

Sonnets from the Portuguese, 43

How do I love thee? Let me count the ways.
I love thee to the depth and breadth and height
My soul can reach, when feeling out of sight
For the ends of Being and ideal Grace.
I love thee to the level of everyday's   5

Most quiet need, by sun and candle-light.
I love thee freely, as men strive for Right;
I love thee purely, as they turn from Praise.
I love thee with the passion put to use
In my old griefs, and with my childhood's faith.   10
I love thee with a love I seemed to lose
With my lost saints—I love thee with the breath,
Smiles, tears, of all my life!—and, if God choose,
I shall but love thee better after death.

—1845–46

Edgar Allan Poe (1809–1849) has survived his own myth as a deranged, drug-crazed genius, despite the wealth of evidence to the contrary that can be gleaned from his brilliant, though erratic, career as a poet, short-story writer, critic, and editor. Poe's brand of romanticism seems at odds with that of other American poets of his day, and is perhaps more in keeping with the spirit of Coleridge than that of Wordsworth. "The Raven" has been parodied perhaps more than any other American poem, yet it still retains a powerful hold on its audience.

Edgar Allan Poe
The Raven

Once upon a midnight dreary, while I pondered, weak and weary,
Over many a quaint and curious volume of forgotten lore—
While I nodded, nearly napping, suddenly there came a tapping,
As of some one gently rapping, rapping at my chamber door.
"'Tis some visitor," I muttered, "tapping at my chamber door—   5
            Only this and nothing more."

Ah, distinctly I remember it was in the bleak December;
And each separate dying ember wrought its ghost upon the floor.
Eagerly I wished the morrow;—vainly I had sought to borrow
From my books surcease of sorrow—sorrow for the lost Lenore—   10
For the rare and radiant maiden whom the angels name Lenore—
            Nameless *here* for evermore.

And the silken, sad, uncertain rustling of each purple curtain
Thrilled me—filled me with fantastic terrors never felt before;
So that now, to still the beating of my heart, I stood repeating   15
"'Tis some visitor entreating entrance at my chamber door;—
Some late visitor entreating entrance at my chamber door;—
        This it is and nothing more."

Presently my soul grew stronger; hesitating then no longer,
"Sir," said I, "or Madam, truly your forgiveness I implore;   20
But the fact is I was napping, and so gently you came rapping,
And so faintly you came tapping, tapping at my chamber door,
That I scarce was sure I heard you"—here I opened wide the door;—
        Darkness there and nothing more.

Deep into that darkness peering, long I stood there wondering,
    fearing,   25
Doubting, dreaming dreams no mortal ever dared to dream before;
But the silence was unbroken, and the stillness gave no token,
And the only word there spoken was the whispered word, "Lenore?"
This I whispered, and an echo murmured back the word, "Lenore!"
        Merely this and nothing more.   30

Back into the chamber turning, all my soul within me burning,
Soon again I heard a tapping somewhat louder than before.
"Surely," said I, "surely that is something at my window lattice;
Let me see, then, what thereat is, and this mystery explore—
Let my heart be still a moment and this mystery explore;—   35
        'Tis the wind and nothing more!"

Open here I flung the shutter, when, with many a flirt and flutter,
In there stepped a stately Raven of the saintly days of yore;
Not the least obeisance made he; not a minute stopped or stayed he;
But, with mien of lord or lady, perched above my chamber door—   40
Perched upon a bust of Pallas° just above my chamber door—
        Perched, and sat, and nothing more.

41 **Pallas** Athena, goddess of wisdom

Then this ebony bird beguiling my sad fancy into smiling,
By the grave and stern decorum of the countenance it wore,
"Though thy crest be shorn and shaven, thou," I said, "art sure no
    craven,   *45*
Ghastly grim and ancient Raven wandering from the Nightly shore—
Tell me what thy lordly name is on the Night's Plutonian° shore!"
             Quoth the Raven, "Nevermore."

Much I marvelled this ungainly fowl to hear discourse so plainly,
Though its answer little meaning—little relevancy bore;   *50*
For we cannot help agreeing that no living human being
Ever yet was blessed with seeing bird above his chamber door—
Bird or beast upon the sculptured bust above his chamber door,
             With such name as "Nevermore."

But the Raven, sitting lonely on the placid bust, spoke only   *55*
That one word, as if his soul in that one word he did outpour.
Nothing farther then he uttered—not a feather then he fluttered—
Till I scarcely more than muttered, "Other friends have flown
    before—
On the morrow *he* will leave me, as my Hopes have flown before."
             Then the bird said, "Nevermore."   *60*

Startled at the stillness broken by reply so aptly spoken,
"Doubtless," said I, "what it utters is its only stock and store
Caught from some unhappy master whom unmerciful Disaster
Followed fast and followed faster till his songs one burden bore—
Till the dirges of his Hope that melancholy burden bore   *65*
             Of 'Never—nevermore.'"

But the Raven still beguiling all my sad fancy into smiling,
Straight I wheeled a cushioned seat in front of bird and bust and
    door;
Then, upon the velvet sinking, I betook myself to linking
Fancy unto fancy, thinking what this ominous bird of yore—   *70*
What this grim, ungainly, ghastly, gaunt, and ominous bird of yore
             Meant in croaking "Nevermore."

47 Plutonian after Pluto, Roman god of the underworld

This I sat engaged in guessing, but no syllable expressing
To the fowl whose fiery eyes now burned into my bosom's core;
This and more I sat divining, with my head at ease reclining 75
On the cushion's velvet lining that the lamp-light gloated o'er,
But whose velvet-violet lining with the lamp-light gloating o'er,
    She shall press, ah, nevermore!

Then, methought, the air grew denser, perfumed from an unseen censer
Swung by seraphim whose foot-falls tinkled on the tufted floor. 80
"Wretch," I cried, "thy God hath lent thee—by these angels he hath sent thee.
Respite—respite and nepenthe° from thy memories of Lenore;
Quaff, oh quaff this kind nepenthe and forget this lost Lenore!"
    Quoth the Raven, "Nevermore."

"Prophet!" said I, "thing of evil!—prophet still, if bird or devil!— 85
Whether Tempter sent, or whether tempest tossed thee here ashore,
Desolate yet all undaunted, on this desert land enchanted—
On this home by Horror haunted—tell me truly, I implore—
Is there—*is* there balm in Gilead?—tell me—tell me, I implore!"
    Quoth the Raven, "Nevermore." 90

"Prophet!" said I, "thing of evil!—prophet still, if bird or devil!
By that Heaven that bends above us—by that God we both adore—
Tell this soul with sorrow laden if, within the distant Aidenn,°
It shall clasp a sainted maiden whom the angels name Lenore—
Clasp a rare and radiant maiden whom the angels name Lenore." 95
    Quoth the Raven, "Nevermore."

"Be that word our sign of parting, bird or fiend!" I shrieked, upstarting—
"Get thee back into the tempest and the Night's Plutonian shore!
Leave no black plume as a token of that lie thy soul hath spoken!
Leave my loneliness unbroken!—quit the bust above my door! 100
Take thy beak from out my heart, and take thy form from off my door!"
    Quoth the Raven, "Nevermore."

---

82 nepenthe drug causing forgetfulness **93 Aidenn** Eden

And the Raven, never flitting, still is sitting, *still* is sitting
On the pallid bust of Pallas just above my chamber door;
And his eyes have all the seeming of a demon's that is dreaming,⁣   *105*
And the lamp-light o'er him streaming throws his shadow on
    the floor;
And my soul from out that shadow that lies floating on the floor
                 Shall be lifted—nevermore!

                             —1845

To Helen

Helen, thy beauty is to me
    Like those Nicean° barks of yore,
That gently, o'er a perfumed sea
    The weary, way-worn wanderer bore
    To his own native shore.⁣   *5*

On desperate seas long wont to roam,
    Thy hyacinth° hair, thy classic face
Thy Naiad° airs have brought me home
    To the glory that was Greece
And the grandeur that was Rome.⁣   *10*

Lo! in yon brilliant window-niche
    How statue-like I see thee stand!
    The agate lamp within thy hand,
Ah! Psyche,° from the regions which
    Are Holy Land!⁣   *15*

                             —1831

---

2 Nicean possibly of Nice (in the South of France); or Phoenician   **7 hyacinth** reddish, like the flower of Greek myth   **8 Naiad** water nymph   **14 Psyche** the soul

Alfred Lord Tennyson (1809–1892) became the most famous English poet of his era with the 1850 publication of In Memoriam, *a sequence of poems on the death of his friend Arthur Hallam. As poet laureate, he was an official apologist for Victorian England, but he often returned to the past for inspiration—to classical Greece for poems such as "Ulysses" and to Arthurian England for "The Lady of Shalott," a poem that has inspired many painters, including the Pre-Raphaelites.*

Alfred Lord Tennyson

The Lady of Shalott

I

On either side the river lie
Long fields of barley and of rye,
That clothe the wold° and meet the sky;
And thro' the field the road runs by
    To many-tower'd Camelot;°   5
And up and down the people go,
Gazing where the lilies blow
Round an island there below,
    The island of Shalott.

Willows whiten, aspens quiver,   10
Little breezes dusk and shiver
Thro' the wave that runs forever
By the island in the river
    Flowing down to Camelot.
Four gray walls, and four gray towers,   15
Overlook a space of flowers,
And the silent isle imbowers
    The Lady of Shalott.

By the margin, willow-veil'd
Slide the heavy barges trail'd   20
By slow horses; and unhail'd

3 wold rolling uplands   **5 Camelot** King Arthur's legendary castle

The shallop° flitteth silken-sail'd
    Skimming down to Camelot:
But who hath seen her wave her hand?
Or at the casement seen her stand?   25
Or is she known in all the land,
    The Lady of Shalott?

Only reapers, reaping early
In among the bearded barley,
Hear a song that echoes cheerly   30
From the river winding clearly,
    Down to tower'd Camelot:
And by the moon the reaper weary,
Piling sheaves in uplands airy,
Listening, whispers "'Tis the fairy   35
    Lady of Shalott."

II

There she weaves by night and day
A magic web with colors gay.
She has heard a whisper say,
A curse is on her if she stay   40
    To look down to Camelot.
She knows not what the curse may be,
And so she weaveth steadily,
And little other care hath she,
    The Lady of Shalott.   45

And moving thro' a mirror clear
That hangs before her all the year,
Shadows of the world appear.
There she sees the highway near
    Winding down to Camelot: 50
There the river eddy whirls,
And there the surly village churls,
And the red cloaks of market girls,
    Pass onward from Shalott.

22 shallop open boat propelled by oars or sail

Sometimes a troop of damsels glad,   55
An abbot on an ambling pad,°
Sometimes a curly shepherd lad,
Or long-hair'd page in crimson clad,
    Goes by to tower'd Camelot;
And sometimes through the mirror blue   60
The knights come riding two and two:
She hath no loyal knight and true,
    The Lady of Shalott.

But in her web she still delights
To weave the mirror's magic sights,   65
For often thro' the silent nights
A funeral, with plumes and lights
    And music, went to Camelot;
Or when the moon was overhead,
Came two young lovers lately wed: 70
"I am half-sick of shadows," said
    The Lady of Shalott.

III

A bow-shot from her bower-eaves,
He rode between the barley-sheaves,
The sun came dazzling thro' the leaves,   75
And flamed upon the brazen greaves°
    Of bold Sir Lancelot.
A red-cross knight for ever kneel'd
To a lady in his shield,
That sparkled on the yellow field,   80
    Beside remote Shalott.

The gemmy bridle glitter'd free,
Like to some branch of stars we see
Hung in the golden Galaxy.
The bridle bells rang merrily   85
    As he rode down to Camelot:

---

56 **ambling pad** horse moving leisurely   76 **greaves** armour for the shins

And from his blazon'd baldric° slung
A mighty silver bugle hung,
And as he rode his armour rung,
 Beside remote Shalott.   *90*

All in the blue unclouded weather
Thick-jewel'd shone the saddle-leather,
The helmet and the helmet-feather
Burn'd like one burning flame together,
 As he rode down to Camelot.   *95*
As often thro' the purple night,
Below the starry clusters bright,
Some bearded meteor, trailing light,
 Moves over still Shalott.

His broad clear brow in sunlight glow'd;   *100*
On burnish'd hooves his war-horse trode;
From underneath his helmet flow'd
His coal-black curls as on he rode,
 As he rode down to Camelot.
From the bank and from the river   *105*
He flash'd into the crystal mirror,
"Tirra lirra," by the river
 Sang Sir Lancelot.

She left the web, she left the loom,
She made three paces thro' the room,
She saw the water-lily bloom,   *110*
She saw the helmet and the plume,
 She look'd down to Camelot.
Out flew the web and floated wide;
The mirror crack'd from side to side;
"The curse is come upon me," cried   *115*
 The Lady of Shalott.

---

87 baldric ornamented sash worn diagonally across the chest

IV

In the stormy east wind straining,
The pale yellow woods were waning,
The broad stream in his banks complaining,   *120*
Heavily the low sky raining
    Over tower'd Camelot;
Down she came and found a boat
Beneath a willow left afloat,
And round about the prow she wrote   *125*
    The Lady of Shalott.

And down the river's dim expanse
Like some bold seër in a trance,
Seeing all his own mischance—
With a glassy countenance   *130*
    Did she look to Camelot.
And at the closing of the day
She loosed the chain, and down she lay;
The broad stream bore her far away,
    The Lady of Shalott.   *135*

Lying, robed in snowy white
That loosely flew to left and right—
The leaves upon her falling light—
Thro' the noises of the night
    She floated down to Camelot;   *140*
And as the boat-head wound along
The willowy hills and fields among,
They heard her singing her last song,
    The Lady of Shalott.

Heard a carol, mournful, holy,   *145*
Chanted loudly, chanted lowly,
Till her blood was frozen slowly,
And her eyes were darken'd wholly,
    Turn'd to tower'd Camelot.

For ere she reach'd upon the tide   *150*
The first house by the waterside,
Singing in her song she died,
    The Lady of Shalott.

Under tower and balcony,
By garden wall and gallery,   *155*
A gleaming shape she floated by,
Dead-pale between the houses high,
    Silent into Camelot.
Out upon the wharfs they came,
Knight and burgher,° lord and dame,   *160*
And round the prow they read her name,
    The Lady of Shalott.

Who is this? and what is here?
And in the lighted palace near
Died the sound of royal cheer;   *165*
And they cross'd themselves for fear,
    All the knights at Camelot:
But Lancelot mused a little space;
He said, "She has a lovely face;
God in his mercy lend her grace,   *170*
    The Lady of Shalott."

—1832

---

160 burgher citizen

Robert Browning (1812–1889) wrote many successful dramatic monologues that are his lasting legacy, for he brings the genre to a level of achievement rarely equalled. Less regarded during his lifetime than his contemporary Tennyson, he has consistently risen in the esteem of modern readers. Often overlooked in his gallery of often grotesque characters are his considerable metrical skills and ability to simulate speech while working in demanding poetic forms.

Robert Browning
My Last Duchess

FERRARA°

That's my last duchess painted on the wall,
Looking as if she were alive. I call
That piece a wonder, now: Frà Pandolf's° hands
Worked busily a day, and there she stands.
Will't please you sit and look at her? I said   5
"Frà Pandolf" by design, for never read
Strangers like you that pictured countenance,
The depth and passion of its earnest glance,
But to myself they turned (since none puts by
The curtain I have drawn for you, but I)   10
And seemed as they would ask me, if they durst,
How such a glance came there; so, not the first
Are you to turn and ask thus. Sir, 'twas not
Her husband's presence only, called that spot
Of joy into the Duchess' cheek: perhaps   15
Frà Pandolf chanced to say "Her mantle laps
Over my lady's wrist too much," or "Paint
Must never hope to reproduce the faint
Half-flush that dies along her throat": such stuff
Was courtesy, she thought, and cause enough   20
For calling up that spot of joy. She had
A heart—how shall I say?—too soon made glad,
Too easily impressed; she liked whate'er

Ferrara The speaker is probably Alfonso II d'Este, Duke of Ferrara (1533–158?).   **3 Frà Pandolf** an imaginary painter

She looked on, and her looks went everywhere.
Sir, 'twas all one! My favor at her breast,   25
The dropping of the daylight in the West,
The bough of cherries some officious fool
Broke in the orchard for her, the white mule
She rode with round the terrace—all and each
Would draw from her alike the approving speech,   30
Or blush, at least. She thanked men—good! but thanked
Somehow—I know not how—as if she ranked
My gift of a nine-hundred-years-old name
With anybody's gift. Who'd stoop to blame
This sort of trifling? Even had you skill   35
In speech—which I have not—to make your will
Quite clear to such an one, and say, "Just this
Or that in you disgusts me; here you miss,
Or there exceed the mark"—and if she let
Herself be lessoned so, nor plainly set   40
Her wits to yours, forsooth, and made excuse,
—E'en then would be some stooping; and I choose
Never to stoop. Oh sir, she smiled, no doubt,
Whene'er I passed her; but who passed without
Much the same smile? This grew; I gave commands;   45
Then all smiles stopped together. There she stands
As if alive. Will't please you rise? We'll meet
The company below, then. I repeat,
The Count your master's° known munificence
Is ample warrant that no just pretense   50
Of mine for dowry will be disallowed;
Though his fair daughter's self, as I avowed
At starting, is my object. Nay, we'll go
Together down, sir. Notice Neptune, though,
Taming a sea horse, thought a rarity,   55
Which Claus of Innsbruck cast in bronze for me!

—1842

---

49 Count your master's The auditor is apparently an envoy sent to arrange a marriage between the Duke of Ferrara and a count's daughter.

Emily Brontë *(1818–1848)* *Although best known for her fiercely passionate novel,* Wuthering Heights *(1847), set on the Yorkshire moors of England where she was raised, Brontë also wrote poetry that, according to her sister Charlotte, possessed "a peculiar music—wild, melancholy and elevating." The poetry of Charlotte, Emily, and Anne Brontë first appeared in* Poems by Currer, Ellis, and Acton Bell *(1846), but the book's poor reception inspired the three sisters to try writing novels.*

Emily Brontë

[Ah! why, because the dazzling sun]

Ah! why, because the dazzling sun
Restored my earth to joy
Have you° departed, every one,
And left a desert sky?

All through the night, your glorious eyes   5
Were gazing down in mine,
And with a full heart's thankful sighs
I blessed that watch divine!

I was at peace, and drank your beams
As they were life to me   10
And revelled in my changeful dreams
Like petrel° on the sea.

Thought followed thought—star followed star
Through boundless regions on,
While one sweet influence, near and far,   15
Thrilled through and proved us one.

Why did the morning rise to break
So great, so pure a spell,
And scorch with fire the tranquil cheek
Where your cool radiance fell?   20

3 you The poet is addressing the stars.   **12 petrel** small seabirds

Blood-red he rose, and arrow-straight
His fierce beams struck my brow:
The soul of Nature sprang elate,
But mine sank sad and low!

My lids closed down—yet through their veil   25
I saw him blazing still;
And bathe in gold the misty dale,
And flash upon the hill.

I turned me to the pillow then
To call back Night, and see   30
Your worlds of solemn light, again
Throb with my heart and me!

It would not do—the pillow glowed
And glowed both roof and floor,
And birds sang loudly in the wood,   35
And fresh winds shook the door.

The curtains waved, the wakened flies
Were murmuring round my room,
Imprisoned there, till I should rise
And give them leave to roam.   40

O Stars and Dreams and Gentle Night;
O Night and Stars return!
And hide me from the hostile light
That does not warm, but burn—

That drains the blood of suffering men;   45
Drinks tears, instead of dew:
Let me sleep through his blinding reign,
And only wake with you!

—1845

Alexander McLachlan (1818–1896) Known as the "Burns of Canada," McLachlan immigrated from Scotland to Ontario in 1840. He struggled as a farmer, eventually returning to tailoring, the profession for which he had trained. He also wrote five books of poetry between 1846 and 1874. Though he often celebrated the beauty of his adopted country, in this poem, he reveals the plight of the poor and the hypocrisy of those who fail to help.

Alexander McLachlan

We Live in a Rickety House

We live in a rickety house,
　　In a dirty dismal street,
Where the naked hide from day,
　　And thieves and drunkards meet.

And pious folks with their tracts,°　　　　　　　　　　5
　　When our dens they enter in,
They point to our shirtless backs,
　　As the fruits of beer and gin.

And they quote us texts, to prove
　　That our hearts are hard as stone;　　　　　　　10
And they feed us with the fact,
　　That the fault is all our own.

And the parson comes and prays—
　　He's very concerned 'bout our souls;
But he never asks, in the coldest days,　　　　　　　15
　　How we may be off for coals.

It will be long ere the poor
　　Will learn their grog° to shun;
While it's raiment, food and fire,
　　And religion all in one.　　　　　　　　　　　　20

5 tracts short pamphlets on religious topics　**18 grog** alcohol

I wonder some pious folks
    Can look us straight in the face,
For our ignorance and crime
    Are the Church's shame and disgrace.

We live in a rickety house,   25
    In a dirty dismal street,
Where the naked hide from day,
    And thieves and drunkards meet.

                                   —1861

Walt Whitman (1819–1892) pioneered the use of free verse, which established him as one of the forebears of modern poetry, but his subject matter, often dealing with sexual topics, and his unsparing realism were equally controversial in his day. An admirer of Emerson, he adapted many of the ideas of transcendentalism in Song of Myself, *his first major sequence, and also incorporated many of Emerson's calls for poets to use American subjects and patterns of speech.* Leaves of Grass, *which he revised from 1855 until his death, expanded to include virtually all of his poems, including the graphic poems he wrote while serving as a volunteer in Civil War army hospitals.*

Walt Whitman
from Song of Myself

1

I celebrate myself, and sing myself,
And what I assume you shall assume,
For every atom belonging to me as good belongs to you.

I loaf and invite my soul,
I lean and loaf at my ease observing a spear of summer grass.   5

My tongue, every atom of my blood, formed from this soil,
    this air,
Born here of parents born here from parents the same, and their
    parents the same,

I, now thirty-seven years old in perfect health begin,
Hoping to cease not till death.

Creeds and schools in abeyance,   *10*
Retiring back a while sufficed at what they are, but never forgotten,
I harbor for good or bad, I permit to speak at every hazard,
Nature without check with original energy.

52

The spotted hawk swoops by and accuses me, he complains of my gab and
    my loitering.   *1331*

I too am not a bit tamed, I too am untranslatable,
I sound my barbaric yawp° over the roofs of the world.

The last scud of day holds back for me,
It flings my likeness after the rest and true as any on the shadowed
    wilds,   *1335*
It coaxes me to the vapor and the dusk.

I depart as air, I shake my white locks at the runaway sun,
I effuse my flesh in eddies, and drift it in lacy jags.

I bequeath myself to the dirt to grow from the grass I love,
If you want me again look for me under your boot-soles.   *1340*

You will hardly know who I am or what I mean,
But I shall be good health to you nevertheless,
And filter and fiber your blood.

Failing to fetch me at first keep encouraged,
Missing me one place search another,   *1345*
I stop somewhere waiting for you.

—1881

1333 yawp harsh hoarse cry

Matthew Arnold (1822–1888) was the son of the headmaster of Rugby School and himself served as an inspector of schools during much of his adult life. An influential essayist as well as a poet, Arnold was unsparing in his criticism of middle-class "Philistinism." At least part of "Dover Beach" is thought to date from his honeymoon in 1851.

Matthew Arnold

Dover Beach

The sea is calm tonight.
The tide is full, the moon lies fair
Upon the straits; on the French coast the light
Gleams and is gone; the cliffs of England stand,
Glimmering and vast, out in the tranquil bay.   5
Come to the window, sweet is the night-air!
Only, from the long line of spray
Where the sea meets the moon-blanched land,
Listen! you hear the grating roar
Of pebbles which the waves draw back, and fling,   10
At their return, up the high strand,
Begin, and cease, and then again begin,
With tremulous cadence slow, and bring
The eternal note of sadness in.

Sophocles° long ago   15
Heard it on the Aegean, and it brought
Into his mind the turbid ebb and flow
Of human misery; we
Find also in the sound a thought,
Hearing it by this distant northern sea.   20

The Sea of Faith
Was once, too, at the full, and round earth's shore
Lay like the folds of a bright girdle° furled.
But now I only hear

15 Sophocles Athenian tragic poet (496–406 B.C.)   **23 girdle** sash

Its melancholy, long, withdrawing roar,   *25*
Retreating, to the breath
Of the night-wind, down the vast edges drear
And naked shingles° of the world.

Ah, love, let us be true
To one another! for the world, which seems   *30*
To lie before us like a land of dreams,
So various, so beautiful, so new,
Hath really neither joy, nor love, nor light,
Nor certitude, nor peace, nor help for pain;
And we are here as on a darkling plain   *35*
Swept with confused alarms of struggle and flight,
Where ignorant armies clash by night.

—1867

Emily Dickinson (1830–1886) *has been reinvented with each generation, and readers' views of her have ranged between two extremes — one perceiving her as the abnormally shy "Belle of Amherst" making poetry out of her own neuroses and another seeing her as a protofeminist carving out a world of her own in self-willed isolation. What remains is her brilliant poetry — unique, original, and marked with the stamp of individual talent. Dickinson published only seven poems during her life- time, but left behind hundreds of poems in manuscript at her death. Published by her relatives, they were immediately popular, but it was not until the edition of Thomas Johnson in 1955 that they were read with Dickinson's eccentric punctuation and capitalization intact.*

Emily Dickinson
[I died for Beauty—but was scarce]

I died for Beauty—but was scarce
Adjusted in the Tomb
When One who died for Truth, was lain
In an adjoining Room—

---

28 shingles beach pebbles

He questioned softly "Why I failed?"   5
"For Beauty," I replied—
"And I—for Truth—Themself are One—
We Brethren, are," He said—

And so, as Kinsmen, met a Night—
We talked between the Rooms—   10
Until the Moss had reached our lips—
And covered up—our names—

                                    —*1890*

[I had been hungry, all the Years—]

I had been hungry, all the Years—
My Noon had Come—to dine—
I trembling drew the Table near—
And touched the Curious Wine—

'Twas this on Tables I had seen—   5
When turning, hungry, Home
I looked in Windows, for the Wealth
I could not hope—for Mine—

I did not know the ample Bread—
'Twas so unlike the Crumb   10
The Birds and I, had often shared
In Nature's—Dining Room—

The Plenty hurt me—'twas so new—
Myself felt ill—and odd—
As Berry—of a Mountain Bush—   15
Transplanted—to the Road—

Nor was I hungry—so I found
That Hunger—was a way
Of Persons outside Windows—
The Entering—takes away—

20

—*1891*

Christina Rossetti (1830–1894) *was the younger sister of the Pre-Raphaelite painter Dante Gabriel Rossetti, who illustrated one of her most famous poems, "Goblin Market" (1862). Explored from many critical perspectives (feminist, religious, psychological, economic, creative, etc.), this poem reveals new dimensions of a poet once defined by her invalidism and devotional poetry. Christina Rossetti published six collections of poetry, as well as short stories, works for children, and religious essays.*

Christina Rossetti

Goblin Market

Morning and evening
Maids heard the goblins cry:
"Come buy our orchard fruits,
Come buy, come buy:
Apples and quinces,   5
Lemons and oranges,
Plump unpecked cherries—
Melons and raspberries,
Bloom-down-cheeked peaches,
Swart-headed° mulberries,   10
Wild free-born cranberries,
Crab-apples, dewberries,
Pine-apples, blackberries,
Apricots, strawberries—
All ripe together   15

10 swart-headed dark

In summer weather—
Morns that pass by,
Fair eves that fly;
Come buy, come buy;
Our grapes fresh from the vine,   20
Pomegranates full and fine,
Dates and sharp bullaces,°
Rare pears and greengages,
Damsons and bilberries,
Taste them and try: 25
Currants and gooseberries,
Bright-fire-like barberries,
Figs to fill your mouth,
Citrons from the South,
Sweet to tongue and sound to eye,   30
Come buy, come buy."

Evening by evening
Among the brookside rushes,
Laura bowed her head to hear,
Lizzie veiled her blushes: 35
Crouching close together
In the cooling weather,
With clasping arms and cautioning lips,
With tingling cheeks and finger-tips.
"Lie close," Laura said,   40
Pricking up her golden head:
We must not look at goblin men,
We must not buy their fruits:
Who knows upon what soil they fed
Their hungry thirsty roots?"   45
"Come buy," call the goblins
Hobbling down the glen.
"O! cried Lizzie, Laura, Laura,
You should not peep at goblin men."
Lizzie covered up her eyes   50

---

22 bullaces type of plum as are greengages and damsons

Covered close lest they should look;
Laura reared her glossy head,
And whispered like the restless brook:
"Look, Lizzie, look, Lizzie,
Down the glen tramp little men.   55
One hauls a basket,
One bears a plate,
One lugs a golden dish
Of many pounds' weight.
How fair the vine must grow   60
Whose grapes are so luscious;
How warm the wind must blow
Through those fruit bushes."
"No," said Lizzie, "no, no, no;
Their offers should not charm us,   65
Their evil gifts would harm us."
She thrust a dimpled finger
In each ear, shut eyes and ran:
Curious Laura chose to linger
Wondering at each merchant man.   70
One had a cat's face,
One whisked a tail,
One tramped at a rat's pace,
One crawled like a snail,
One like a wombat prowled obtuse and furry,   75
One like a ratel° tumbled hurry-scurry.
Lizzie heard a voice like voice of doves
Cooing all together:
They sounded kind and full of loves
In the pleasant weather.   80

Laura stretched her gleaming neck
Like a rush-imbedded swan,
Like a lily from the beck,°
Like a moonlit poplar branch,
Like a vessel at the launch   85
When its last restraint is gone.

76 ratel honey badger   **83 beck** stream

Backwards up the mossy glen
Turned and trooped the goblin men,
With their shrill repeated cry,
"Come buy, come buy."   90
When they reached where Laura was
They stood stock still upon the moss,
Leering at each other,
Brother with queer brother;
Signalling each other,   95
Brother with sly brother.
One set his basket down,
One reared his plate;
One began to weave a crown
Of tendrils, leaves, and rough nuts brown   100
(Men sell not such in any town);
One heaved the golden weight
Of dish and fruit to offer her:
"Come buy, come buy," was still their cry.
Laura stared but did not stir,   105
Longed but had no money:
The whisk-tailed merchant bade her taste
In tones as smooth as honey,
The cat-faced purr'd,
The rat-paced spoke a word   110
Of welcome, and the snail-paced even was heard;
One parrot-voiced and jolly
Cried "Pretty Goblin" still for "Pretty Polly";
One whistled like a bird.

But sweet-tooth Laura spoke in haste: 115
"Good folk, I have no coin;
To take were to purloin:
I have no copper in my purse,
I have no silver either,
And all my gold is on the furze°   120
That shakes in windy weather

120 furze bush bearing yellow flowers

Above the rusty heather."
"You have much gold upon your head,"
They answered altogether:
"Buy from us with a golden curl."   *125*
She clipped a precious golden lock,
She dropped a tear more rare than pearl,
Then sucked their fruit globes fair or red:
Sweeter than honey from the rock,
Stronger than man-rejoicing wine,   *130*
Clearer than water flowed that juice;
She never tasted such before,
How should it cloy with length of use?
She sucked and sucked and sucked the more
Fruits which that unknown orchard bore,   *135*
She sucked until her lips were sore;
Then flung the emptied rinds away,
But gathered up one kernel stone,
And knew not was it night or day
As she turned home alone.   *140*

Lizzie met her at the gate
Full of wise upbraidings:
"Dear, you should not stay so late,
Twilight is not good for maidens;
Should not loiter in the glen   *145*
In the haunts of goblin men.
Do you not remember Jeanie,
How she met them in the moonlight,
Took their gifts both choice and many,
Ate their fruits and wore their flowers   *150*
Plucked from bowers
Where summer ripens at all hours?
But ever in the moonlight
She pined and pined away;
Sought them by night and day,   *155*
Found them no more, but dwindled and grew gray;
Then fell with the first snow,
While to this day no grass will grow

Where she lies low:
I planted daisies there a year ago   *160*
That never blow.
You should not loiter so."
"Nay hush," said Laura.
"Nay hush, my sister:
I ate and ate my fill,   *165*
Yet my mouth waters still;
To-morrow night I will
Buy more," and kissed her.
"Have done with sorrow;
I'll bring you plums to-morrow   *170*
Fresh on their mother twigs,
Cherries worth getting;
You cannot think what figs
My teeth have met in,
What melons, icy-cold   *175*
Piled on a dish of gold
Too huge for me to hold,
What peaches with a velvet nap,
Pellucid grapes without one seed:
Odorous indeed must be the mead   *180*
Whereon they grow, and pure the wave they drink,
With lilies at the brink,
And sugar-sweet their sap."

Golden head by golden head,
Like two pigeons in one nest   *185*
Folded in each other's wings,
They lay down, in their curtained bed:
Like two blossoms on one stem,
Like two flakes of new-fallen snow,
Like two wands of ivory   *190*
Tipped with gold for awful° kings.
Moon and stars beamed in at them,
Wind sang to them lullaby,
Lumbering owls forbore to fly,

191 awful inspiring awe

Not a bat flapped to and fro   *195*
Round their rest:
Cheek to cheek and breast to breast
Locked together in one nest.

Early in the morning
When the first cock crowed his warning,   *200*
Neat like bees, as sweet and busy,
Laura rose with Lizzie:
Fetched in honey, milked the cows,
Aired and set to rights the house,
Kneaded cakes of whitest wheat,   *205*
Cakes for dainty mouths to eat,
Next churned butter, whipped up cream,
Fed their poultry, sat and sewed;
Talked as modest maidens should
Lizzie with an open heart,   *210*
Laura in an absent dream,
One content, one sick in part;
One warbling for the mere bright day's delight,
One longing for the night.

At length slow evening came—   *215*
They went with pitchers to the reedy brook;
Lizzie most placid in her look,
Laura most like a leaping flame.
They drew the gurgling water from its deep
Lizzie plucked purple and rich golden flags,   *220*
Then turning homeward said: "The sunset flushes
Those furthest loftiest crags;
Come, Laura, not another maiden lags,
No wilful squirrel wags,
The beasts and birds are fast asleep."   *225*
But Laura loitered still among the rushes
And said the bank was steep.

And said the hour was early still,
The dew not fallen, the wind not chill:
Listening ever, but not catching   *230*

The customary cry,
"Come buy, come buy,"
With its iterated jingle
Of sugar-baited words:
Not for all her watching   235
Once discerning even one goblin
Racing, whisking, tumbling, hobbling;
Let alone the herds
That used to tramp along the glen,
In groups or single,   240
Of brisk fruit-merchant men.

Till Lizzie urged, "O Laura, come,
I hear the fruit-call, but I dare not look:
You should not loiter longer at this brook:
Come with me home.   245
The stars rise, the moon bends her arc,
Each glow-worm winks her spark,
Let us get home before the night grows dark;
For clouds may gather even
Though this is summer weather,   250
Put out the lights and drench us through;
Then if we lost our way what should we do?"

Laura turned cold as stone
To find her sister heard that cry alone,
That goblin cry,   255
"Come buy our fruits, come buy."
Must she then buy no more such dainty fruit?
Must she no more such succous pasture find,
Gone deaf and blind?
Her tree of life drooped from the root: 260
She said not one word in her heart's sore ache;
But peering thro' the dimness, naught discerning,
Trudged home, her pitcher dripping all the way;
So crept to bed, and lay
Silent 'til Lizzie slept;   265

Then sat up in a passionate yearning,
And gnashed her teeth for balked desire, and wept
As if her heart would break.

Day after day, night after night,
Laura kept watch in vain,   270
In sullen silence of exceeding pain.
She never caught again the goblin cry:
"Come buy, come buy,"
She never spied the goblin men
Hawking their fruits along the glen: 275
But when the noon waxed bright
Her hair grew thin and gray;
She dwindled, as the fair full moon doth turn
To swift decay, and burn
Her fire away.   280

One day remembering her kernel-stone
She set it by a wall that faced the south;
Dewed it with tears, hoped for a root,
Watched for a waxing shoot,
But there came none;   285
It never saw the sun,
It never felt the trickling moisture run:
While with sunk eyes and faded mouth
She dreamed of melons, as a traveller sees
False waves in desert drouth   290
With shade of leaf-crowned trees,
And burns the thirstier in the sandful breeze.

She no more swept the house,
Tended the fowls or cows,
Fetched honey, kneaded cakes of wheat,   295
Brought water from the brook:
But sat down listless in the chimney-nook
And would not eat.

Tender Lizzie could not bear
To watch her sister's cankerous° care,   *300*
Yet not to share.
She night and morning
Caught the goblins' cry:
"Come buy our orchard fruits,
Come buy, come buy."   *305*
Beside the brook, along the glen
She heard the tramp of goblin men,
The voice and stir
Poor Laura could not hear;
Longed to buy fruit to comfort her,   *310*
But feared to pay too dear.

She thought of Jeanie in her grave,
Who should have been a bride;
But who for joys brides hope to have
Fell sick and died   *315*
In her gay prime,
In earliest winter-time,
With the first glazing rime,
With the first snow-fall of crisp winter-time.

Till Laura, dwindling,   *320*
Seemed knocking at Death's door:
Then Lizzie weighed no more
Better and worse,
But put a silver penny in her purse,
Kissed Laura, crossed the heath with clumps of furze   *325*
At twilight, halted by the brook,
And for the first time in her life
Began to listen and look.

Laughed every goblin
When they spied her peeping: *330*
Came towards her hobbling,
Flying, running, leaping,
Puffing and blowing,

300 cankerous eating away

Chuckling, clapping, crowing,
Clucking and gobbling,   335
Mopping and mowing,
Full of airs and graces,
Pulling wry faces,
Demure grimaces,
Cat-like and rat-like,   340
Ratel and wombat-like,
Snail-paced in a hurry,
Parrot-voiced and whistler,
Helter-skelter, hurry-skurry,
Chattering like magpies,   345
Fluttering like pigeons,
Gliding like fishes,—
Hugged her and kissed her;
Squeezed and caressed her;
Stretched up their dishes,   350
Panniers and plates:
"Look at our apples
Russet and dun,
Bob at our cherries
Bite at our peaches,   355
Citrons and dates,
Grapes for the asking,
Pears red with basking
Out in the sun,
Plums on their twigs;   360
Pluck them and suck them,
Pomegranates, figs."

"Good folk," said Lizzie,
Mindful of Jeanie,
"Give me much and many";—   365
Held out her apron,
Tossed them her penny.
"Nay, take a seat with us,
Honor and eat with us,"

They answered grinning; 370
"Our feast is but beginning.
Night yet is early,
Warm and dew-pearly,
Wakeful and starry:
Such fruits as these 375
No man can carry;
Half their bloom would fly,
Half their dew would dry,
Half their flavor would pass by.
Sit down and feast with us, 380
Be welcome guest with us,
Cheer you and rest with us."
"Thank you," said Lizzie; "but one waits
At home alone for me:
So, without further parleying, 385
If you will not sell me any
Of your fruits though much and many,
Give me back my silver penny
I tossed you for a fee."
They began to scratch their pates, 390
No longer wagging, purring,
But visibly demurring,
Grunting and snarling.
One called her proud,
Cross-grained, uncivil; 395
Their tones waxed loud,
Their looks were evil.
Lashing their tails
They trod and hustled her,
Elbowed and jostled her, 400
Clawed with their nails,
Barking, mewing, hissing, mocking,
Tore her gown and soiled her stocking,
Twitched her hair out by the roots,
Stamped upon her tender feet, 405
Held her hands and squeezed their fruits
Against her mouth to make her eat.

White and golden Lizzie stood,
Like a lily in a flood,
Like a rock of blue-veined stone   410
Lashed by tides obstreperously,—
Like a beacon left alone
In a hoary roaring sea,
Sending up a golden fire,—
Like a fruit-crowned orange-tree   415
White with blossoms honey-sweet
Sore beset by wasp and bee,—
Like a royal virgin town
Topped with gilded dome and spire
Close beleaguered by a fleet   420
Mad to tear her standard down.

One may lead a horse to water,
Twenty cannot make him drink.
Though the goblins cuffed and caught her,
Coaxed and fought her,   425
Bullied and besought her,
Scratched her, pinched her black as ink,
Kicked and knocked her,
Mauled and mocked her,
Lizzie uttered not a word;   430
Would not open lip from lip
Lest they should cram a mouthful in;
But laughed in heart to feel the drip
Of juice that syruped all her face,
And lodged in dimples of her chin,   435
And streaked her neck which quaked like curd.
At last the evil people,
Worn out by her resistance,
Flung back her penny, kicked their fruit
Along whichever road they took,   440
Not leaving root or stone or shoot.
Some writhed into the ground,
Some dived into the brook
With ring and ripple.

Some scudded on the gale without a sound,   445
Some vanished in the distance.

In a smart, ache, tingle,
Lizzie went her way;
Knew not was it night or day;
Sprang up the bank, tore through the furze,   450
Threaded copse and dingle,
And heard her penny jingle
Bouncing in her purse,—
Its bounce was music to her ear.
She ran and ran   455
As if she feared some goblin man
Dogged her with gibe or curse
Or something worse:
But not one goblin skurried after,
Nor was she pricked by fear;   460
The kind heart made her windy-paced
That urged her home quite out of breath with haste
And inward laughter.

She cried "Laura," up the garden,
"Did you miss me?   465
Come and kiss me.
Never mind my bruises,
Hug me, kiss me, suck my juices
Squeezed from goblin fruits for you,
Goblin pulp and goblin dew.   470
Eat me, drink me, love me;
Laura, make much of me:
For your sake I have braved the glen
And had to do with goblin merchant men."

Laura started from her chair,   475
Flung her arms up in the air,
Clutched her hair:
"Lizzie, Lizzie, have you tasted
For my sake the fruit forbidden?
Must your light like mine be hidden,   480

Your young life like mine be wasted,
Undone in mine undoing,
And ruined in my ruin;
Thirsty, cankered, goblin-ridden?"
She clung about her sister,   485
Kissed and kissed and kissed her:
Tears once again
Refreshed her shrunken eyes,
Dropping like rain
After long sultry drouth;   490
Shaking with anguish, fear, and pain,
She kissed and kissed her with a hungry mouth.

Her lips began to scorch,
That juice was wormwood to her tongue,
She loathed the feast: 495
Writhing as one possessed she leaped and sung,
Rent all her robe, and wrung
Her hands in lamentable haste,
And beat her breast.
Her locks streamed like the torch   500
Borne by a racer at full speed,
Or like the mane of horses in their flight,
Or like an eagle when she stems° the light
Straight toward the sun,
Or like a caged thing freed,   505
Or like a flying flag when armies run.

Swift fire spread through her veins, knocked at her heart,
Met the fire smouldering there
And overbore its lesser flame,
She gorged on bitterness without a name: 510
Ah! fool, to choose such part
Of soul-consuming care!
Sense failed in the mortal strife:
Like the watch-tower of a town
Which an earthquake shatters down,   515

503 stems makes headway against

Like a lightning-stricken mast,
Like a wind-uprooted tree
Spun about,
Like a foam-topped water-spout
Cast down headlong in the sea,   520
She fell at last;
Pleasure past and anguish past,
Is it death or is it life ?

Life out of death.
That night long Lizzie watched by her,   525
Counted her pulse's flagging stir,
Felt for her breath,
Held water to her lips, and cooled her face
With tears and fanning leaves:
But when the first birds chirped about their eaves,   530
And early reapers plodded to the place
Of golden sheaves,
And dew-wet grass
Bowed in the morning winds so brisk to pass,
And new buds with new day   535
Opened of cup-like lilies on the stream,
Laura awoke as from a dream,
Laughed in the innocent old way,
Hugged Lizzie but not twice or thrice;
Her gleaming locks showed not one thread of gray,   540
Her breath was sweet as May,
And light danced in her eyes.

Days, weeks, months, years
Afterwards, when both were wives
With children of their own;   545
Their mother-hearts beset with fears,
Their lives bound up in tender lives;
Laura would call the little ones
And tell them of her early prime,
Those pleasant days long gone   550
Of not-returning time:
Would talk about the haunted glen,

The wicked, quaint fruit-merchant men,
Their fruits like honey to the throat,
But poison in the blood;   555
(Men sell not such in any town);
Would tell them how her sister stood
In deadly peril to do her good,
And win the fiery antidote:
Then joining hands to little hands   560
Would bid them cling together,
"For there is no friend like a sister,
In calm or stormy weather,
To cheer one on the tedious way,
To fetch one if one goes astray,   565
To lift one if one totters down,
To strengthen whilst one stands."

—*1830*

Thomas Hardy (1840–1928), after the disappointing response to his novel Jude
the Obscure *in 1895, returned to his first love, writing poetry for the last thirty years
of his long life. The language and life of Hardy's native Wessex inform both his novels
and poems. His subject matter is very much of the nineteenth century, but his ironic,
disillusioned point of view marks him as one of the chief predecessors of modernism.*

Thomas Hardy

The Convergence
of the Twain

LINES ON THE LOSS OF THE TITANIC

1

    In a solitude of the sea
    Deep from human vanity,
And the Pride of Life that planned her, stilly couches she.

2

    Steel chambers, late the pyres
    Of her salamadrine fires,°   5
Cold currents thrid,° and turn to rhythmic tidal lyres.

3

    Over the mirrors meant
    To glass the opulent
The sea-worm crawls—grotesque, slimed, dumb, indifferent.

4

    Jewels in joy designed   10
    To ravish the sensuous mind
Lie lightless, all their sparkles bleared and black and blind.

5

    Dim moon-eyed fishes near
    Gaze at the gilded gear
And query: "What does this vaingloriousness down here?"   15

6

    Well: while was fashioning
    This creature of cleaving wing,
The Immanent Will° that stirs and urges everything

7

    Prepared a sinister mate
    For her—so gaily great—   20
A Shape of Ice, for the time far and dissociate.

8

    And as the smart ship grew
    In stature, grace, and hue,
In shadowy silent distance grew the Iceberg too.

---

5 salamandrine fires The salamander, according to legend, could live in fire. **6 thrid** thread
18 Immanent Will term used by Hardy for fate

9

> Alien they seemed to be: *25*
> No mortal eye could see
The intimate welding of their later history,

10

> Or sign that they were bent
> By paths coincident
On being anon twin halves of one august event,   *30*

11

> Till the Spinner of the Years
> Said "Now!" And each one hears,
And consummation comes, and jars two hemispheres.

—1912

Gerard Manley Hopkins (1844–1889) was an English Jesuit priest who developed elaborate theories of poetic metre (what he called "sprung rhythm") and language to express his own spiritual ardour. Most of his work was posthumously printed through the efforts of his Oxford friend and later correspondent Robert Bridges, who was poet laureate.

Gerard Manley Hopkins
God's Grandeur

The world is charged with the grandeur of God.
   It will flame out, like shining from shook foil;°
   It gathers to a greatness, like the ooze of oil
Crushed.° Why do men then now not reck his rod?
Generations have trod, have trod, have trod;   *5*
   And all is seared with trade; bleared, smeared with toil;
   And wears man's smudge and shares man's smell: the soil
Is bare now, nor can foot feel, being shod.

2 foil gold leaf   **4 Crushed** Hopkins is referring to olive oil.

And for all this, nature is never spent;
    There lives the dearest freshness deep down things;   *10*
And though the last lights off the black West went
    Oh, morning, at the brown brink eastward, springs—
Because the Holy Ghost over the bent
    World broods with warm breast and with ah! bright wings.

                                              —1877

Pied Beauty

Glory be to God for dappled things—
    For skies of couple-color as a brinded° cow;
        For rose-moles all in stipple upon trout that swim;
Fresh-firecoal chestnut-falls;° finches' wings;
    Landscape plotted and pieced—fold, fallow, and plough;   *5*
        And all trades, their gear and tackle and trim.
All things counter, original, spare, strange;
    Whatever is fickle, freckled (who knows how?)
        With swift, slow; sweet, sour; adazzle, dim;
He fathers-forth whose beauty is past change: *10*
        Praise him.

                                              —1877

---

2 brinded streaked   **4 Fresh-firecoal chestnut-falls** According to the poet, chestnuts have a red colour.

Isabella Valancy Crawford (1850–1887) Born in Dublin, Ireland, Crawford came with her family to Canada in 1858, and lived in various Ontario locations, finally settling in Toronto, where she published her only book of verse, Old Spookses' Pass, Malcolm's Katie, and Other Poems *(1884). Long dismissed, she is now considered an important and versatile early Canadian poet. Though Crawford published "The Dark Stag" separately, the lyric is part of a long unfinished poem known as "Hugh and Ion."*

Isabella Valancy Crawford
The Dark Stag

A startl'd stag the blue grey night
Leaps down beyond dark pines
Behind, a length of yellow light,
    The Hunter's arrow shines
His moccasins are stain'd with red   5
    He bends upon his knee
From cov'ring peaks his shafts are sped
The blue mists plume his mighty head!
    Well may the dark stag flee!

The pale moon like a snow-white doe   10
    Bounds by his dappl'd flank;
They beat the stars down as they go
    As wood-bells growing rank.
The winds lift dew-laps from the ground
    Leap from dry shaking reeds   15
Their hoarse bays shake the cedars round—
With keen cries on the trail they bound—
    Swift, swift the dark stag speeds!

Roar the rent lakes, as through the waves
    Their silver warriors plunge   20
As vaults from core of crystal caves
    The vast, fierce Maskelonge.°
Red torches of the sumach glow
    Fall's council fires are lit

22 **Maskelonge** a large pike prized by fishermen

The bittern, squaw-like scolds the air   25
The wild duck splashes loudly, where
   The waving rice-spears knit.

Shaft after shaft the red sun speeds—
   Rent the stag's dappl'd side,
His breast to fangs of hoarse winds bleeds   30
   He staggers on the tide.
He feels the hungry waves of space
   Rush at him high and blue
The white spray smites his dusky face
Swifter the sun's swift arrows race   35
   And pierce his strong heart through.

Away! his white doe far behind
   Lies wounded on the plain
Yells at his flank the nimblest wind—
   His large tears fall like rain   40
Like lily-pads shall clouds grow white
   About his darkling way
From her bald nest upon the height
The red-ey'd eagle sees his flight
He falters—turns—the antler'd night   45
   The black stag stands at bay!

His feet are in the waves of space
   His antlers broad and dun,
He low'rs, and turns his velvet face
   To front the hunter sun,   50
He stamps the lilied clouds and high,
   His branches fill the west—
The lean stork sails across the sky—
The shy loon shrieks to see him die
   The winds leap at his breast.   55

His antlers fall—once more he spurns
   The hoarse hounds of the day
His blood upon the crisp blue burns
   Reddens the mounting spray.

His branches smite the wave—with cries   *60*
    The shrill winds pausing, flag
He sinks in space—red glow the skies;
The brown earth crimsons as he dies,
    The stout and lusty stag!

                                                    —1883

Charles G. D. Roberts (1860–1943) Born in New Brunswick, Roberts was raised by the Tantramar Marshes, which are the subject of this poem on the theme of change, written in the tradition of Wordsworth. One of the most prolific of the "Confederation Poets," who included Archibald Lampman and Duncan Campbell Scott, Roberts was also known for his sonnets and animal stories.

Charles G. D. Roberts
Tantramar° Revisited

Summers and summers have come, and gone with the flight of the
    swallow;
Sunshine and thunder have been, storm, and winter, and frost;
Many and many a sorrow has all but died from remembrance,
Many a dream of joy fall'n in the shadow of pain.
Hands of chance and change have marred, or moulded, or
    broken,   *5*
Busy with spirit or flesh, all I most have adored;
Even the bosom of Earth is strewn with heavier shadows,—
Only in these green hills, aslant to the sea, no change!
Here where the road that has climbed from the inland valleys and
    woodlands,
Dips from the hill-tops down, straight to the base of the hills,— *10*
Here, from my vantage-ground, I can see the scattering houses,
Stained with time, set warm in orchards, meadows, and wheat,
Dotting the broad bright slopes outspread to southward and
    eastward,
Wind-swept all day long, blown by the south-east wind.

Tantramar a fertile area of marshes and rivers flowing into Chignecto Bay and the Bay of Fundy
where New Brunswick and Nova Scotia join, near the childhood home of Charles G. D. Roberts

Skirting the sunbright uplands stretches a riband° of meadow,   *15*
Shorn of the labouring grass, bulwarked well from the sea,
Fenced on its seaward border with long clay dikes from
    the turbid
Surge and flow of the tides vexing the Westmoreland shores.
Yonder, toward the left, lie broad the Westmoreland
    marshes,—
Miles on miles they extend, level, and grassy, and dim,   *20*
Clear from the long red sweep of flats to the sky in the
    distance,
Save for the outlying heights, green-rampired° Cumberland
    Point;
Miles on miles outrolled, and the river-channels divide them,—
Miles on miles of green, barred by the hurtling gusts.

Miles on miles beyond the tawny bay is Minudie.°   *25*
There are the low blue hills; villages gleam at their feet.
Nearer a white sail shines across the water, and nearer
Still are the slim, grey masts of fishing boats dry on the flats.
Ah, how well I remember those wide red flats, above
    tide-mark
Pale with scurf° of the salt, seamed and baked in the sun!   *30*
Well I remember the piles of blocks and ropes, and the net-reels
Wound with the beaded nets, dripping and dark from the sea!
Now at this season the nets are unwound; they hang from
    the rafters
Over the fresh-stowed hay in upland barns, and the wind
Blows all day through the chinks, with the streaks of sunlight,
    and sways them   *35*
Softly at will; or they lie heaped in the gloom of a loft.

Now at this season the reels are empty and idle; I see them
Over the lines of the dikes, over the gossiping grass.
Now at this season they swing in the long strong wind,
    thro' the lonesome
Golden afternoon, shunned by the foraging gulls.   *40*

---

15 riband ribbon   **22 green-rampired** The green slopes are like ramparts or fortifications.
25 Minudie village that lies across the Bay of Fundy in Nova Scotia   **30 scurf** flaky deposits

Near about sunset the crane will journey homeward above
    them;
Round them, under the moon, all the calm night long,
Winnowing soft grey wings of marsh-owls wander and wander,
Now to the broad, lit marsh, now to the dusk of the dike.
Soon, thro' their dew-wet frames, in the live keen freshness of
    morning,   *45*
Out of the teeth of the dawn blows back the awakening wind.
Then, as the blue day mounts, and the low-shot shafts of the
    sunlight
Glance from the tide to the shore, gossamers jewelled with dew
Sparkle and wave, where late sea-spoiling fathoms of drift-net
Myriad-meshed, uploomed sombrely over the land.   *50*

Well I remember it all. The salt, raw scent of the margin;
While, with men at the windlass, groaned each reel, and the net,
Surging in ponderous lengths, uprose and coiled in its station;
Then each man to his home,—well I remember it all!

Yet, as I sit and watch, this present peace of the landscape,—   *55*
Stranded boats, these reels empty and idle, the hush,
One grey hawk slow-wheeling above yon cluster of haystacks,—
More than the old-time stir this stillness welcomes me home.
Ah, the old-time stir, how once it stung me with rapture,—
Old-time sweetness, the winds freighted with honey and salt!   *60*
Yet will I stay my steps and not go down to the marshland,—
Muse and recall far off, rather remember than see,—
Lest on too close sight I miss the darling illusion,
Spy at their task even here the hands of chance and change.

                                                           —*1886*

Pauline Johnson (1861–1913) Born on the Six Nations Reserve near Brantford, Ontario, Johnson was the daughter of an Englishwoman and a Mohawk chief, a mixed heritage that defined her poetry and her performance career, which included extensive touring across Canada and internationally. Her collections include The White Wampum *(1895),* Canadian Born *(1903), and* Flint and Feather *(1912).*

Pauline Johnson
The Idlers

The sun's red pulses beat,
Full prodigal of heat,
Full lavish of its lustre unrepressed;
But we have drifted far
From where his kisses are,   5
And in this landward-lying shade we let our paddles rest.

The river, deep and still,
The maple-mantled hill,
The little yellow beach whereon we lie,
The puffs of heated breeze,   10
All sweetly whisper—These
Are days that only come in a Canadian July.

So, silently we two
Lounge in our still canoe,
Nor fate, nor fortune matters to us now: 15
So long as we alone
May call this dream our own,
The breeze may die, the sail may droop, we care not
     when or how.

Against the thwart, near by,
Inactively you lie,   20
And all too near my arm your temple bends.
Your indolently crude,
Abandoned attitude,
Is one of ease and art, in which a perfect languor blends.

Your costume, loose and light,   25
Leaves unconcealed your might
Of muscle, half-suspected, half defined;
And falling well aside,
Your vesture opens wide,
Above your splendid sunburnt throat that pulses unconfined.   30

With easy unreserve,
Across the gunwale's curve,
Your arm superb is lying, brown and bare;
Your hand just touches mine
With import firm and fine,   35
(I kiss the very wind that blows about your tumbled hair).

Ah! Dear, I am unwise
In echoing your eyes
Whene'er they leave their far-off gaze, and turn
To melt and blur my sight;   40
For every other light
Is servile to your cloud-grey eyes, wherein cloud shadows burn.

But once the silence breaks,
But once your ardour wakes
To words that humanize this lotus-land;°   45
So perfect and complete
Those burning words and sweet,
So perfect is the single kiss your lips lay on my hand.

The paddles lie disused,
The fitful breeze abused,   50
Has dropped to slumber, with no after-blow;
And hearts will pay the cost,
For you and I have lost
More than the homeward blowing wind that died an hour ago.

                                                                  —1890

---

45 lotus-land In Homer's *Odyssey* (9.82–87) veterans of the Trojan War become forgetful of the
homeward way after eating the fruit of the lotus, an episode also explored in Alfred Tennyson's poem
"The Lotos-Eaters."

Archibald Lampman (1861–1899) Born in Morpeth, Canada West, Lampman worked in the Post Office in Ottawa, and wrote several fine collections of poetry, including Among the Millet *(1888),* Lyrics of Earth *(1895), and* Alcyone *(1899), in which this grim vision of an urban dystopia appears.*

Archibald Lampman

The City of the End of Things°

Beside the pounding cataracts
Of midnight streams unknown to us
'Tis builded in the leafless tracts
And valleys huge of Tartarus.°
Lurid and lofty and vast it seems;   *5*
It hath no rounded name that rings,
But I have heard it called in dreams
The City of the End of Things.

Its roofs and iron towers have grown
None knoweth how high within the night,   *10*
But in its murky streets far down
A flaming terrible and bright
Shakes all the stalking shadows there,
Across the walls, across the floors,
And shifts upon the upper air   *15*
From out a thousand furnace doors;
And all the while an awful sound
Keeps roaring on continually,
And crashes in the ceaseless round
Of a gigantic harmony.   *20*
Through its grim depths re-echoing
And all its weary height of walls,

The City of the End of Things Originally the poem was titled "The Issue of Things That Are."
4 Tartarus in Greek mythology, the lowest part of Hades, or hell

With measured roar and iron ring,
The inhuman music lifts and falls.
Where no thing rests and no man is,   25
And only fire and night hold sway;
The beat, the thunder and the hiss
Cease not, and change not, night nor day.

And moving at unheard commands,
The abysses and vast fires between,   30
Flit figures that with clanking hands
Obey a hideous routine;
They are not flesh, they are not bone,
They see not with the human eye,
And from their iron lips is blown   35
A dreadful and monotonous cry;
And whoso of our mortal race
Should find that city unaware,
Lean Death would smite him face to face,
And blanch him with its venomed air: 40
Or caught by the terrific spell,
Each thread of memory snapt and cut,
His soul would shrivel and its shell
Go rattling like an empty nut.

It was not always so, but once,   45
In days that no man thinks upon,
Fair voices echoed from its stones,
The light above it leaped and shone:
Once there were multitudes of men,
That built that city in their pride,   50
Until its might was made, and then
They withered age by age and died.
But now of that prodigious race,
Three only in an iron tower,
Set like carved idols face to face,   55
Remain the masters of its power;
And at the city gate a fourth,
Gigantic and with dreadful eyes,

Sits looking toward the lightless north,
Beyond the reach of memories;   60
Fast rooted to the lurid floor,
A bulk that never moves a jot,
In his pale body dwells no more,
Or mind or soul,—an idiot!
But sometime in the end those three   65
Shall perish and their hands be still,
And with the master's touch shall flee
Their incommunicable skill.
A stillness absolute as death
Along the slacking wheels shall lie,   70
And, flagging at a single breath,
The fires shall moulder out and die.
The roar shall vanish at its height,
And over that tremendous town
The silence of eternal night   75
Shall gather close and settle down.
All its grim grandeur, tower and hall,
Shall be abandoned utterly,
And into rust and dust shall fall
From century to century;   80
Nor ever living thing shall grow,
Nor trunk of tree, nor blade of grass;
No drop shall fall, no wind shall blow,
Nor sound of any foot shall pass:
Alone of its accursèd state,   85
One thing the hand of Time shall spare,
For the grim Idiot at the gate
Is deathless and eternal there.

—*1895*

Duncan Campbell Scott (1862–1947) *Born in Ottawa, Scott began to write after meeting Archibald Lampman, producing seven volumes of poetry, including* The Magic House *(1893) and* The Green Cloister *(1935), as well as collections of short stories. Many of his poems reflect his experiences in his controversial work as an official with the Department of Indian Affairs.*

Duncan Campbell Scott

The Forsaken

I

Once in the winter
Out on a lake
In the heart of the north-land,
Far from the Fort
And far from the hunters,   5
A Chippewa woman
With her sick baby,
Crouched in the last hours
Of a great storm.
Frozen and hungry,   10
She fished through the ice
With a line of the twisted
Bark of the cedar,
And a rabbit-bone hook
Polished and barbed;   15
Fished with the bare hook
All through the day,
Fished and caught nothing;
While the young chieftain
Tugged at her breasts,   20
Or slept in the lacings
Of the warm *tikanagan.*°
All the lake-surface
Streamed with the hissing
Of millions of iceflakes,   25
Hurled by the wind;

22 **tikanagan** Cree word for a cradle board used to carry an infant

Behind her the round
Of a lonely island
Roared like a fire
With the voice of the storm   30
In the deeps of the cedars.
Valiant, unshaken,
She took of her own flesh,
Baited the fish-hook,
Drew in a grey-trout,   35
Drew in his fellows,
Heaped them beside her,
Dead in the snow.
Valiant, unshaken,
She faced the long distance,   40
Wolf-haunted and lonely,
Sure of her goal
And the life of her dear one;
Tramped for two days,
On the third in the morning,   45
Saw the strong bulk
Of the Fort by the river,
Saw the wood-smoke
Hang soft in the spruces,
Heard the keen yelp   50
Of the ravenous huskies
Fighting for whitefish:
Then she had rest.

           II

Years and years after,
When she was old and withered,   55
When her son was an old man
And his children filled with vigour,
They came in their northern tour on the verge of winter,
To an island in a lonely lake.
There one night they camped, and on the morrow   60
Gathered their kettles and birch-bark°

61 birch-bark waterproof birch-bark bowls or buckets

Their rabbit-skin robes and their mink-traps,
Launched their canoes and slunk away through the islands,
Left her alone forever,
Without a word of farewell,   65
Because she was old and useless,
Like a paddle broken and warped,
Or a pole that was splintered.
Then, without a sigh,
Valiant, unshaken,   70
She smoothed her dark locks under her kerchief,
Composed her shawl in state,
Then folded her hands ridged with sinews and corded
     with veins,
Folded them across her breasts spent with the nourishing
     of children,
Gazed at the sky past the tops of the cedars,   75
Saw two spangled nights arise out of the twilight,
Saw two days go by filled with the tranquil sunshine,
Saw, without pain, or dread, or even a moment of longing:
Then on the third great night there came thronging and
     thronging
Millions of snowflakes out of a windless cloud;   80
They covered her close with a beautiful crystal shroud,
Covered her deep and silent.
But in the frost of the dawn,
Up from the life below,
Rose a column of breath   85
Through a tiny cleft in the snow,
Fragile, delicately drawn,
Wavering with its own weakness,
In the wilderness a sign of the spirit,
Persisting still in the sight of the sun   90
Till day was done.
Then all light was gathered up by the hand of God and hid in His
     breast,
Then there was born a silence deeper than silence,
Then she had rest.

                                                        —*1905*

William Butler Yeats (1865–1939) is considered the greatest Irish poet and provides an important link between the late romantic era and early modernism. His early poetry, focusing on Irish legend and landscape, is regional in the best sense of the term, but his later work, with its prophetic tone and symbolist texture, moves on a larger stage. Yeats lived in London for many years and was at the centre of British literary life. He was awarded the Nobel Prize in 1923.

William Butler Yeats

Sailing to Byzantium°

1

That is no country for old men. The young
In one another's arms, birds in the trees
—Those dying generations—at their song,
The salmon-falls, the mackerel-crowded seas,
Fish, flesh, or fowl, commend all summer long   5
Whatever is begotten, born, and dies.
Caught in that sensual music all neglect
Monuments of unaging intellect.

2

An aged man is but a paltry thing,
A tattered coat upon a stick, unless   10
Soul clap its hands and sing, and louder sing
For every tatter in its mortal dress,
Nor is there singing school but studying
Monuments of its own magnificence;
And therefore I have sailed the seas and come   15
To the holy city of Byzantium.

3

O sages standing in God's holy fire
As in the gold mosaic of a wall,
Come from the holy fire, perne in a gyre,°
And be the singing-masters of my soul.   20

Byzantium Constantinople or Istanbul, capital of the Eastern Roman Empire   **19 perne in a gyre**
descend in a spiral; the gyre for Yeats was a private symbol of historical cycles

Consume my heart away; sick with desire
And fastened to a dying animal
It knows not what it is; and gather me
Into the artifice of eternity.

4

Once out of nature I shall never take   25
My bodily form from any natural thing,
But such a form as Grecian goldsmiths make
Of hammered gold and gold enameling
To keep a drowsy Emperor awake;
Or set upon a golden bough to sing   30
To lords and ladies of Byzantium
Of what is past, or passing, or to come.

—*1927*

The Second Coming

Turning and turning in the widening gyre°
The falcon cannot hear the falconer;
Things fall apart; the center cannot hold;
Mere anarchy is loosed upon the world,
The blood-dimmed tide is loosed, and everywhere   5
The ceremony of innocence is drowned;
The best lack all conviction, while the worst
Are full of passionate intensity.

Surely some revelation is at hand;
Surely the Second Coming is at hand.   10
The Second Coming! Hardly are those words out
When a vast image out of *Spiritus Mundi*°
Troubles my sight: somewhere in the sands of the desert
A shape with lion body and the head of a man,
A gaze blank and pitiless as the sun,   15
Is moving its slow thighs, while all about it

1 gyre see note to "Sailing to Byzantium"   **12 Spiritus Mundi** World-Spirit

Reel shadows of the indignant desert birds.
The darkness drops again; but now I know
That twenty centuries of stony sleep
Were vexed to nightmare by a rocking cradle,   *20*
And what rough beast, its hour come round at last,
Slouches towards Bethlehem to be born?

—*1921*

Sophia Almon Hensley (1866–1946) Born in Bridgetown, Nova Scotia, Hensley was encouraged by Charles G. D. Roberts to develop as a poet. She published five collections of poetry, including The Way of a Woman *(1928), in which this World War I poem, first published in 1918, appeared, as well as a novel and non-fiction studies of social issues affecting women.*

Sophia Almon Hensley
Courage°

Leave me alone here, proudly, with my dead,
    Ye mothers of brave sons adventurous;
He who once prayed: "If it be possible°
    Let this cup pass," will arbitrate for us.
Your boy with iron nerves and careless smile   5
    Marched gaily by, and dreamed of glory's goal;
Mine had blanched cheek, straight mouth, and close-
        gripped hands,
    And prayed that somehow he might save his soul.
I do not grudge your ribbon or your cross,°
    The price of these my soldier, too, has paid;   10
I hug a prouder knowledge to my heart,
    The mother of the boy who was afraid!

He was a tender child with nerves so keen
    They doubled pain and magnified the sad,

Courage This poem was first published under the title "Somewhere in France."   **3 If it be possible** the prayer of Jesus in the Garden of Gethsemane on the night before he was crucified (Matthew 26:39)   **9 ribbon or your cross** military medals for courage, such as the Victoria Cross

He hated cruelty and things obscene,   15
   And in all high and holy things was glad.
And so he gave what others could not give,
   The one supremest sacrifice he made,

A thing your brave boy could not understand;
   He gave his all because he was afraid.   20
Like a machine he fed the shining shell
   Into a hungry maw from sun to sun;
And when at last the hour struck, and he fell,
   He smiled, and murmured: "Thank God, it is done."
Ye glory well, ye mothers of brave sons   25
   Eager and sinewy, in the part they played;
And England will remember, and repay,
   And history will see their names arrayed.
But God looked down upon my soldier-boy
   Who set his teeth, and did his bit, and prayed,   30
And understands why I am proud to be
   The mother of the boy who was afraid!

—*1918*

---

*Edwin Arlington Robinson (1869–1935) wrote many poems set in "Tilbury,"
a re-creation of his hometown of Gardiner, Maine. These poems continue to present
readers with a memorable cast of eccentric characters who somehow manifest universal human desires. Robinson languished in poverty and obscurity for many years
before his reputation began to flourish as a result of the interest taken in his work by
President Theodore Roosevelt, who obtained a government job for Robinson and wrote
a favourable review of one of his books.*

Edwin Arlington Robinson

Richard Cory

Whenever Richard Cory went down town,
We people on the pavement looked at him:
He was a gentleman from sole to crown,
Clean favored, and imperially slim.

And he was always quietly arrayed,   5
And he was always human when he talked;
But still he fluttered pulses when he said,
"Good-morning," and he glittered when he walked.

And he was rich—yes, richer than a king—
And admirably schooled in every grace: 10
In fine, we thought that he was everything
To make us wish that we were in his place.

So on we worked, and waited for the light,
And went without the meat, and cursed the bread;
And Richard Cory, one calm summer night,   15
Went home and put a bullet through his head.

—*1896*

Paul Laurence Dunbar (1872–1906), *a native of Dayton, Ohio, was one of the first Black poets to make a mark in American literature. Many of his dialect poems reflect a sentimentalized view of life in the South, which he did not know directly. However, he was also capable of powerful expressions of racial protest. The last line of his poem "Sympathy" appears as the title of Maya Angelou's autobiography.*

Paul Laurence Dunbar
Sympathy

I know what the caged bird feels, alas!
    When the sun is bright on the upland slopes;
When the wind stirs soft through the springing grass,
And the river flows like a stream of glass;
    When the first bird sings and the first bud opens,   5
And the faint perfume from its chalice steals—
I know what the caged bird feels!

I know why the caged bird beats his wing
    Till its blood is red on the cruel bars;
For he must fly back to his perch and cling   10

When he fain would be on the bough a-swing;
   And a pain still throbs in the old, old scars
And they pulse again with a keener sting—
I know why he beats his wing!

I know why the caged bird sings, ah me,   *15*
   When his wing is bruised and his bosom sore,—
When he beats his bars and he would be free;
It is not a carol of joy or glee,
   But a prayer that he sends from his heart's deep core,
But a plea, that upward to Heaven he flings—   *20*
I know why the caged bird sings!

—1893

Robert Frost (1874–1963), during the second half of his long life, was a public figure who attained a popularity unmatched by any American poet of the last century. His reading at the inauguration of John F. Kennedy in 1961 capped an impressive career that included four Pulitzer Prizes. Unattracted by the more exotic aspects of modernism, Frost nevertheless remains a poet who speaks eloquently to contemporary uncertainties about humanity's place in a universe that does not seem to care much for its existence. While Frost is rarely directly an autobiographical poet, his work always bears the stamp of his powerful personality and identification with the New England landscape.

Robert Frost

Neither Out Far nor In Deep

The people along the sand
All turn and look one way.
They turn their back on the land.
They look at the sea all day.

As long as it takes to pass   *5*
A ship keeps raising its hull;

The wetter ground like glass
Reflects a standing gull.

The land may vary more;
But wherever the truth may be—   *10*
The water comes ashore,
And the people look at the sea.

They cannot look out far.
They cannot look in deep.
But when was that ever a bar   *15*
To any watch they keep?

—1936

Stopping by Woods on a Snowy Evening

Whose woods these are I think I know.
His house is in the village though;
He will not see me stopping here
To watch his woods fill up with snow.

My little horse must think it queer   *5*
To stop without a farmhouse near
Between the woods and frozen lake
The darkest evening of the year.

He gives his harness bells a shake
To ask if there is some mistake.   *10*
The only other sound's the sweep
Of easy wind and downy flake.

The woods are lovely, dark and deep,
But I have promises to keep,
And miles to go before I sleep,   *15*
And miles to go before I sleep.

—1923

Katherine Hale (1878–1956) Born Amelia Beers Warnock in Galt, Ontario, Hale published widely under her pen name. She wrote six collections of poetry, including Morning in the West *(1923) and* The Island and Other Poems *(1934), a book about Isabella Valancy Crawford, and several prose works on Canadian history.*

Katherine Hale

This Oblivion

One dear to him is moving towards the river;
Her broad-brimmed hat and dress of faded blue,
Her sketch book under a protecting arm.
Slowly she disappears, hid by the grasses,
Fading in light of the dim, blue-grey day.   5
Ah, so he faded as his tie with earth
Was loosed, and he slipped down
Hidden, as she is now. But the dim green
That floats and weaves above his secret place
Will not return him, not for any grace   10
Of wildest supplication. Yet she comes,
Risen from the grasses, back along the road,
Her little disappearance traced in form,
Her morning told in colour and in line.
Self-tranced she walks into the world again   15
Renewed by this oblivion.
But, oh, for him, bound in a blinding sleep,
What recompense?
I see no recompense that such negation brings
Or—is there song that endless silence sings   20
Faintly, below these grasses strong and deep?

—1950

Émile Nelligan (1879–1941) *Influenced by the symbolist poets of France, the Montreal-born Nelligan made a significant contribution to poetry in Quebec, though most of his poems were written in a three-year period before 1899, when a mental breakdown led to institutionalization for the remainder of his life. The first collection of his poetry,* Émile Nelligan et son oeuvre, *was published in 1903.*

Émile Nelligan
Evening Bells

Some evenings I roamed the moors, beyond the bounds
Of my home village, lost in the great rosy hills'
Calm pride, and down the wind the Angels shook the bells
Of churches in long waves of melancholy sound.

And in a shepherd-poet's dreamy, romantic mood   5
In the perfume of roses I used to breathe their prayer,
While in the dying gold my flocks of mania
Aimlessly wandered through forests of sandalwood.

Thus in this life where I follow my lonely path
I have kept in my mind a corner of old earth,   10
That evening countryside whose glow I see again;

While you, my heart, within your private reach of moor,
Recall the long-ago angelus, voiceless, faint:
That winging of bronze birds flown from the chapel towers.

—1903

Translated by P. F. Widdows.

Wallace Stevens (1879–1955) was a lawyer specializing in surety bonds and rose to be a vice-president of the Hartford Accident and Indemnity Company. His poetry was collected for the first time in Harmonium when he was forty-five, and while he published widely during his lifetime, his poetry was only slowly recognized as the work of a major modernist whose originality has not been surpassed. Stevens's idea of poetry as a force taking the place of religion has had a profound influence on poets and critics of this century.

Wallace Stevens

Thirteen Ways of Looking at a Blackbird

I

Among twenty snowy mountains,
The only moving thing
Was the eye of the blackbird.

II

I was of three minds,
Like a tree   5
In which there are three blackbirds.

III

The blackbird whirled in the autumn winds.
It was a small part of the pantomime.

IV

A man and a woman
Are one.   10
A man and a woman and a blackbird
Are one.

V

I do not know which to prefer,
The beauty of inflections
Or the beauty of innuendoes,   15
The blackbird whistling
Or just after.

VI

Icicles filled the long window
With barbaric glass.
The shadow of the blackbird   20
Crossed it, to and fro.
The mood
Traced in the shadow
An indecipherable cause.

VII

O thin men of Haddam,°   25
Why do you imagine golden birds?
Do you not see how the blackbird
Walks around the feet
Of the women about you?

VIII

I know noble accents   30
And lucid, inescapable rhythms;
But I know, too,
That the blackbird is involved
In what I know.

IX

When the blackbird flew out of sight,   35
It marked the edge
Of one of many circles.

X

At the sight of blackbirds
Flying in a green light,
Even the bawds of euphony   40
Would cry out sharply.

XI

He rode over Connecticut
In a glass coach.
Once, a fear pierced him,
In that he mistook   45

25 Haddam town in Connecticut

The shadow of his equipage
For blackbirds.

XII
The river is moving.
The blackbird must be flying.

XIII
It was evening all afternoon.   *50*
It was snowing
And it was going to snow.
The blackbird sat
In the cedar-limbs.

—1923

The Motive for Metaphor

You like it under the trees in autumn,
Because everything is half dead.
The wind moves like a cripple among the leaves
And repeats words without meaning.

In the same way, you were happy in spring,   *5*
With the half colors of quarter-things,
The slightly brighter sky, the melting clouds,
The single bird, the obscure moon—

The obscure moon lighting an obscure world
Of things that would never be quite expressed,   *10*
Where you yourself were never quite yourself
And did not want nor have to be,

Desiring the exhilarations of changes:
The motive for metaphor, shrinking from
The weight of primary noon,   *15*
The A B C of being,

The ruddy temper, the hammer
Of red and blue, the hard sound—
Steel against intimation—the sharp flash,
The vital, arrogant, fatal, dominant X.   *20*

                                                                          —1947

E. J. Pratt (1882–1964) *Born in Western Bay, Newfoundland, Pratt went on to teach at Victoria College, University of Toronto. The publication of his second volume,* Newfoundland Verse *(1923), marked a new direction in Canadian poetry. Pratt also published several long poems that deal with pivotal events in Canadian history, including* Brébeuf and His Brethren *(1940) and* Towards the Last Spike *(1952).*

E. J. Pratt
From Stone to Steel

From stone to bronze, from bronze to steel
Along the road-dust of the sun,
Two revolutions of the wheel
From Java to Geneva° run.

The snarl Neanderthal is worn   *5*
Close to the smiling Aryan lips,
The civil polish of the horn
Gleams from our praying finger tips.

The evolution of desire
Has but matured a toxic wine,   *10*
Drunk long before its heady fire
Reddened Euphrates or the Rhine.

Between the temple and the cave
The boundary lies tissue-thin:
The yearlings still the altars crave   *15*
As satisfaction for a sin.

---

4 Java to Geneva Java was then the site of the discovery of the oldest human fossils. Geneva is the Swiss city associated with peace and humane conduct during war.

The road goes up, the road goes down—
Let Java or Geneva be—
But whether to the cross or crown,
The path lies through Gethsemane.° 20

—*1932*

William Carlos Williams (1883–1963), like his friend Wallace Stevens, followed an unconventional career for a poet, working until his death as a pediatrician in Rutherford, New Jersey. Williams is modern poetry's greatest proponent of the American idiom. His plain-spoken poems have been more widely imitated than those of any other American poet of the twentieth century, perhaps because he represents a homegrown modernist alternative to the intellectualized Europeanism of T. S. Eliot and Ezra Pound (a friend of his from college days). In his later years, Williams assisted many younger poets, among them Allen Ginsberg, for whose controversial book Howl *he wrote an introduction.*

William Carlos Williams
The Red Wheelbarrow

so much depends
upon

a red wheel
barrow

glazed with rain 5
water

beside the white
chickens.

—*1923*

---

20 Gethsemane the garden where Christ prayed before his crucifixion, asking to be released from the suffering to come

To a Poor Old Woman

munching a plum on
the street a paper bag
of them in her hand

They taste good to her
They taste good   5
to her. They taste
good to her

You can see it by
the way she gives herself
to the one half   10
sucked out in her hand

Comforted
a solace of ripe plums
seeming to fill the air
They taste good to her   15

—1935

Ezra Pound (1885–1972) *was the greatest international proponent of modern poetry. Born in Idaho and reared in Philadelphia, he emigrated to England in 1909, where he befriended Yeats, promoted the early work of Frost, and discovered Eliot. Pound's early promotion of the imagist movement assisted a number of important poetic principles and reputations, including those of H. D. (Hilda Doolittle) and, later, William Carlos Williams. Pound's support of Mussolini during World War II, expressed in controversial radio broadcasts, caused him to be held for over a decade after the war as a mental patient in the United States, after which he returned to Italy for the final years of his long and controversial life.*

Ezra Pound
In a Station of the Metro

The apparition of these faces in the crowd;
Petals on a wet, black bough.

—1916

The River-Merchant's Wife: A Letter°

While my hair was still cut straight across my forehead
I played about the front gate, pulling flowers.
You came by on bamboo stilts, playing horse,
You walked about my seat, playing with blue plums.
And we went on living in the village of Chokan: 5
Two small people, without dislike or suspicion.
At fourteen I married My Lord you.
I never laughed, being bashful.
Lowering my head, I looked at the wall.
Called to, a thousand times, I never looked back.   10

At fifteen I stopped scowling,
I desired my dust to be mingled with yours
Forever and forever and forever.
Why should I climb the lookout?

At sixteen you departed,   15
You went into far Ku-to-yen, by the river of swirling eddies,
And you have been gone five months.
The monkeys make sorrowful noise overhead.

You dragged your feet when you went out.
By the gate now, the moss is grown, the different mosses,   20
Too deep to clear them away!
The leaves fall early this autumn, in wind.
The paired butterflies are already yellow with August
Over the grass in the West garden;
They hurt me. I grow older.   25
If you are coming down through the narrows of the river Kiang,
Please let me know beforehand,
And I will come out to meet you
    As far as Cho-Fu-Sa.

—1915

The River-Merchant's Wife: A Letter imitation of a poem by Li-Po (A.D. 701–762)

H. D. (Hilda Doolittle) (1886–1961) was born in Bethlehem, Pennsylvania. Hilda Doolittle was a college friend of both William Carlos Williams and Ezra Pound and moved to Europe permanently in 1911. With her husband, Richard Aldington, H. D. was an important member of the imagist group promoted by Pound.

H. D. (Hilda Doolittle)

Helen°

All Greece hates
the still eyes in the white face,
the lustre as of olives
where she stands,
and the white hands.   5

All Greece reviles
the wan face when she smiles,
hating it deeper still
when it grows wan and white,
remembering past enchantments   10
and past ills.

Greece sees unmoved,
God's daughter, born of love,
the beauty of cool feet
and slenderest knees,   15
could love indeed the maid,
only if she were laid,
white ash amid funereal cypresses.

                                                                  —1924

Helen The beautiful daughter of Leda and Zeus, who was given to Paris, the Prince of Troy, by Aphrodite. Her husband, the Greek leader Menelaus, waged the Trojan War to bring her back.

Marianne Moore (1887–1972) called her own work poetry—unconventional and marked with the stamp of a rare personality—because, as she put it, there was no other category for it. For four years she was editor of the Dial, one of the chief modernist periodicals. Moore's wide range of reference, which can leap from the commonplace to the wondrous within a single poem, reflects her unique set of personal interests—which range from exotic natural species to baseball.

Marianne Moore

The Fish

wade
through black jade.
    Of the crow-blue mussel-shells, one keeps
    adjusting the ash-heaps;
        opening and shutting itself like   5

an
injured fan.
    The barnacles which encrust the side
    of the wave, cannot hide
        there for the submerged shafts of the   10

sun,
split like spun
    glass, move themselves with spotlight swiftness
    into the crevices—
        in and out, illuminating   15

the
turquoise sea
    of bodies. The water drives a wedge
    of iron through the iron edge
        of the cliff; whereupon the stars,   20

pink
rice-grains, ink-
    bespattered jelly-fish, crabs like green
    lilies, and submarine
        toadstools, slide each on the other.   25

All
external
marks of abuse are present on this
defiant edifice—
all the physical features of   *30*

ac-
cident—lack
of cornice, dynamite grooves, burns, and
hatchet strokes, these things stand
out on it; the chasm-side is   *35*

dead.
Repeated
evidence has proved that it can live
on what can not revive
its youth. The sea grows old in it.

—1921

T. S. Eliot (1888–1965) *was the author of* The Waste Land, *one of the most famous and difficult modernist poems, and became an international figure. Born in St. Louis and educated at Harvard, he moved to London in 1914, where he remained for the rest of his life, becoming a British subject in 1927. This chief prophet of modern despair turned to the Church of England in later life and wrote successful dramas on religious themes. As a critic and influential editor, Eliot dominated poetic taste in England and America for over twenty-five years. He was awarded the Nobel Prize in 1948.*

T. S. Eliot
Journey of the Magi°

'A cold coming we had of it,
Just the worst time of the year
For a journey, and such a long journey:
The ways deep and the weather sharp,
The very dead of winter.'°   *5*

Magi Wise Men mentioned in Matthew 2:1–2   **1–5 'A cold . . . winter'** The quotation marks indicated Eliot's source, a sermon by Lancelot Andrewes (1555–1626).

And the camels galled, sore-footed, refractory,
Lying down in the melting snow.
There were times we regretted
The summer palaces on slopes, the terraces,
And the silken girls bringing sherbet.   *10*
Then the camel men cursing and grumbling
And running away, and wanting their liquor and women,
And the night-fires going out, and the lack of shelters,
And the cities hostile and the towns unfriendly
And the villages dirty and charging high prices: *15*
A hard time we had of it.
At the end we preferred to travel all night,
Sleeping in snatches,
With the voices singing in our ears, saying
That this was all folly.   *20*

Then at dawn we came down to a temperate valley,
Wet, below the snow line, smelling of vegetation;
With a running stream and a water-mill beating the darkness,
And three trees on the low sky.
And an old white horse galloped away in the meadow.   *25*
Then we came to a tavern with vine-leaves over the lintel,
Six hands at an open door dicing for pieces of silver,
And feet kicking the empty wine-skins.
But there was no information, and so we continued
And arrived at evening, not a moment too soon   *30*
Finding the place; it was (you may say) satisfactory.

All this was a long time ago, I remember,
And I would do it again, but set down
This° set down
This: were we led all that way for   *35*
Birth or Death? There was a Birth, certainly,
We had evidence and no doubt. I had seen birth and death,
But had thought they were different; this Birth was
Hard and bitter agony for us, like Death, our death.

33–34 set down . . . This The Magus is dictating his memoirs to a scribe.

We returned to our places, these Kingdoms,   *40*
But no longer at ease here, in the old dispensation,°
With an alien people clutching their gods.
I should be glad of another death.

—1927

The Love Song of
J. Alfred Prufrock

S'io credesse che mia risposta fosse
A persona che mai tornasse al mondo,
Questa fiamma staria senza più scosse.
Ma perciocche giammai di questo fondo
Non tornò vivo alcun, s'i'odo il vero,
Senza tema d'infamia ti rispondo.°

Let us go then, you° and I,
When the evening is spread out against the sky
Like a patient etherised upon a table;
Let us go, through certain half-deserted streets,
The muttering retreats   *5*
Of restless nights in one-night cheap hotels
And sawdust restaurants with oyster-shells:
Streets that follow like a tedious argument
Of insidious intent
To lead you to an overwhelming question . . .   *10*
Oh, do not ask, "What is it?"
Let us go and make our visit.

In the room the women come and go
Talking of Michelangelo.°

---

41 old dispensation world before the birth of Christ
S'io credesse . . . rispondo From Dante's *Inferno* (Canto 27). The speaker is Guido da Montefeltro:
"If I thought I spoke to someone who would return to the world, this flame would tremble no longer.
But, if what I hear is true, since no one has ever returned alive from this place I can answer you with-
out fear of infamy."   **1 you** Eliot said that the auditor of the poem was a male friend of Prufrock.
14 Michelangelo Italian painter and sculptor (1475–1564)

The yellow fog that rubs its back upon the window-panes,   *15*
The yellow smoke that rubs its muzzle on the window-panes,
Licked its tongue into the corners of the evening,
Lingered upon the pools that stand in drains,
Let fall upon its back the soot that falls from chimneys,
Slipped by the terrace, made a sudden leap,   *20*
And seeing that it was a soft October night,
Curled once about the house, and fell asleep.

And indeed there will be time
For the yellow smoke that slides along the street,
Rubbing its back upon the window-panes;   *25*
There will be time, there will be time
To prepare a face to meet the faces that you meet;
There will be time to murder and create,
And time for all the works and days of hands
That lift and drop a question on your plate: *30*
Time for you and time for me,
And time yet for a hundred indecisions,
And for a hundred visions and revisions,
Before the taking of a toast and tea.

In the room the women come and go   *35*
Talking of Michelangelo.

And indeed there will be time
To wonder, "Do I dare?" and, "Do I dare?"—
Time to turn back and descend the stair,
With a bald spot in the middle of my hair—   *40*
(They will say: "How his hair is growing thin!")
My morning coat, my collar mounting firmly to the chin,
My necktie rich and modest, but asserted by a simple pin—
(They will say: "But how his arms and legs are thin!")
Do I dare   *45*
Disturb the universe?
In a minute there is time
For decisions and revisions which a minute will reverse.

For I have known them all already, known them all:
Have known the evenings, mornings, afternoons,   50
I have measured out my life with coffee spoons;
I know the voices dying with a dying fall
Beneath the music from a farther room.
      So how should I presume?

And I have known the eyes already, known them all—   55
The eyes that fix you in a formulated phrase,
And when I am formulated, sprawling on a pin,
When I am pinned and wriggling on the wall,
Then how should I begin
To spit out all the butt-ends of my days and ways?   60
      And how should I presume?

And I have known the arms already, known them all—
Arms that are braceleted and white and bare
(But in the lamplight, downed with light brown hair!)
Is it perfume from a dress   65
That makes me so digress?
Arms that lie along a table, or wrap about a shawl.
    And should I then presume?
    And how should I begin?

    . . . . .

Shall I say, I have gone at dusk through narrow streets,   70
And watched the smoke that rises from the pipes
Of lonely men in shirtsleeves, leaning out of windows? . . .

I should have been a pair of ragged claws
Scuttling across the floors of silent seas.

    . . . . .

And the afternoon, the evening, sleeps so peacefully!   75
Smoothed by long fingers,
Asleep . . . tired . . . or it malingers,
Stretched on the floor, here beside you and me.
Should I, after tea and cakes and ices,
Have the strength to force the moment to its crisis?   80
But though I have wept and fasted, wept and prayed,

Though I have seen my head (grown slightly bald) brought in
    upon a platter,
I am no prophet°—and here's no great matter;
I have seen the moment of my greatness flicker,
And I have seen the eternal Footman hold my coat, and
    snicker,   *85*
    And in short, I was afraid.

And would it have been worth it, after all,
After the cups, the marmalade, the tea,
Among the porcelain, among some talk of you and me,
Would it have been worth while,   *90*
To have bitten off the matter with a smile,
To have squeezed the universe into a ball
To roll it towards some overwhelming question,
To say: "I am Lazarus,° come from the dead,
Come back to tell you all, I shall tell you all"—   *95*
If one, settling a pillow by her head,
    Should say: "That is not what I meant at all;
    That is not it, at all."

And would it have been worth it, after all,
Would it have been worth while,   *100*
After the sunsets and the dooryards and the sprinkled streets,
After the novels, after the teacups, after the skirts that trail
    along the floor—
And this, and so much more?—
It is impossible to say just what I mean!
But as if a magic lantern° threw the nerves in patterns on
    a screen: *105*
Would it have been worth while
If one, settling a pillow or throwing off a shawl,
And turning toward the window, should say:
    "That is not it at all,
    That is not what I meant, at all."   *110*

      . . . . .

82–83 my head . . . no prophet allusion to John the Baptist   **94 Lazarus** raised from the dead in
John 11:1–44   **105 magic lantern** old-fashioned slide projector

No! I am not Prince Hamlet, nor was meant to be;
Am an attendant lord, one that will do
To swell a progress, start a scene or two,
Advise the prince; no doubt, an easy tool,
Deferential, glad to be of use,   115
Politic, cautious, and meticulous;
Full of high sentence, but a bit obtuse;
At times, indeed, almost ridiculous—
Almost, at times, the Fool.°

I grow old . . . I grow old . . .   120
I shall wear the bottoms of my trousers rolled.

Shall I part my hair behind? Do I dare to eat a peach?
I shall wear white flannel trousers, and walk upon the beach.
I have heard the mermaids singing, each to each.

I do not think that they will sing to me.   125

I have seen them riding seaward on the waves
Combing the white hair of the waves blown back
When the wind blows the water white and black.
We have lingered in the chambers of the sea
By sea-girls wreathed with seaweed red and brown   130
Till human voices wake us, and we drown.

—*1917*

111–119 not Prince Hamlet . . . the Fool The allusion is probably to Polonius, a character in
Hamlet.

Edna St. Vincent Millay (1892–1950) was extremely popular in the 1920s, when her sonnets seemed the ultimate expression of the liberated sexuality of what was then called the New Woman. Neglected for many years, her poems have recently generated renewed interest, and it seems likely that she will eventually regain her status as one of the most important female poets of the twentieth century.

Edna St. Vincent Millay

What Lips My Lips Have Kissed, and Where, and Why

What lips my lips have kissed, and where, and why,
I have forgotten, and what arms have lain
Under my head till morning; but the rain
Is full of ghosts tonight, that tap and sigh
Upon the glass and listen for reply,   *5*
And in my heart there stirs a quiet pain
For unremembered lads that not again
Will turn to me at midnight with a cry.
Thus in the winter stands the lonely tree,
Nor knows what birds have vanished one by one,   *10*
Yet knows its boughs more silent than before:
I cannot say what loves have come and gone,
I only know that summer sang in me
A little while, that in me sings no more.

—*1923*

Wilfred Owen (1893–1918) was killed in the trenches only a few days before the armistice that ended World War I. Owen showed more promise than any other English poet of his generation. A decorated officer whose nerves broke down after exposure to battle, he met Siegfried Sassoon at Craiglockhart military hospital. His work was posthumously collected by his friend. A novel by Pat Barker, Regeneration *(also made into a film), deals with their poetic and personal relationship.*

Wilfred Owen

Dulce et Decorum Est°

Bent double, like old beggars under sacks,
Knock-kneed, coughing like hags, we cursed through sludge,
Till on the haunting flares we turned our backs
And towards our distant rest began to trudge.
Men marched asleep. Many had lost their boots   5
But limped on, blood-shod. All went lame; all blind;
Drunk with fatigue; deaf even to the hoots
Of tired, outstripped Five-Nines° that dropped behind.

Gas! Gas! Quick, boys!—An ecstasy of fumbling
Fitting the clumsy helmets just in time;   10
But someone still was yelling out and stumbling
And flound'ring like a man in fire or lime . . .
Dim, through the misty panes and thick green light,°
As under a green sea, I saw him drowning.

In all my dreams, before my helpless sight,   15
He plunges at me, guttering, choking, drowning.

If in some smothering dreams you too could pace
Behind the wagon that we flung him in,
And watch the white eyes writhing in his face,
His hanging face, like a devil's sick of sin;   20
If you could hear, at every jolt, the blood
Come gargling from the froth-corrupted lungs,

Dulce et Decorum Est (pro patria mori) from the Roman poet Horace: "It is sweet and proper to die for one's country"   **8 Five-Nines** German artillery shells (59 mm)   **13 misty panes and thick green light** i.e., through the gas mask

Obscene as cancer, bitter as the cud
Of vile, incurable sores on innocent tongues,—
My friend,° you would not tell with such high zest   *25*
To children ardent for some desperate glory,
The old Lie: Dulce et decorum est
Pro patria mori.

                                                                    —1920

Disabled

He sat in a wheeled chair, waiting for dark,
And shivered in his ghastly suit of grey,
Legless, sewn short at elbow. Through the park
Voices of boys rang saddening like a hymn,
Voices of play and pleasure after day,   *5*
Till gathering sleep had mothered them from him.

About this time Town used to swing so gay
When glow-lamps budded in the light blue trees,
And girls glanced lovelier as the air grew dim,—
In the old times, before he threw away his knees.   *10*
Now he will never feel again how slim
Girls' waists are, or how warm their subtle hands;
All of them touch him like some queer disease.

There was an artist silly for his face,
For it was younger than his youth, last year.   *15*
Now, he is old; his back will never brace;
He's lost his color very far from here,
Poured it down shell-holes till the veins ran dry,
And half his lifetime lapsed in the hot race,
And leap of purple spurted from his thigh.   *20*

25 my friend The poem was originally addressed to Jessie Pope, a writer of patriotic verse.

One time he liked a blood-smear down his leg,
After the matches,° carried shoulder-high
It was after football, when he'd drunk a peg,°
He thought he'd better join.—He wonders why.
Someone had said he'd look a god in kilts,   25
That's why; and may be, too, to please his Meg;
Aye, that was it, to please the giddy jilts°
He asked to join. He didn't have to beg;
Smiling they wrote his lie; aged nineteen years.

Germans he scarcely thought of; all their guilt,   30
And Austria's, did not move him. And no fears
Of Fear came yet. He thought of jeweled hilts
For daggers in plaid socks; of smart salutes;
And care of arms; and leave; and pay arrears;
Esprit de corps; and hints for young recruits.   35
And soon, he was drafted out with drums and cheers.

Some cheered him home, but not as crowds cheer Goal.
Only a solemn man who brought him fruits
Thanked him; and then inquired about his soul.
Now, he will spend a few sick years in Institutes,   40
And do what things the rules consider wise,
And take whatever pity they may dole.
Tonight he noticed how the women's eyes
Passed from him to the strong men that were whole.
How cold and late it is! Why don't they come   45
And put him into bed? Why don't they come?

—*1917*

---

22 **matches** soccer, called "football" in England   23 **peg** drink, usually brandy and soda
27 **jilts** contemptuous term for girls or young women

Bertolt Brecht (1898–1956) is the German poet and playwright best known for his epic drama using "alienation effects" that reminded audiences they were viewing theatre and not reality. Born in Bavaria, he studied medicine and served in an army hospital in 1918. His greatest plays were written while in exile from Nazi Germany, first in Scandinavia (1933–1941) and then in the United States (1941–1947). Arguing that "all great poems have the quality of documents," he wrote over 1500 poems about the public and private upheavals of the tumultuous first half of the twentieth century.

Bertolt Brecht
The God of War

I saw the old god of war stand in a bog between chasm and
   rockface.
He smelled of free beer and carbolic and showed his testicles to
adolescents, for he had been rejuvenated by several professors.
In a hoarse wolfish voice he declared his love for everything
young. Nearby stood a pregnant woman, trembling.   *5*

   And without shame he talked on and presented himself as
a great one for order. And he described how everywhere he
put barns in order, by emptying them.
And as one throws crumbs to sparrows, he fed poor people
with crusts of bread which he had taken away from poor   *10*
people.

   His voice was now loud, now soft, but always hoarse.

   In a loud voice he spoke of great times to come, and in a soft voice
he taught the women how to cook crows and sea-gulls. Meanwhile
his back was unquiet, and he kept looking round, as though   *15*
afraid of being stabbed.

   And every five minutes he assured his public that he would
take up very little of their time.

—1939

Translated by Michael Hamburger.

Dorothy Parker (1893–1967), *as a humorist, journalist, and poet, was for many years associated with* The New Yorker *as both author and critic. Along with Robert Benchley, James Thurber, and E. B. White, she epitomizes the hard-edged humour that made that magazine unique among American periodicals.*

Dorothy Parker

One Perfect Rose

A single flow'r he sent me, since we met.
All tenderly his messenger he chose;
Deep-hearted, pure, with scented dew still wet—
One perfect rose.

I knew the language of the floweret;   5
"My fragile leaves," it said, "his heart enclose."
Love long has taken for his amulet
One perfect rose.

Why is it no one sent me yet
One perfect limousine, do you suppose?   10
Ah no, it's always just my luck to get
One perfect rose.

                                                       —1926

e. e. cummings (1894–1962) was the son of a Harvard professor and Unitarian clergyman. Edward Estlin Cummings served as a volunteer ambulance driver in France during World War I. Cummings's experimentation with the typographical aspects of poetry reveals his serious interest in cubist painting, which he studied in Paris in the 1920s. A brilliant satirist, he also excelled as a writer of lyrical poems whose unusual appearance and idiosyncratic grammar, spelling, and punctuation often overshadow their traditional themes.

e. e. cummings

[pity this busy monster,manunkind]

pity this busy monster,manunkind,

not. Progress is a comfortable disease:
your victim (death and life safely beyond)

plays with the bigness of his littleness
—electrons° deify one razorblade   5
into a mountainrange; lenses extend

unwish through curving wherewhen till unwish
returns on its unself.
                           A world of made
is not a world of born—pity poor flesh

and trees,poor stars and stones,but never this   10
fine specimen of hypermagical

ultraomnipotence. We doctors know

a hopeless case if—listen: there's a hell
of a good universe next door; let's go

—1944

---

5 electrons in an electron microscope

[l(a]

l(a

le
af
fa

ll

s)
one
l

iness

—1958

F. R. Scott (1899–1985) was born in Quebec City, settling eventually in Montreal, where he was a professor at McGill's faculty of law. Influential in politics, poetry, and translation, he helped to shape Canadian culture while exposing it to satire. The Collected Poems of F. R. Scott *(1981) was awarded the Governor General's Award.*

F. R. Scott
Laurentian Shield

Hidden in wonder and snow, or sudden with summer,
This land stares at the sun in a huge silence
Endlessly repeating something we cannot hear.
Inarticulate, arctic,
Not written on by history, empty as paper,   5
It leans away from the world with songs in its lakes
Older than love, and lost in the miles.

This waiting is wanting.
It will choose its language

When it has chosen its technic,   *10*
A tongue to shape the vowels of its productivity.

A language of flesh and of roses.°

Now there are pre-words,
Cabin syllables,
Nouns of settlement   *15*
Slowly forming, with steel syntax,
The long sentence of its exploitation.

The first cry was the hunter, hungry for fur,
And the digger for gold, nomad, no-man, a particle;
Then the bold commands of monopoly, big with machines,   *20*
Carving their kingdoms out of the public wealth;
And now the drone of the plane, scouting the ice,
Fills all the emptiness with neighbourhood
And links our future over the vanished pole.

But a deeper note is sounding, heard in the mines,   *25*
The scattered camps and the mills, a language of life,
And what will be written in the full culture of occupation
Will come, presently, tomorrow,
From millions whose hands can turn this rock into children.

                                                         —1954

12 *A language of flesh and of roses* a line from British poet Stephen Spender

A. J. M. Smith (1902–1980) was born in Montreal and became a founder of the Canadian modernist movement through his work as a poet, editor, and critic. This poem, originally subtitled "Group of Seven," first appeared in the McGill Fortnightly Review, *which Smith began with F. R. Scott. His poetry collections include* News of the Phoenix *(1943) and* The Classic Shade *(1978).*

A. J. M. Smith

The Lonely Land

Cedar and jagged fir
uplift sharp barbs
against the gray
and cloud-piled sky;
and in the bay   5
blown spume and windrift
and thin, bitter spray
snap
at the whirling sky;
and the pine trees   10
lean one way.

A wild duck calls
to her mate,
and the ragged
and passionate tones   15
stagger and fall,
and recover,
and stagger and fall,
on these stones—
are lost   20
in the lapping of water
on smooth, flat stones.

This is a beauty
of dissonance,
this resonance   25
of stony strand,
this smoky cry

curled over a black pine
like a broken
and wind-battered branch   *30*
when the wind
bends the tops of the pines
and curdles the sky
from the north.

This is the beauty   *35*
of strength
broken by strength
and still strong.

—*1926*

Earle Birney *(1904–1995) was born in Alberta and travelled extensively
throughout his life. A Chaucerian scholar and a poetic innovator, he published over
fifteen collections of poetry, including the award-winning* David and Other
Poems *(1945),* Collected Poems *(1975), and* Last Makings *(1991), as well as
two novels and various non-fiction works on writing and writers.*

Earle Birney

El Greco: *Espolio* °

The carpenter is intent on the pressure of his hand

on the awl   and the trick of pinpointing his strength
through the awl to the wood   which is tough
He has no effort to spare for despoilings
or to worry if he'll be cut in on the dice   5
His skill is vital to the scene   and the safety of the state
Anyone can perform the indignities   It's his hard arms
and craft that hold the eyes of the convict's women
There is the problem of getting the holes exact

El Greco: *Espolio* The Spanish painter known as El Greco (1541–1614) was famous for painting
intensely expressive religious scenes like *Espolio* (from the Latin for "despoiling"), which shows Christ
just before his clothes are torn away and he is crucified. Birney focuses on the figure of the
carpenter in the right foreground, who is preparing the cross.

(in the middle of this elbowing crowd)   *10*
and deep enough to hold the spikes
after they've sunk through those bared feet
and inadequate wrists he knows are waiting behind him
He doesn't sense perhaps that one of the hands
Is held in a curious gesture over him—   *15*
giving   or asking   forgiveness?—
but he'd scarcely take time to be puzzled by poses
Criminals come in all sorts
as anyone knows who makes crosses
are as mad or sane as those who decide on their killings   *20*
Our one at least has been quiet so far
though they say he talked himself into this trouble
a carpenter's son who got notions of preaching
Well here's a carpenter's son who'll have carpenter sons
God willing   and build what's wanted   *25*
temples or tables   mangers or crosses
and shape them decently
working alone in that firm and profound abstraction
which blots out the bawling of rag-snatchers
To construct with hands   knee-weight   braced thigh   *30*
keeps the back turned from death

But it's too late now for the other carpenter's boy
to return to this peace before the nails are hammered

Point Grey 1960
—1962

Pablo Neruda (1904–1973) *Born in Parral, Chile, as Neftali Ricardo Reyes y Basoalto, Neruda helped to shape Latin American literature and politics, winning the Nobel Prize in 1971. From 1948 until 1952, when Chile lifted its ban on communism, Neruda lived in exile in the USSR, Europe, and Mexico. Considered the people's poet, he published several accessible collections, including* Residence on Earth *(tr. 1946),* The Elementary Odes *(tr. 1961), and a volume of love poems.*

Pablo Neruda

In Praise of Ironing

Poetry is pure white:
it emerges from the water covered with drops,
all wrinkled, in a heap.
It has to be spread out, the skin of this planet,
has to be ironed, the sea in its whiteness;   5
and the hands keep on moving,
smoothing the holy surfaces.
So are things accomplished.
Each day, hands re-create the world,
fire is married to steel,   10
and the canvas, the linens and the cottons return
from the skirmishing of the laundries;
and out of light is born a dove.
Out of the froth once more comes chastity.

—1962

Translated by Alastair Reid.

*W. H. Auden (1907–1973) was already established as an important younger
British poet before he moved to America in 1939 (he later became a U.S. citizen). As
an important transatlantic link between two literary cultures, Auden was one of the
most important literary figures and cultural spokespersons in the English-speaking
world for almost forty years, giving a name to the post-war era when he dubbed it
"The Age of Anxiety" in a poem. In his last years he returned briefly to Oxford,
where he occupied the poetry chair.*

W. H. Auden
Musée des Beaux Arts°

About suffering they were never wrong,
The Old Masters: how well they understood
Its human position; how it takes place
While someone else is eating or opening a window or just
    walking dully along;
How, when the aged are reverently, passionately waiting   5
For the miraculous birth, there always must be
Children who did not specially want it to happen, skating
On a pond at the edge of the wood:
They never forgot
That even the dreadful martyrdom must run its course   10
Anyhow in a corner, some untidy spot
Where the dogs go on with their doggy life and the torturer's
    horse
Scratches its innocent behind on a tree.

In Brueghel's *Icarus,*° for instance: how everything turns away
Quite leisurely from the disaster; the ploughman may   15
Have heard the splash, the forsaken cry,
But for him it was not an important failure; the sun shone
As it had to on the white legs disappearing into the green
Water; and the expensive delicate ship that must have seen
Something amazing, a boy falling out of the sky,   20
Had somewhere to get to and sailed calmly on.

—1938

Musée des Beaux Arts Museum of Fine Arts   **14 Brueghel's *Icarus*** In this painting (c. 1550) the
famous event from Greek myth is almost inconspicuous among the other details Auden mentions.

Theodore Roethke (1908–1963) *was born in Michigan. Roethke was an influential teacher of poetry at the University of Washington for many years. His father was the owner of a greenhouse, and Roethke's childhood closeness to nature was an important influence on his mature poetry. His periodic nervous breakdowns, the result of bipolar manic-depression, presaged his early death.*

Theodore Roethke
Root Cellar

Nothing would sleep in that cellar, dank as a ditch,
Bulbs broke out of boxes hunting for chinks in the dark,
Shoots dangled and drooped,
Lolling obscenely from mildewed crates,
Hung down long yellow evil necks, like tropical snakes.   5
And what a congress of stinks!—
Roots ripe as old bait,
Pulpy stems, rank, silo-rich,
Leaf-mold, manure, lime, piled against slippery planks.
Nothing would give up life: 10
Even the dirt kept breathing a small breath.

—*1948*

Louis Zukofsky (1904–1978) *was born in New York to Jewish immigrants. Though once influential through his association with the Objectivist movement of the 1930s and his impact on the Black Mountain Poets, Zukofsky's own work is now experiencing a critical revival. His major achievement is the long poem "A," which he worked on throughout his life, but he also published numerous volumes of short poems and critical essays.*

Louis Zukofsky
Mantis

Mantis! praying mantis! since your wings' leaves
And your terrified eyes, pins, bright, black and poor
Beg—"Look, take it up" (thoughts' torsion)! "save it!"
I who can't bear to look, cannot touch,—You—

You can—but no one sees you steadying lost   5
In the cars' drafts on the lit subway stone.

Praying mantis, what wind-up brought you, stone
On which you sometimes prop, prey among leaves
(Is it love's food your raised stomach prays?), lost
Here, stone holds only seats on which the poor   10
Ride, who rising from the news may trample you—
The shops' crowds a jam with no flies in it.

Even the newsboy who now sees knows it
No use, papers make money, makes stone, stone,
Banks, "it is harmless," he says moving on—You?   15
Where will he put *you*? There are no safe leaves
To put you back in here, here's news! too poor
Like all the separate poor to save the lost.

Don't light on my chest, mantis! do—you're lost,
Let the poor laugh at my fright, then see it: 20
My shame and theirs, you whom old Europe's poor
Call spectre, strawberry, by turns; a stone—
You point—they say—you lead lost children—leaves
Close in the paths men leave, saved, safe with you.

Killed by thorns (once men), who now will save you   25
Mantis? what male love bring a fly, be lost
Within your mouth, prophetess, harmless to leaves
And hands, faked flower,—the myth is: dead, bones, it
Was assembled, apes wing in wind: On stone,
Mantis, you will die, touch, beg, of the poor.   30

Android, loving beggar, dive to the poor
As your love would even without head to you,
Graze like machined wheels, green, from off this stone
And preying on each terrified chest, lost
Say, I am old as the globe, the moon, it   35
Is my old shoe, yours, be free as the leaves.

Fly, mantis, on the poor, arise like leaves
The armies of the poor, strength: stone on stone
And build the new world in your eyes, Save it!

—1934

A. M. Klein (1909–1972) Born in the Ukraine, Klein came as an infant to Montreal with his family and went on to become a lawyer and poet. His collections Hath Not a Jew . . . *(1940) and the satiric* Hitleriad *(1944), and his novel* The Second Scroll *(1951), draw on his Jewish heritage, whereas the award-winning* The Rocking Chair *(1948) also explores French Quebec. After a breakdown in 1954, he withdrew from writing and public activity for the remainder of his life.*

A. M. Klein

Portrait of the Poet as Landscape

I

Not an editorial-writer, bereaved with bartlett,°
mourns him, the shelved Lycidas.°
No actress squeezes a glycerine tear for him.
The radio broadcast lets his passing pass.
And with the police, no record. Nobody, it appears,   5
either under his real name or his alias,
missed him enough to report.

It is possible that he is dead, and not discovered.
It is possible that he can be found some place
in a narrow closet, like the corpse in a detective story,   10
standing, his eyes staring, and ready to fall on his face.
It is also possible that he is alive
and amnesiac, or mad, or in retired disgrace,
or beyond recognition lost in love.

We are sure only that from our real society   15
he has disappeared; he simply does not count,
except in the pullulation° of vital statistics—
somebody's vote, perhaps, an anonymous taunt

---

1 bartlett *Bartlett's Familiar Quotations*   **2 Lycidas** In his poem "Lycidas" (1637), John Milton mourns the drowning death of his Cambridge schoolmate Edward King (1612–1637).
17 pullulation breeding, rapid increase

of the Gallup poll, a dot in a government table—
but not felt, and certainly far from eminent—   20
in a shouting mob, somebody's sigh.

O, he who unrolled our culture from his scroll—
the prince's quote, the rostrum-rounding roar—
who under one name made articulate
heaven, and under another the seven-circled air,°   25
is, if he is at all, a number, an x,
a Mr Smith in a hotel register,—
incognito, lost, lacunal.°

　　II

The truth is he's not dead, but only ignored—
like the mirroring lenses forgotten on a brow   30
that shine with the guilt of their unnoticed world.
The truth is he lives among neighbours, who, though
　　they will allow
him a passable fellow, think him eccentric, not solid,
a type that one can forgive, and for that matter, forgo.

Himself he has his moods, just like a poet.   35
Sometimes, depressed to nadir, he will think all lost,
will see himself as throwback, relict,° freak,
his mother's miscarriage, his great-grandfather's ghost,
and he will curse his quintuplet senses, and their tutors
in whom he put, as he should not have put, his trust.   40

Then he will remember his travels over that body—
the torso verb, the beautiful face of the noun,
and all those shaped and warm auxiliaries!
A first love it was, the recognition of his own.
Dear limbs adverbial, complexion of adjective,   45
dimple and dip of conjugation!

And then remember how this made a change in him
affecting for always the glow and growth of his being;

---

25 seven-circled air Before Copernicus, Ptolemy's system of the universe showed circles around the
earth for the moon, the five known planets, and the sun. Perhaps also an allusion to the Muslim belief
that Allah created seven heavens.　**28 lacunal** resembling an empty space　**37 relict** leftover organ-
ism surviving in a changed environment

how suddenly was aware of the air, like shaken tinfoil,°
of the patents of nature, the shock of belated seeing,   *50*
the lonelinesses peering from the eyes of crowds;
the integers of thought; the cube-roots of feeling.

Thus, zoomed to zenith, sometimes he hopes again,
and sees himself as a character, with a rehearsed role:
the Count of Monte Cristo,° come for his revenges;   *55*
the unsuspected heir, with papers; the risen soul;
or the chloroformed prince awaking from his flowers;
or—deflated again—the convict on parole.

III

He is alone; yet not completely alone.
Pins on a map of a colour similar to his,   *60*
each city has one, sometimes more than one;
here, caretakers of art, in colleges;
in offices, there, with arm-bands, and green-shaded;
and there, pounding their catalogued beats in libraries,—

everywhere menial, a shadow's shadow.   *65*
And always for their egos—their outmoded art.
Thus, having lost the bevel in the ear,
they know neither up nor down, mistake the part
for the whole, curl themselves in a comma,
talk technics, make a colon their eyes. They distort—   *70*

such is the pain of their frustration—truth
to something convolute and cerebral.
How they do fear the slap of the flat of the platitude!
Now Pavlov's victims,° their mouths water at bell,
the platter empty.   *75*
        See they set twenty-one jewels
into their watches; the time they do not tell!

---

49 tinfoil See Gerard Manley Hopkins's poem "God's Grandeur" (p. 131).   **55 Count of Monte Cristo** *The Count of Monte Cristo* (1844) is a novel by Alexandre Dumas, in which a wrongfully imprisoned man escapes to take revenge on those who made him suffer.   **74 Pavlov's victims** Russian physiologist Ivan Pavlov (1849–1936) was famous for his experiments on the conditioned reflex, including making a dog salivate at the sound of a bell.

Some, patagonian° in their own esteem,
and longing for the multiplying word,
join party and wear pins, now have a message,   *80*
an ear, and the convention-hall's regard.
Upon the knees of ventriloquists, they own,
of their dandled brightness, only the paint and board.

And some go mystical, and some go mad.
One stares at a mirror all day long, as if   *85*
to recognize himself; another courts
angels,—for here he does not fear rebuff;
and a third, alone, and sick with sex, and rapt,
doodles him symbols convex and concave.

O schizoid solitudes! O purities   *90*
curdling upon themselves! Who live for themselves,
or for each other, but for nobody else;
desire affection, private and public loves;
are friendly, and then quarrel and surmise
the secret perversions of each other's lives.   *95*

IV

He suspects that something has happened, a law
been passed, a nightmare ordered. Set apart,
he finds himself, with special haircut and dress,
as on a reservation. Introvert.
He does not understand this; sad conjecture   *100*
muscles and palls thrombotic on his heart.

He thinks an imposter, having studied his personal
    biography,
his gestures, his moods, now has come forward to pose
in the shivering vacuums his absence leaves.
Wigged with his laurel, that other, and faked with his face,   *105*
he pats the heads of his children, pecks his wife,
and is at home, and slippered, in his house.

---

78 patagonian Natives of the Patagonia area in Argentina were described by early explorers as the
world's tallest people.

So he guesses at the impertinent silhouette
that talks to his phone-piece and slits open his mail.
Is it the local tycoon who for a hobby   *110*
plays poet, he so epical in steel?
The orator, making a pause? Or is that man
he who blows his flash of brass in the jittering hall?

Or is he cuckolded by the troubadour
rich and successful out of celluloid?   *115*
Or by the don who unrhymes atoms? Or
the chemist death built up? Pride, lost impostor'd pride,
it is another, another, whoever he is,
who rides where he should ride.

         V

Fame, the adrenalin: to be talked about;   *120*
to be a verb; to be introduced as *The*:
to smile with endorsement from slick paper; make
caprices anecdotal; to nod to the world; to see
one's name like a song upon the marquees played;
to be forgotten with embarrassment; to be—   *125*
to be.

It has its attractions, but is not the thing;
nor is it the ape mimesis° who speaks from the tree
ancestral; nor the merkin° joy . . .
Rather it is stark infelicity   *130*
which stirs him from his sleep, undressed, asleep
to walk upon roofs and window-sills and defy
the gape of gravity.

         VI

Therefore he seeds illusions. Look, he is
the nth Adam taking a green inventory   *135*
in world but scarcely uttered, naming, praising,
the flowering fiats° in the meadow, the

---

128 mimesis imitation   **129 merkin** pubic wig for women; also slang for "American"
137 fiats commands from the Latin, "let it be done"

syllabled fur, stars aspirate, the pollen
whose sweet collision sounds eternally.   140
For to praise

the world—he, solitary man—is breath
to him. Until it has been praised, that part
has not been. Item by exciting item—
air to his lungs, and pressured blood to his heart.—   145
they are pulsated, and breathed, until they map,
not the world's, but his own body's chart!

And now in imagination he has climbed
another planet, the better to look
with single camera view upon this earth—   150
its total scope, and each afflated° tick,
its talk, its trick, its tracklessness—and this,
this, he would like to write down in a book!

To find a new function for the *déclassé* craft
archaic like the fletcher's;° to make a new thing;   155
to say the word that will become sixth sense;
perhaps by necessity and indirection bring
new forms to life, anonymously, new creeds—
O, somehow pay back the daily larcenies of the lung!

These are not mean ambitions. It is already something   160
merely to entertain them. Meanwhile, he
makes of his status as zero a rich garland,
a halo of his anonymity,
and lives alone, and in his secret shines
like phosphorus. At the bottom of the sea.   165

—*1948*

---

151 afflated breathed upon, inspired   **155 fletcher's** arrow maker's

Dorothy Livesay (1909–1996) Born in Winnipeg, Livesay lived and worked in Montreal, Vancouver, and Zambia. The publication of Green Pitcher *(1928) and the many collections that followed marked her as an important contributor to modern Canadian poetry. Her style ranged from imagism to what she called the "documentary" poem that creates dialogue between historical material and the poet's own thoughts.*

Dorothy Livesay

The Three Emilys°

These women crying in my head
Walk alone, uncomforted:
The Emilys, these three
Cry to be set free—
And others whom I will not name   5
Each different, each the same.

Yet they had liberty!
Their kingdom was the sky:
They batted clouds with easy hand,
Found a mountain for their stand;   10
From wandering lonely they could catch
The inner magic of a heath—
A lake their palette, any tree
Their brush could be.

And still they cry to me   15
As in reproach—
I, born to hear their inner storm
Of separate man in woman's form,
I yet possess another kingdom, barred
To them, these three, this Emily.   20
I move as mother in a frame,
My arteries

The Three Emilys British poet and novelist Emily Brontë (1818–1878), American poet Emily Dickinson (1830–1886), and Canadian painter Emily Carr (1871–1945). Unlike Livesay, none of the three married or had children.

Flow the immemorial way
Towards the child, the man;
And only for a brief span   25
Am I an Emily on mountain snows
And one of these.

And so the whole that I possess
Is still much less—
They move triumphant through my head: 30
I am the one
Uncomforted.

—1953

Charles Olson (1910–1970) *was born in Worcester, Massachusetts, and educated at Harvard. In his influential essay "Projective Verse" (1950), he argued that "a poem is energy transferred from where the poet got it . . . to the reader" and that the ear and the breath are essential to poetry. He and other avant-garde poets associated with North Carolina's Black Mountain College were known as the "Black Mountain Poets."*

Charles Olson

The Ring of

it was the west wind caught her up, as
she° rose
from the genital
wave, and bore her from the delicate
foam, home   5
to her isle

and those lovers
of the difficult, the hours
of the golden day welcomed her, clad her, were
as though they had made her, were wild   10

---

2 she Aphrodite, goddess of love in Greek mythology and Botticelli's *Birth of Venus* (1485)

to bring this new thing born
of the ring of the sea pink
& naked, this girl, brought her
to the face of the gods, violets
in her hair   15

Beauty, and she
said no to zeus & them all, all were not or
was it she chose the ugliest
to bed with, or was it straight
and to expiate the nature of beauty, was it?   20

knowing hours, anyway,
she did not stay long, or the lame
was only one part, & the handsome
mars had her   And the child
had that name, the arrow of   25
as the flight of, the move of
his mother who adorneth

with myrtle the dolphin and words
they rise, they do who
are born of like   30
elements

—*1953*

Elizabeth Bishop (1911–1979) was from Worcester, Massachusetts, but time spent with maternal grandparents in a Nova Scotia coastal village inspired some memorable poems. Always highly regarded as a "poet's poet," she won the Pulitzer Prize in 1956, but her reputation has continued to increase since the publication of The Complete Poems 1927–1979 (1983). *She travelled widely and lived in Brazil for many years before returning to the United States to teach at Harvard during the last years of her life.*

Elizabeth Bishop
At the Fishhouses

Although it is a cold evening,
down by one of the fishhouses
an old man sits netting,
his net, in the gloaming almost invisible
a dark purple-brown,   5
and his shuttle worn and polished.
The air smells so strong of codfish
it makes one's nose run and one's eyes water.
The five fishhouses have steeply peaked roofs
and narrow, cleated gangplanks slant up   10
to storerooms in the gables
for the wheelbarrows to be pushed up and down on.
All is silver: the heavy surface of the sea,
swelling slowly as if considering spilling over,
is opaque, but the silver of the benches,   15
the lobster pots, and masts, scattered
among the wild jagged rocks,
is of an apparent translucence
like the small old buildings with an emerald moss
growing on their shoreward walls.   20
The big fish tubs are completely lined
with layers of beautiful herring scales
and the wheelbarrows are similarly plastered
with creamy iridescent coats of mail,
with small iridescent flies crawling on them.   25

Up on the little slope behind the houses,
set in the sparse bright sprinkle of grass,
is an ancient wooden capstan,°
cracked, with two long bleached handles
and some melancholy stains, like dried blood,   *30*
where the ironwork has rusted.
The old man accepts a Lucky Strike.°
He was a friend of my grandfather.
We talk of the decline in the population
and of codfish and herring   *35*
while he waits for a herring boat to come in.
There are sequins on his vest and on his thumb.
He has scraped the scales, the principal beauty,
from unnumbered fish with that black old knife,
the blade of which is almost worn away.   *40*

Down at the water's edge, at the place
where they haul up the boats, up the long ramp
descending into the water, thin silver
tree trunks are laid horizontally
across the gray stones, down and down   *45*
at intervals of four or five feet.

Cold dark deep and absolutely clear,
element bearable to no mortal,
to fish and to seals . . . One seal particularly
I have seen here evening after evening.   *50*
He was curious about me. He was interested in music;
like me a believer in total immersion,
so I used to sing him Baptist hymns.
I also sang "A Mighty Fortress Is Our God."
He stood up in the water and regarded me   *55*
steadily, moving his head a little.
Then he would disappear, then suddenly emerge
almost in the same spot, with a sort of shrug
as if it were against his better judgment.
Cold dark deep and absolutely clear,   *60*

---

28 capstan mechanism for winding cable   **32 Lucky Strike** brand of American cigarettes

the clear gray icy water . . . Back, behind us,
the dignified tall firs begin.
Bluish, associating with their shadows,
a million Christmas trees stand
waiting for Christmas. The water seems suspended   65
above the rounded gray and blue-gray stones.
I have seen it over and over, the same sea, the same,
slightly, indifferently swinging above the stones,
icily free above the stones,
above the stones and then the world.   70
If you should dip your hand in,
your wrist would ache immediately,
your bones would begin to ache and your hand would burn
as if the water were a transmutation of fire
that feeds on stones and burns with a dark gray flame.   75
If you tasted it, it would first taste bitter,
then briny, then surely burn your tongue.
It is like what we imagine knowledge to be:
dark, salt, clear, moving, utterly free,
drawn from the cold hard mouth   80
of the world, derived from the rocky breasts
forever, flowing and drawn, and since
our knowledge is historical, flowing, and flown.

—1955

One Art

The art of losing isn't hard to master;
so many things seem filled with the intent
to be lost that their loss is no disaster.

Lose something every day. Accept the fluster
of lost door keys, the hour badly spent.   5
The art of losing isn't hard to master.

Then practice losing farther, losing faster:
places, and names, and where it was you meant
to travel. None of these will bring disaster.

I lost my mother's watch. And look! my last, or   *10*
next-to-last, of three loved houses went.
The art of losing isn't hard to master.

I lost two cities, lovely ones. And, vaster,
some realms I owned, two rivers, a continent.
I miss them, but it wasn't a disaster.   *15*

—Even losing you (the joking voice, a gesture
I love) I shan't have lied. It's evident
the art of losing's not too hard to master
though it may look like *(Write* it!) like disaster.

                                                      —1976

---

*Allen Curnow (1911–2001) was born in Timaru, New Zealand, and is considered
one of that country's leading poets. In poems like "Landfall in Unknown Seas" he
explores the history of his island homeland. His numerous books of poetry span a
long career from* Valley of Decision *(1933) to* Bells of Saint Babel's *(2001).*

Allen Curnow
Landfall in Unknown Seas

THE 300TH ANNIVERSARY OF THE DISCOVERY OF NEW ZEALAND
BY ABEL TASMAN, 13 DECEMBER 1642

I

Simply by sailing in a new direction
You could enlarge the world.
                              You picked your captain,
Keen on discoveries, tough enough to make them,
Whatever vessels could be spared from other   *5*
More urgent service for a year's adventure;
Took stock of the more probable conjectures
About the Unknown to be traversed, all
Guesses at golden coasts and tales of monsters
To be digested into plain instructions   *10*
For likely and unlikely situations.

All this resolved and done, you launched the whole
On a fine morning, the best time of year,
Skies widening and the oceanic furies
Subdued by summer illumination; time   15
To go and to be gazed at going
On a fine morning, in the Name of God
Into the nameless waters of the world.

O you had estimated all the chances
Of business in those waters, the world's waters   20
Yet unexploited.
              But more than the sea-empire's
Cannon, the dogs of bronze and iron barking
From Timor to the Straits, backed up the challenge.
Between you and the South an older enmity   25
Lodged in the searching mind, that would not tolerate
So huge a hegemony of ignorance.
There, where your Indies had already sprinkled
Their tribes like ocean rains, you aimed your voyage;
Like them invoked your God, gave seas to history   30
And islands to new hazardous tomorrows.

              II

Suddenly exhilaration
Went off like a gun, the whole
Horizon, the long chase done,
Hove to. There was the seascape   35
Crammed with coast, surprising
As new lands will, the sailor
Moving on the face of the waters,
Watching the earth take shape
Round the unearthly summits, brighter   40
Than its emerging colour.

Yet this, no far fool's errand,
Was less than the heart desired,
In its old Indian dream
The glittering gulfs ascending   45

Past palaces and mountains
Making one architecture.
Here the uplifted structure,
Peak and pillar of cloud—
O splendour of desolation—reared   *50*
Tall from the pit of the swell,
With a shadow, a finger of wind, forbade
Hopes of a lucky landing.

Always to islanders danger
Is what comes over the sea;   *55*
Over the yellow sands and the clear
Shallows, the dull filament
Flickers, the blood of strangers:
Death discovered the Sailor
O in a flash, in a flat calm,   *60*
A clash of boats in the bay
And the day marred with murder.
The dead required no further
Warning to keep their distance;
The rest, noting the failure,   *65*
Pushed on with a reconnaissance
To the north; and sailed away.

III

Well, home is the Sailor, and that is a chapter
In a schoolbook, a relevant yesterday
We thought we knew all about, being much apter   *70*
      To profit, sure of our ground,
No murderers mooring in our Golden Bay.

But now there are no more islands to be found
And the eye scans risky horizons of its own
In unsettled weather, and murmurs of the drowned   *75*
      Haunt their familiar beaches—
Who navigates us towards what unknown

But not improbable provinces? Who reaches
A future down for us from the high shelf

Of spiritual daring? Not those speeches   80
    Pinning on the Past like a decoration
For merit that congratulates itself,

O not the self-important celebration
Or most painstaking history, can release
The current of a discoverer's elation   85
    And silence the voices saying,
'Here is the world's end where wonders cease.'

Only by a more faithful memory, laying
On him the half-light of a diffident glory,
The Sailor lives, and stands beside us, paying   90
    Out into our time's wave
The stain of blood that writes an island story.

                                             —*1943*

Irving Layton (1912–2006) was born in Romania to a Jewish family but came to Montreal as an infant, eventually changing his name from Lazarovitch to Layton. He is one of Canada's best-known poets as much for his feisty personality as for his exuberant poetry. In more than forty collections, including the award-winning A Red Carpet for the Sun *(1959) and* Collected Poems *(1971), he has explored his hope that love and imagination are two ways to dominate reality.*

Irving Layton
The Fertile Muck

There are brightest apples on those trees
    but until I, fabulist, have spoken
they do not know their significance
or what other legends are hung like garlands
    on their black boughs twisting   5
like a rumour. The wind's noise is empty.

Nor are the winged insects better off
    though they wear my crafty eyes
wherever they alight. Stay here, my love;

you will see how delicately they deposit   10
    me on the leaves of elms
or fold me in the orient dust of summer.

And if in August joiners and bricklayers
    are thick as flies around us
building expensive bungalows for those   15
who do not need them, unless they release
    me roaring from their moth-proofed cupboards
their buyers will have no joy, no ease.

I could extend their rooms for them without cost
    and give them crazy sundials   20
to tell the time with, but I have noticed
how my irregular footprint horrifies them
    evenings and Sunday afternoons:
they spray for hours to erase its shadow.

How to dominate reality? Love is one way;   25
    imagination another. Sit here
beside me, sweet; take my hard hand in yours.
We'll mark the butterflies disappearing over the hedge
    with tiny wristwatches on their wings:
our fingers touching the earth, like two Buddhas.   30

—1956

Muriel Rukeyser (1913–1980) was born and lived in New York, and sought in her poetry to offer a female-centred vision to counteract the violence of Western culture. Her poetic career ranged from Theory of Flight *(1935) to* Collected Poems *(1978).*

Muriel Rukeyser

Myth

Long afterward, Oedipus, old and blinded, walked the
roads.   He smelled a familiar smell.   It was
the Sphinx.   Oedipus said, "I want to ask one question.

Why didn't I recognize my mother?"   "You gave the
wrong answer," said the Sphinx.   "But that was what   5
made everything possible," said Oedipus.   "No," she said.
"When I asked, What walks on four legs in the morning,
two at noon, and three in the evening, you answered,
Man.   You didn't say anything about woman."
"When you say Man," said Oedipus, "you include women   10
too. Everyone knows that."   She said, "That's what
you think."

—1973

Dudley Randall (1914–2000) *was the founder of Broadside Press, a Black-owned
publishing firm that eventually attracted important writers like Gwendolyn Brooks
and Don L. Lee. For most of his life a resident of Detroit, Randall spent many years
working in that city's library system before taking a similar position at the
University of Detroit.*

Dudley Randall
Ballad of Birmingham

ON THE BOMBING OF A CHURCH IN BIRMINGHAM, ALABAMA, 1963°

"Mother dear, may I go downtown
Instead of out to play,
And march the streets of Birmingham
In a Freedom March today?"

"No, baby, no, you may not go,   5
For the dogs are fierce and wild,
And clubs and hoses, guns and jail
Aren't good for a little child."

"But, mother, I won't be alone.
Other children will go with me,   10

Birmingham, Alabama, 1963 during the height of the civil rights movement

And march the streets of Birmingham
To make our country free."

"No, baby, no, you may not go,
For I fear those guns will fire.
But you may go to church instead   15
And sing in the children's choir."

She has combed and brushed her night-dark hair,
And bathed rose petal sweet,
And drawn white gloves on her small brown hands,
And white shoes on her feet.   20

The mother smiled to know her child
Was in the sacred place,
But that smile was the last smile
To come upon her face.

For when she heard the explosion,   25
Her eyes grew wet and wild.
She raced through the streets of Birmingham
Calling for her child.

She clawed through bits of glass and brick,
Then lifted out a shoe.   30
"O, here's the shoe my baby wore,
But, baby, where are you?"

—1969

William Stafford (1914–1993) was one of the most prolific poets of the post-war era. Stafford published in virtually every magazine in the United States. Raised in Kansas as a member of the pacifist Church of the Brethren, Stafford served in a camp for conscientious objectors during World War II. His first book did not appear until he was in his forties, but he published over thirty collections before his death at age seventy-nine.

William Stafford

Traveling Through the Dark

Traveling through the dark I found a deer
dead on the edge of the Wilson River road.
It is usually best to roll them into the canyon:
that road is narrow; to swerve might make more dead.

By glow of the tail-light I stumbled back of the car   5
and stood by the heap, a doe, a recent killing;
she had stiffened already, almost cold.
I dragged her off; she was large in the belly.

My fingers touching her side brought me the reason—
her side was warm; her fawn lay there waiting,   10
alive, still, never to be born.
Beside that mountain road I hesitated.

The car aimed ahead its lowered parking lights;
under the hood purred the steady engine.
I stood in the glare of the warm exhaust turning red;   15
around our group I could hear the wilderness listen.

I thought hard for us all—my only swerving—
then pushed her over the edge into the river.

—1960

Dylan Thomas (1914–1953) *was a legendary performer of his and others' poetry. His popularity in the United States led to several collegiate reading tours, punctuated with outrageous behaviour and self-destructive drinking that led to his early death in New York City, the victim of what the autopsy report labelled "insult to the brain." The Wales of his childhood remained a constant source of inspiration for his poetry and for radio dramas like* Under Milk Wood, *which was turned into a film by fellow Welshman Richard Burton and his wife at the time, Elizabeth Taylor.*

Dylan Thomas

Do Not Go Gentle into That Good Night

Do not go gentle into that good night,
Old age should burn and rave at close of day;
Rage, rage against the dying of the light.

Though wise men at their end know dark is right,
Because their words had forked no lightning they   5
Do not go gentle into that good night.

Good men, the last wave by, crying how bright
Their frail deeds might have danced in a green bay,
Rage, rage against the dying of the light.

Wild men who caught and sang the sun in flight,   10
And learn, too late, they grieved it on its way,
Do not go gentle into that good night.

Grave men, near death, who see with blinding sight
Blind eyes could blaze like meteors and be gay,
Rage, rage against the dying of the light.   15

And you, my father, there on the sad height,
Curse, bless, me now with your fierce tears, I pray,
Do not go gentle into that good night.
Rage, rage against the dying of the light.

—*1952*

Fern Hill

Now as I was young and easy under the apple boughs
About the lilting house and happy as the grass was green,
   The night above the dingle starry,
     Time let me hail and climb
   Golden in the heydays of his eyes,   5
And honored among wagons I was prince of the apple towns
And once below a time I lordly had the trees and leaves
   Trail with daisies and barley
   Down the rivers of the windfall light.

And as I was green and carefree, famous among the barns   10
About the happy yard and singing as the farm was home,
   In the sun that is young once only,
     Time let me play and be
   Golden in the mercy of his means,
And green and golden I was huntsman and herdsman, the calves 15
Sang to my horn, the foxes on the hills barked clear and cold,
   And the sabbath rang slowly
   In the pebbles of the holy streams.

All the sun long it was running, it was lovely, the hay
Fields high as the house, the tunes from the chimneys, it was air 20
   And playing, lovely and watery
     And fire green as grass.
   And nightly under the simple stars
As I rode to sleep the owls were bearing the farm away,
All the moon long I heard, blessed among stables, the night-jars 25
   Flying with the ricks, and the horses
   Flashing into the dark.

And then to awake, and the farm, like a wanderer white
With the dew, come back, the cock on his shoulder: it was all
   Shining, it was Adam and maiden,   30
     The sky gathered again
   And the sun grew round that very day.
So it must have been after the birth of the simple light
In the first, spinning place, the spellbound horses walking warm

Out of the whinnying green stable   35
    On to the fields of praise.

And honored among foxes and pheasants by the gay house
Under the new made clouds and happy as the heart was long,
    In the sun born over and over,
        I ran my heedless ways,   40
    My wishes raced through the house high hay
And nothing I cared, at my sky blue trades, that time allows
In all his tuneful turning so few and such morning songs
    Before the children green and golden
        Follow him out of grace,   45

Nothing I cared, in the lamb white days, that time would take me
Up to the swallow thronged loft by the shadow of my hand,
    In the moon that is always rising,
        Nor that riding to sleep
    I should hear him fly with the high fields   50
And wake to the farm forever fled from the childless land.
Oh as I was young and easy in the mercy of his means,
        Time held me green and dying
    Though I sang in my chains like the sea.

—1946

Randall Jarrell (1914–1965) excelled as both a poet and a (sometimes brutally honest) reviewer of poetry. Ironically, the author of what is perhaps the best-known poem to have emerged from World War II did not see combat during the war: He served as a control tower officer in stateside bases. A native of Nashville, Kentucky, Jarrell studied at Vanderbilt University and followed his mentor, John Crowe Ransom, to Kenyon College in 1937, where he befriended another student, Robert Lowell.

Randall Jarrell
The Death of the Ball Turret° Gunner

From my mother's sleep I fell into the State,
And I hunched in its belly till my wet fur froze.
Six miles from earth, loosed from its dream of life,
I woke to black flak and the nightmare fighters.
When I died they washed me out of the turret with a hose.   *5*

—*1945*

John Ciardi (1916–1986) was born in Boston, the son of Italian immigrants. He was an aerial gunner with the U.S. Army Air Corps (1942–1945), returning to teach at Harvard and other universities until 1961. He has written over forty collections of poetry for adults and children, a critically acclaimed translation of Dante's Divine Comedy, *and several prose works that have helped to make poetry more widely accessible.*

John Ciardi
To Lucasta,° About That War

A long winter from home the gulls blew
  on their brinks, the tankers slid
  over the hump where the wolf packs hid

Ball Turret A Plexiglas sphere set into the belly of a heavy bomber; Jarrell noted the similarity between the gunner and a fetus in the womb.
Lucasta See Richard Lovelace's poem of 1649.

like voodoo talking, the surf threw
bundles with eyes ashore. I did   5
what booze brought me, and it wasn't you.

I was almost bored. I watched and told time
as enforced, a swag-man
under the clock. The bloat-bags ran
wet from nowhere, selling three-for-a-dime   10
and nobody buying. Armies can
type faster than men die, I'm

told, and can prove. Didn't I find
time there, and more, to count
all, triplicate, and still walk guard-mount   15
on the gull- and drum-wind
over the hump? I did, and won't
deny several (or more) pig-blind

alleys with doors, faces, dickers,
which during, the ships slid   20
over the humps where the packs hid.
And talking voodoo and snickers
over the edge of their welts, I did
what I could with (they called them) knickers;

and it was goddam good,   25
and not bad either. It
was war (they called it) and it lit
a sort of skyline somehow in the blood,
and I typed the dead out a bit
faster than they came, or anyone should,   30

and the gulls blew high on their brinks,
and the ships slid, and the surf threw,
and the army initialled, and you
were variously, and straight and with kinks,
raped, fondled, and apologized to—   35
which is called (as noted) war. And it stinks.

—1959

Anne Hébert (1916–2000) was born in a small village not far from Quebec City and is one of Quebec's best known writers, though she lived for many years in Paris. She is probably best known for her novels, including Kamouraska *(1970) and* Un Habit de lumière *(1998), but has also written plays and poems, including this one translated by F. R. Scott.*

Anne Hébert

Snow

Snow puts us in a dream on vast plains without track or colour

Beware, my heart, snow puts us in the saddle on steeds of foam

Proclaim the coronation of childhood, snow consecrates us on high seas, dreams fulfilled, all sails set

Snow puts us in a trance, a widespread whiteness, flaring plumes pierced by the red eye of this bird

My heart; a point of fire under palms of frost flows the marvelling blood.   5

—1960

Translated by F.R. Scott.

P. K. Page (b. 1916) was born in England and raised on the Canadian prairies. She lived abroad in Australia and Brazil, settling finally in British Columbia. A visual artist and a poet, she has published over a dozen books, including the two-volume collected poems The Hidden Room *(1997) and* Hand Luggage *(2006). "Planet Earth" is based on lines from Pablo Neruda's poem "In Praise of Ironing."*

P. K. Page

Planet Earth

It has to be spread out, the skin of this planet,
has to be ironed, the sea in its whiteness;
and the hands keep on moving,
smoothing the holy surfaces.

In Praise of Ironing, *Pablo Neruda*

It has to be loved the way a laundress loves her linens,
the way she moves her hands caressing the fine muslins
knowing their warp and woof,
like a lover coaxing, or a mother praising.
It has to be loved as if it were embroidered   5
with flowers and birds and two joined hearts upon it.
It has to be stretched and stroked.
It has to be celebrated.
O this great beloved world and all the creatures in it.
It has to be spread out, the skin of this planet.   10

The trees must be washed, and the grasses and mosses.
They have to be polished as if made of green brass.
The rivers and little streams with their hidden cresses
and pale-coloured pebbles
and their fool's gold   15
must be washed and starched or shined into brightness,.
the sheets of lake water
smoothed with the hand
and the foam of the oceans pressed into neatness.
It has to be ironed, the sea in its whiteness.   20

and pleated and goffered, the flower-blue sea
the protean, wine-dark, grey, green, sea
with its metres of satin and bolts of brocade.
And sky—such an O! overhead—night and day
must be burnished and rubbed   25
by hands that are loving
so the blue blazons forth
and the stars keep on shining
within and above
and the hands keep on moving.   30

It has to be made bright, the skin of this planet
till it shines in the sun like gold leaf.
Archangels then will attend to its metals
and polish the rods of its rain.
Seraphim will stop singing hosannas   35

to shower it with blessings and blisses and praises
and, newly in love,
we must draw it and paint it
our pencils and brushes and loving caresses
smoothing the holy surfaces.   40

                                                           —1994

Robert Lowell (1917–1977) was born into a prominent Boston family and became known for his autobiographical poetry and his political activism. His poetry collections include the Pulitzer Prize–winning Lord Weary's Castle *(1947) and* The Dolphin *(1973), as well as the influential* Life Studies *(1959). He was repeatedly hospitalized for severe manic depression.*

Robert Lowell
Water

It was a Maine lobster town—
each morning boatloads of hands
pushed off for granite
quarries on the islands,

and left dozens of bleak   5
white frame houses stuck
like oyster shells
on a hill of rock,

and below us, the sea lapped
the raw little match-stick   10
mazes of a weir,
where the fish for bait were trapped.

Remember? We sat on a slab of rock.
From this dance in time,
it seems the color   15
of iris, rotting and turning purpler,

but it was only
the usual gray rock
turning the usual green
when drenched by the sea.   *20*

The sea drenched the rock
at our feet all day,
and kept tearing away
flake after flake.

One night you dreamed   *25*
you were a mermaid clinging to a wharf-pile,
and trying to pull
off the barnacles with your hands.

We wished our two souls
might return like gulls   *30*
to the rock. In the end,
the water was too cold for us.

—1964

Gwendolyn Brooks (1917–2000) was the first African American to win a Pulitzer Prize for poetry. Brooks reflected many changes in Black culture during her long career, and she wrote about the stages of her own life candidly in From the Mecca, *her literary autobiography. Brooks was the last poetry consultant of the Library of Congress before that position became poet laureate of the United States. At the end of her life Brooks was one of the most honoured and beloved of American poets.*

Gwendolyn Brooks
First Fight. Then Fiddle.

First fight. Then fiddle. Ply the slipping string
With feathery sorcery; muzzle the note
With hurting love; the music that they wrote
Bewitch, bewilder. Qualify to sing
Threadwise. Devise no salt, no hempen thing   *5*

For the dear instrument to bear. Devote
The bow to silks and honey. Be remote
A while from malice and from murdering.
But first to arms, to armor. Carry hate
In front of you and harmony behind.   10
Be deaf to music and to beauty blind.
Win war. Rise bloody, maybe not too late
For having first to civilize a space
Wherein to play your violin with grace.

—*1949*

Margaret Avison (b. 1918) was born in Galt, Ontario, and grew up on the prairies. Her conversion to Christianity in 1963 is reflected in collections like The Dumfounding *(1966) and* Sunblue *(1978). Her other collections include the award-winning* Winter Sun *(1960),* No Time *(1989),* Concrete and Wild Carrot *(2002),* Always Now *(in three volumes), and* Momentary Dark *(2006).*

Margaret Avison
Snow

Nobody stuffs the world in at your eyes.
The optic heart must venture: a jail-break
And re-creation. Sedges and wild rice
Chase rivery pewter. The astonished cinders quake
With rhizomes.° All ways through the electric air   5
Trundle candy-bright disks; they are desolate
Toys if the soul's gates seal, and cannot bear,
Must shudder under, creation's unseen freight.
But soft, there is snow's legend: colour of mourning
Along the yellow Yangtze° where the wheel   10

---

5 rhizomes plant stems that run along the ground and send out both roots and leaves   **10 Yangtze** longest river in China

Spins an indifferent stasis that's death's warning.
Asters of tumbled quietness reveal
Their petals. Suffering this starry blur
The rest may ring your change,° sad listener.

—1960

Al Purdy (1918–2000) *Identified as the People's Poet and the Voice of the Land, Purdy was born in Wooler, Ontario, but travelled widely across Canada, celebrating its places and people in memorable poems such as "Lament for the Dorsets" and "The Country North of Belleville." His collections include* The Cariboo Horses *(1965),* Collected Poems *(1986), and* Beyond Remembering *(2000).*

Al Purdy
A Handful of Earth

TO RENÉ LÉVESQUE°

Proposal:
let us join Quebec
if Quebec won't join us
I don't mind in the least
being governed from Quebec City   5
by Canadiens instead of Canadians
in fact the fleur-de-lis
                and maple leaf
are only symbols
and our true language   10
speaks from inside
the land itself

---

14 ring your change To ring the changes is to go through all the changes in ringing a peal of bells; to go through all the possible variations of a process.
René Lévesque (1922–1987) became leader of the separatist Parti Québécois in 1967 and served as premier of Quebec from 1976 to 1985.

Listen:
you can hear soft wind blowing
among tall fir trees on Vancouver Island   15
it is the same wind we knew
whispering along Côte des Neiges
on the island of Montreal
when we were lovers and had no money
Once flying in a little Cessna 180   20
above that great spine of mountains
where a continent attempts the sky
I wondered who owns this land
and knew that no one does
for we are tenants only   25

Go back a little:
to hip-roofed houses on the Isle d'Orléans
and scattered along the road to Chicoutimi
the remaining few log houses in Ontario
sod huts of sunlit prairie places   30
dissolved in rain long since
the stones we laid atop of one another
a few of which still stand
those origins
in which children were born   35
in which we loved and hated
in which we built a place to stand on
and now must tear it down?
—and here I ask all the oldest questions
of myself   40
the reasons for being alive
the way to spend this gift and thank the giver
but there is no way

I think of the small dapper man
chain-smoking at PQ headquarters   45
Lévesque
on Avenue Christophe Colomb in Montreal
where we drank coffee together six years past

I say to him now: my place is here
whether Côte des Neiges Avenue Christophe Colomb   50
Yonge Street Toronto Halifax or Vancouver
this place is where I stand
where all my mistakes were made
when I grew awkwardly and knew what I was
and that is Canadian or Canadien   55
it doesn't matter which to me

Sod huts break the prairie skyline
then melt in rain
the hip-roofed houses of New France as well
but French no longer   60
nor are we any longer English
—limestone houses
lean-tos and sheds our fathers built
in which our mothers died
before the forests tumbled down   65
ghost habitations
only this handful of earth
for a time at least
I have no other place to go

—1977, rev. 1978

Lawrence Ferlinghetti (b. 1919) *Born in Yonkers, New York, Ferlinghetti received a doctorate from the Sorbonne and settled in San Francisco, where he established the City Lights Bookstore. He has published* A Far Rockaway of the Heart *(1997) and* Loud Prayer *(1998), but it is* A Coney Island of the Mind *(1958), from which this poem is taken, that remains one of the quintessential documents of the Beat Generation.*

Lawrence Ferlinghetti

In Goya's° greatest scenes we seem to see

In Goya's greatest scenes we seem to see
                              the people of the world
    exactly at the moment when
          they first attained the title of
                              'suffering humanity'   5
    They writhe upon the page
                    in a veritable rage
                              of adversity
        Heaped up
              groaning with babies and bayonets   10
                          under cement skies
        in an abstract landscape of blasted trees
          bent statues bats wings and beaks
                slippery gibbets
          cadavers and carnivorous cocks   15
    and all the final hollering monsters
          of the
                'imagination of disaster'
    they are so bloody real
                it is as if they really still existed   20

    And they do

          Only the landscape is changed

Goya Goya y Lucientes (1746–1828), Spanish painter known for his tortured paintings and etchings of violence and madness, including a series entitled "The Disasters of War"

They still are ranged along the roads
    plagued by legionaires
                false windmills and demented roosters   *25*
They are the same people
             only further from home
  on freeways fifty lanes wide
        on a concrete continent
            spaced with bland billboards   *30*
      illustrating imbecile illusions of happiness
The scene shows fewer tumbrils°
        but more maimed citizens
             in painted cars
  and they have strange license plates   *35*
and engines
      that devour America

                                       —1958

Oodgeroo of the Tribe Noonuccal (1920–1993) was born Kath Walker on Stradbroke Island off the Queensland coast of Australia. Taking her Aboriginal name, she became a prominent activist for Aboriginal rights and a poet whose collections include We Are Going *(1964) and* Stradbroke Dreaming *(1972).*

Oodgeroo of the Tribe Noonuccal (Kath Walker)

We Are Going

For Grannie Coolwell

They came in to the little town
A semi-naked band subdued and silent,
All that remained of their tribe.
They came here to the place of their old bora ground°
Where now the many white men hurry about like ants.   *5*

---

32 tumbrils dung carts or instruments of punishment
4 bora ground site of Aboriginal initiation ceremony in which a boy is admitted to manhood

Notice of estate agent reads: "Rubbish May Be Tipped Here."
Now it half covers the traces of the old bora ring.
They sit and are confused, they cannot say their thoughts:
"We are as strangers here now, but the white tribe are the
    strangers.
We belong here, we are of the old ways.   *10*
We are the corroboree° and the bora ground,
We are the old sacred ceremonies, the laws of the elders.
We are the wonder tales of Dream Time,° the tribal legends
    told.
We are the past, the hunts and the laughing games, the
    wandering camp fires.
We are the lightning-bolt over Gaphembah Hill°   *15*
Quick and terrible,
And the Thunderer after him, that loud fellow.
We are the quiet daybreak paling the dark lagoon.
We are the shadow-ghosts creeping back as the camp fires
    burn low.
We are nature and the past, all the old ways   *20*
Gone now and scattered.
The scrubs are gone, the hunting and the laughter.
The eagle is gone, the emu° and the kangaroo are gone
    from this place.
The bora ring is gone.
The corroboree is gone.   *25*
And we are going."

—1964

---

11 corroboree public performance of songs and dances celebrating Aboriginal mythology and
spirituality   **13 Dream Time** the time beyond living memory, when the world came into being
15 Gaphembah Hill hill near Moongalba on Stradbroke Island, home of the author, off southeastern
Queensland in Australia   **23 emu** large flightless bird of Australia

Richard Wilbur (b. 1921) will be remembered by posterity as perhaps the most skillful metricist and exponent of wit that American poetry has produced. His highly polished poetry—against the grain of much contemporary writing—is a monument to his craftsmanship and intelligence. Perhaps the most honoured of all living American poets, Wilbur served as poet laureate of the United States in 1987. His translations of the verse dramas of Molière and Racine are regularly performed throughout the world.

Richard Wilbur

The Writer

In her room at the prow of the house
Where light breaks, and the windows are tossed with linden,
My daughter is writing a story.

I pause in the stairwell, hearing
From her shut door a commotion of typewriter-keys   5
Like a chain hauled over a gunwale.

Young as she is, the stuff
Of her life is a great cargo, and some of it heavy:
I wish her a lucky passage.

But now it is she who pauses,   10
As if to reject my thought and its easy figure.
A stillness greatens, in which

The whole house seems to be thinking,
And then she is at it again with a bunched clamor
Of strokes, and again is silent.   15

I remember the dazed starling
Which was trapped in that very room, two years ago;
How we stole in, lifted a sash

And retreated, not to affright it;
And how for a helpless hour, through the crack of the door,   20
We watched the sleek, wild, dark

And iridescent creature
Batter against the brilliance, drop like a glove
To the hard floor, or the desk-top.

And wait then, humped and bloody,   25
For the wits to try it again; and how our spirits
Rose when, suddenly sure,

It lifted off from a chair-back,
Beating a smooth course for the right window
And clearing the sill of the world.   30

It is always a matter, my darling,
Of life or death, as I had forgotten. I wish
What I wished you before, but harder.

                                        —1976

Philip Larkin (1922–1985) *was perhaps the last British poet to establish a significant body of readers in the United States. The general pessimism of his work is mitigated by a wry sense of irony and brilliant formal control. For many years he was a librarian at the University of Hull, and he was also a dedicated fan and critic of jazz.*

Philip Larkin
Water

If I were called in
To construct a religion
I should make use of water.

Going to church
Would entail a fording   5
To dry, different clothes;

My liturgy would employ
Images of sousing,
A furious devout drench,

And I should raise in the east   10
A glass of water
Where any-angled light
Would congregate endlessly.

—*1954*

---

*Denise Levertov (1923–1999) was an outspoken opponent of U.S. involvement in
the Vietnam War, an activity that has tended to overshadow her accomplishments as
a lyric poet. Born of Jewish and Welsh parents in England, she emigrated to the
United States during World War II.*

Denise Levertov
In Mind

There's in my mind a woman
of innocence, unadorned but

fair-featured, and smelling of
apples or grass. She wears

a utopian smock or shift, her hair   5
is light brown and smooth, and she

is kind and very clean without
ostentation—
                but she has
no imagination.   10

                And there's a
turbulent moon-ridden girl

or old woman, or both,
dressed in opals and rags, feathers

and torn taffeta,   15
who knows strange songs—

but she is not kind.

—*1964*

Maxine Kumin (b. 1925) was born in Philadelphia and educated at Radcliffe. Kumin was an early literary ally and friend of Anne Sexton, with whom she co-authored several children's books. The winner of the 1973 Pulitzer Prize, Kumin has preferred a rural life raising horses for some years. Her increased interest in the natural world has paralleled the environmental awareness of many of her readers.

Maxine Kumin
Noted in the *New York Times*

[handwritten: flight of sparrow is more miraculous than blast of rocket into space]

Lake Buena Vista, Florida, June 16, 1987

Death claimed the last pure dusky seaside sparrow
today, whose coastal range was narrow,
as narrow as its two-part buzzy song.
From hummocks lost to Cape Canaveral
this mouselike skulker in the matted grass,   5
a six-inch bird, plain brown, once thousands strong,
sang *toodle-raeee azhee*, ending on a trill
before the air gave way to rocket blasts.

It laid its dull white eggs (brown specked) in small
neat cups of grass on plots of pickleweed,   10
bulrushes, or salt hay. It dined
on caterpillars, beetles, ticks, the seeds
of sedges. Unremarkable
the life it led with others of its kind.

Tomorrow we can put it on a stamp,   15
a first-day cover with Key Largo rat,
Schaus swallowtail, Florida swamp
crocodile, and fading cotton mouse.

[handwritten: extinct and put on postage stamps]

How simply symbols replace habitat!
The tower frames of Aerospace   20
quiver in the flush of another shot
where, once indigenous, the dusky sparrow
soared trilling twenty feet above its burrow.

—1989

Allen Ginsberg (1926–1997) became the chief poetic spokesman of the Beat Generation. He was a force —as poet and celebrity —who continued to outrage and delight four decades after the appearance of Howl, *the monumental poem describing how Ginsberg saw: "the best minds of my generation destroyed by madness." Ginsberg's poems are cultural documents that provide a key to understanding the radical changes in American life, particularly among youth, that began in the mid-1950s.*

Allen Ginsberg

A Supermarket in California

What thoughts I have of you tonight, Walt Whitman, for I walked down the sidestreets under the trees with a headache self-conscious looking at the full moon.

In my hungry fatigue, and shopping for images, I went into the neon fruit supermarket, dreaming of your enumerations!

What peaches and what penumbras?° Whole families shopping at night! Aisles full of husbands! Wives in the avocados, babies in the tomatoes!—and you, García Lorca,° what were you doing down by the watermelons?

I saw you, Walt Whitman, childless, lonely old grubber, poking among the meats in the refrigerator and eyeing the grocery boys.

I heard you asking questions of each: Who killed the pork chops? What price bananas? Are you my Angel?   5

I wandered in and out of the brilliant stacks of cans following you, and followed in my imagination by the store detective.

We strode down the open corridors together in our solitary fancy tasting artichokes, possessing every frozen delicacy, and never passing the cashier.

---

3 penumbras shadows   **3 García Lorca** Federico García Lorca, Spanish poet (1899–1936)

Where are we going, Walt Whitman? The doors close in an
hour. Which way does your beard point tonight?
  (I touch your book and dream of our odyssey in the supermarket and feel absurd.)
  Will we walk all night through solitary streets? The trees add
shade to shade, lights out in the houses, we'll both be lonely.   *10*
  Will we stroll dreaming of the lost America of love past blue
automobiles in driveways, home to our silent cottage?
  Ah, dear father, graybeard, lonely old courage-teacher, what
America did you have when Charon° quit poling his ferry and
you got out on a smoking bank and stood watching the boat
disappear on the black waters of Lethe?°

                                                    —*1956*

---

*Robert Kroetsch (b. 1927) was born in Heisler, Alberta, and has explored life on
the prairies and Canada's north through a variety of playful postmodern novels,
including* The Studhorse Man *(1969) and* The Man from the Creeks *(1998),
and long poems collected in* Completed Field Notes *(1989).*

Robert Kroetsch
Stone Hammer Poem

1

This stone
become a hammer
of stone, this maul
is the colour
of bone (no,   *5*
bone is the colour
of this stone maul).

---

12 Charon ferryman of Hades **Lethe** river in Hades, means forgetfulness

The rawhide loops
are gone, the
hand is gone, the   *10*
buffalo's skull
is gone;

the stone is
shaped like the skull
of a child.   *15*

    2

This paperweight on my desk

where I begin
this poem   was

found in a wheatfield
lost (this hammer,   *20*
this poem).

Cut to a function,
this stone was
(the hand is   gone—

    3

Grey, two-headed,   *25*
the pemmican maul°

fell from the travois° or
a boy playing   lost it in
the prairie wool or
a squaw   left it in   *30*
the brain of a buffalo or

It is a million
years older than
the hand that
chipped stone or   *35*
raised slough
water (or blood) or

26 **pemmican maul** stone hammer used by Natives to make pemmican, a preparation of lean meat dried, pounded, and pressed into cakes   27 **travois** type of Native sledge

4

This stone maul
was found.

In the field   *40*
my grandfather
thought
was his

my father
thought was his   *45*

5

It is a stone
old as the last
Ice Age, the
retreating/the
recreating ice,   *50*
the retreating
buffalo, the
retreating Indians

(the saskatoons bloom
white (infrequently   *55*
the chokecherries the
highbush cranberries the
pincherries bloom
white along the barbed
wire fence (the   *60*
pemmican winter

6

This stone maul
stopped a plow
long enough for one
Gott im Himmel.°   *65*

The Blackfoot (the
Cree?) not

65 *Gott im Himmel* German for "God in Heaven"

finding the maul
cursed.

? did he curse   70
? did he try to
go back
? what happened
I have to/I want
to know (not know)   75
? WHAT HAPPENED

    7

The poem
is the stone
chipped and hammered
until it is shaped   80
like the stone
hammer, the maul.

    8

Now the field is
mine because
I gave it   85
(for a price)

to a young man
(with a growing son)
who did not

notice that the land   90
did not belong

to the Indian who
gave it to the Queen
(for a price) who
gave it to the CPR°   95
(for a price) which

95 **CPR** The Canadian Pacific Railway laid rail from east to west and promoted commerce by selling
land along the tracks to farmers.

gave it to my grandfather
(for a price) who
gave it to my father
(50 bucks an acre
Gott im Himmel I cut   100
down all the trees I
picked up all the stones) who

gave it to his son
(who sold it)   105

9

This won't
surprise you.

My grandfather
lost the stone maul.

10

My father (retired)   110
grew raspberries.
He dug in his potato patch.
He drank one glass of wine
each morning.
He was lonesome   115
for death.

He was lonesome for the
hot wind on his face, the smell
of horses, the distant
hum of a threshing machine,   120
the oilcan he carried, the weight
of a crescent wrench in his hind pocket.

He was lonesome for his absent
sons and his daughters,
for his wife, for his own   125
brothers and sisters and

his own mother and father.

He found the stone maul
on a rockpile in the
north-west corner of what
he thought of
as his wheatfield.

130

He kept it (the
stone maul) on the railing
of the back porch in
a raspberry basket.

135

    11

I keep it
on my desk
(the stone).

Sometimes I use it
in the (hot) wind
(to hold down paper)

140

smelling a little of cut
grass or maybe even of
ripening wheat or of
buffalo blood hot
in the dying sun.

145

Sometimes I write
my poems for that

stone hammer.

150

—1975

Phyllis Webb (b. 1927) was born in Victoria. After living in Montreal and Toronto, she eventually moved back to British Columbia. Her poetry—gathered in collections such as Naked Poems *(1965),* Water and Light: Ghazals and Anti-Ghazals *(1984), and the award-winning* Selected Poems: The Vision Tree *(1982)—has been referred to as metaphysical, existential, feminist, and minimalist.*

Phyllis Webb

Leaning

I am half-way up the stairs
of the Leaning Tower of Pisa.

Don't go down. You are in this
with me too.

I am leaning out of the Leaning   5
Tower heading into the middle distance

where a fur-blue star contracts, becomes
the ice-pond Brueghel's° figures are skating on.

North Magnetic pulls me like a flower
out of the perpendicular   10

angles me into outer space
an inch at a time, the slouch

of the ground, do you hear that?
the hiccup of the sludge about the stone.

(Rodin° in Paris, his amanuensis, a torso . . .)   15
   I must change my life or crunch

over in vertigo, hands
bloodying the inside tower walls

lichen and dirt under the fingernails
Parsifal° vocalizing in the crazy night   20

---

8 Brueghel Pieter Brueghel the Elder (1525–1569), Flemish painter known for his landscapes and scenes of peasant life   **15 Rodin** Auguste Rodin (1840–1917), French sculptor famous for *The Thinker*   **20 Parsifal** The composer Richard Wagner (1813–1883) used the story of the Arthurian knight Perceval as the basis for his last opera, *Parsifal* (1882).

my sick head on the table where I write
slumped one degree from the horizontal

the whole culture leaning . . .

the phalloi of Mies,° Columbus returning
stars all shot out—   *25*

And now this. Smelly tourists
shuffling around my ears

climbing into the curvature.
They have paid good lira to get in here.

So have I. So did Einstein and Bohr.°   *30*
Why should we ever come down, ever?

And you, are you still here

tilting in this stranded ark
blind and seeing in the dark.

                                                              —1984

---

*Martin Carter (1927–1997) Considered Guyana's greatest poet, Carter was
involved in politics, the struggle for independence from the British, and the social
well-being of his people, all themes that emerge in his revolutionary poetry gathered
in* Poems of Succession *(1977) and other collections.*

Martin Carter
University of Hunger

is the university of hunger the wide waste.
is the pilgrimage of man the long march.
The print of hunger wanders in the land.
The green tree bends above the long forgotten.
The plains of life rise up and fall in spasms.   *5*
The huts of men are fused in misery.

24 Mies Ludwig Mies van der Rohe (1886–1969), German-born architect who was known for his
skyscrapers   **30 Einstein and Bohr** Albert Einstein (1879–1955) and Neils Bohr (1885–1962) were
quantum physicists who took part in the making of the atomic bomb.

They come treading in the hoofmarks of the mule
passing the ancient bridge
the grave of pride
the sudden flight   10
the terror and the time.

They come from the distant village of the flood
passing from middle air to middle earth
in the common hours of nakedness.
Twin bars of hunger mark their metal brows   15
twin seasons mock them
parching drought and flood.

is the dark ones
the half sunken in the land.
is they who had no voice in the emptiness   20
in the unbelievable
in the shadowless.

They come treading on the mud floor of the year
mingling with dark heavy waters
and the sea sound of the eyeless flitting bat.
O long is the march of men and long is the life   25
and wide is the span.
O cold is the cruel wind blowing.
O cold is the hoe in the ground.

They come like sea birds   30
flapping in the wake of a boat
is the torture of sunset in purple bandages
is the powder of fire spread like dust in the twilight
is the water melodies of white foam on wrinkled sand.

The long streets of night move up and down   35
baring the thighs of a woman
and the cavern of generation.
The beating drum returns and dies away.
The bearded men fall down and go to sleep.
The cocks of dawn stand up and crow like bugles.   40

is they who rose early in the morning
watching the moon die in the dawn.
is they who heard the shell blow and the iron clang.
is they who had no voice in the emptiness
in the unbelievable   45
in the shadowless.
O long is the march of men and long is the life
and wide is the span.

—*1977*

John Ashbery (b. 1927) was born in upstate New York and educated at Harvard University. His first full-length book, Some Trees, *was chosen by W. H. Auden as winner of the Yale Younger Poets Award in 1956. The author of over twenty books of poetry, Ashbery is now seen as the chief inheritor of the symbolist tradition brought to American locales by Wallace Stevens.*

John Ashbery
Paradoxes and Oxymorons

The poem is concerned with language on a very plain level.
Look at it talking to you. You look out a window
Or pretend to fidget. You have it but you don't have it.
You miss it, it misses you. You miss each other.

The poem is sad because it wants to be yours, and cannot.   5
What's a plain level? It is that and other things,
Bringing a system of them into play. Play?
Well, actually, yes, but I consider play to be

A deeper outside thing, a dreamed role-pattern,
As in the division of grace these long August days   10
Without proof. Open-ended. And before you know
It gets lost in the steam and chatter of typewriters.

It has been played once more. I think you exist only
To tease me into doing it, on your level, and then you aren't there
Or have adopted a different attitude. And the poem   15
Has set me softly down beside you. The poem is you.

—1981

Anne Sexton (1928–1974) lived a tortured life of mental illness and family troubles, becoming the model of the confessional poet. A housewife with two small daughters, she began writing poetry as the result of a program on public television, later taking a workshop from Robert Lowell, in which Sylvia Plath was a fellow student. For fifteen years until her suicide, she was a vibrant, exciting presence in American poetry. A controversial biography of Sexton by Diane Wood Middlebrook appeared in 1991.

Anne Sexton
Cinderella

You always read about it:
the plumber with twelve children
who wins the Irish Sweepstakes.
From toilets to riches.
That story.   5

Or the nursemaid,
some luscious sweet from Denmark
who captures the oldest son's heart.
From diapers to Dior.
That story.   10

Or a milkman who serves the wealthy,
eggs, cream, butter, yogurt, milk,
the white truck like an ambulance
who goes into real estate
and makes a pile.   15
From homogenized to martinis at lunch.

Or the charwoman
who is on the bus when it cracks up
and collects enough from the insurance.
From mops to Bonwit Teller.   20
That story.

Once
the wife of a rich man was on her deathbed
and she said to her daughter Cinderella:
Be devout. Be good. Then I will smile   25
down from heaven in the seam of a cloud.
The man took another wife who had
two daughters, pretty enough
but with hearts like blackjacks.
Cinderella was their maid.   30
She slept on the sooty hearth each night
and walked around looking like Al Jolson.
Her father brought presents home from town,
jewels and gowns for the other women
but the twig of a tree for Cinderella.   35
She planted that twig on her mother's grave
and it grew to a tree where a white dove sat.
Whenever she wished for anything the dove
would drop it like an egg upon the ground.
The bird is important, my dears, so heed him.   40

Next came the ball, as you all know.
It was a marriage market.
The prince was looking for a wife.
All but Cinderella were preparing
and gussying up for the big event.   45
Cinderella begged to go too.
Her stepmother threw a dish of lentils
into the cinders and said: Pick them
up in an hour and you shall go.
The white dove brought all his friends;   50
all the warm wings of the fatherland came,
and picked up the lentils in a jiffy.
No, Cinderella, said the stepmother,

you have no clothes and cannot dance.
That's the way with stepmothers.   55

Cinderella went to the tree at the grave
and cried forth like a gospel singer:
Mama! Mama! My turtledove,
send me to the prince's ball!
The bird dropped down a golden dress   60
and delicate little gold slippers.
Rather a large package for a simple bird.
So she went. Which is no surprise.
Her stepmother and sisters didn't
recognize her without her cinder face   65
and the prince took her hand on the spot
and danced with no other the whole day.

As nightfall came she thought she'd
better get home. The prince walked her home
and she disappeared into the pigeon house   70
and although the prince took an axe and broke
it open she was gone. Back to her cinders.
These events repeated themselves for three days.
However on the third day the prince
covered the palace steps with cobbler's wax   75
And Cinderella's gold shoe stuck upon it.
Now he would find whom the shoe fit
and find his strange dancing girl for keeps.
He went to their house and the two sisters
were delighted because they had lovely feet.   80
The eldest went into a room to try the slipper on
but her big toe got in the way so she simply
sliced it off and put on the slipper.
The prince rode away with her until the white dove
told him to look at the blood pouring forth.   85
That is the way with amputations.
They don't just heal up like a wish.
The other sister cut off her heel
but the blood told as blood will.
The prince was getting tired.   90

He began to feel like a shoe salesman.
But he gave it one last try.
This time Cinderella fit into the shoe
like a love letter into its envelope.

At the wedding ceremony   *95*
the two sisters came to curry favor
and the white dove pecked their eyes out.
Two hollow spots were left
like soup spoons.

Cinderella and the prince   *100*
lived, they say, happily ever after,
like two dolls in a museum case
never bothered by diapers or dust,
never arguing over the timing of an egg,
never telling the same story twice,   *105*
never getting a middle-aged spread,
their darling smiles pasted on for eternity
Regular Bobbsey Twins.
That story.

                                                     —1970

The Starry Night

> *That does not keep me from having a terrible*
> *need of—shall I say the word—religion. Then I*
> *go out at night to paint the stars.*
>
>   —Vincent Van Gogh in a letter to his brother

The town does not exist
except where one black-haired tree slips
up like a drowned woman into the hot sky.
The town is silent. The night boils with eleven stars
Oh starry starry night! This is how   *5*
I want to die.

It moves. They are all alive.
Even the moon bulges in its orange irons

to push children, like a god, from its eye.
The old unseen serpent swallows up the stars.   *10*
Oh starry starry night! This is how
I want to die:

into that rushing beast of the night,
sucked up by that great dragon, to split
from my life with no flag,   *15*
no belly,
no cry.

—*1962*

---

*A. K. Ramanujan (1929–1993) was born and educated in Mysore in South India.
He was a poet in both Kannada and English, a scholar, professor, translator, and editor. His poetry collections in English include* The Striders *(1966),* Relations
(1971), Second Sight *(1986), and the posthumous* Collected Poems *(1995).
He also co-edited* The Oxford Anthology of Modern Indian Poetry *(1994).*

A. K. Ramanujan
A River

In Madurai,
            city of temples and poets
who sang of cities and temples:

every summer
a river dries to a trickle   *5*
in the sand,
baring the sand-ribs,
straw and women's hair
clogging the watergates
at the rusty bars   *10*
under the bridges with patches
of repair all over them,
the wet stones glistening like sleepy
crocodiles, the dry ones
shaven water-buffaloes lounging in the sun.   *15*

The poets sang only of the floods.

He was there for a day
when they had the floods.
People everywhere talked
of the inches rising,   20
of the precise number of cobbled steps
run over by the water, rising
on the bathing places,
and the way it carried off three village houses,
one pregnant woman   25
and a couple of cows
named Gopi and Brinda, as usual.

The new poets still quoted
the old poets, but no one spoke
in verse   30
of the pregnant woman
drowned, with perhaps twins in her,
kicking at blank walls
even before birth.

He said: 35
the river has water enough
to be poetic
about only once a year
and then
it carries away   40
in the first half-hour
three village houses,
a couple of cows
named Gopi and Brinda
and one pregnant woman   45
expecting identical twins
with no moles on their bodies,
with different-coloured diapers

to tell them apart.

—1966

Adrienne Rich (b. 1929) was born in Baltimore, Maryland, of Jewish heritage. Her first book of poetry, A Change of World *(1951), was introduced by W. H. Auden. After dedicating time to marriage and motherhood, she returned to writing powerful poetry and prose that was increasingly political and concerned with feminist and lesbian themes. In all, she has written over twenty books of poetry, including the landmark work* Diving into the Wreck *(1973),* An Atlas of the Difficult World *(1991),* Midnight Salvage *(1999), and* The School Among the Ruins *(2004). Her work has earned her many awards, including the Lannan Foundation Lifetime Achievement Award. She lives in California.*

Adrienne Rich
Power

Living   in the earth-deposits   of our history
Today a backhoe divulged   out of a crumbling flank of earth
one bottle   amber   perfect   a hundred-year-old
cure for fever   or melancholy   a tonic
for living on this earth   in the winters of this climate   5

Today I was reading about Marie Curie:
she must have known she suffered   from radiation sickness
her body bombarded for years   by the element
she had purified
It seems she denied to the end   10
the source of the cataracts on her eyes
the cracked and suppurating skin   of her finger-ends
till she could no longer hold   a test-tube or a pencil

She died   a famous woman   denying
her wounds   15
denying
her wounds   came   from the same source as her power

—*1978*

D. G. Jones (b. 1929) *was born in Ontario but has spent much of his life in Quebec. He has earned Governor General's Awards both for his translations and for his own poetry, of which he has published over ten collections. In his complex suite of thirteen acrostic poems, Jones celebrates the love between early Canadian poet Archibald Lampman and Katherine Waddell.*

D. G. Jones

Kate, These Flowers . . .

(THE LAMPMAN POEMS)

I

You picked the dead bloom
expertly, leaving one star
lifting, long-stemmed, above cascading
leaves
    my day's star   5

Oh, Archie, you're a fool, she said

What colours are the vireo?°
Deep garden lights, the reflected lights of
apple leaves
    my dear   10
your shadowed flesh

like grave eyes in the afternoon
it is, under all pain, silent
laughter
    bird, flower   15
you, Kate, briefly on a day in June

II

Kisses are knowledge, Kate
aphasia confounds us with a new
tongue
    too Pentecostal; too   20

7 vireo small songbirds

Eleusinian,° perhaps, for us
moderate Anglicans

You blush and the immoderate blood
riots like a rose
                    we are both   25
exposed
           I who hate Sundays

dream how I will boldly
rush out and overnight paint
Ottawa crimson   30
              I come
secretly to the fold, would find
election° in your mouth

                                                    —1977

Ted Hughes (1930–1998) was a native of Yorkshire, England. He never ventured far from the natural world of his childhood for his subject matter. Hughes was married to Sylvia Plath until her death in 1963; Birthday Letters, a book of poems about their troubled relationship, appeared in 1998. At the time of his death, Hughes was the British poet laureate.

Ted Hughes
The Thought-Fox

I imagine this midnight moment's forest:
Something else is alive
Beside the clock's loneliness
And this blank page where my fingers move.

Through the window I see no star; — no image of spirituality   5
Something more near
Though deeper within darkness — alliteration
Is entering the loneliness:

21 **Eleusinian** celebrations near Athens in honour of the fertility goddess Demeter
33 **election** to be chosen

Cold, delicately as the dark snow,
A fox's nose touches twig, leaf;   *10*
Two eyes serve a movement, that now
And again now, and now, and now

[handwritten: — print of fox's paw each "now"]

Sets neat prints into the snow
Between trees, and warily a lame
Shadow lags by stump and in hollow   *15*
Of a body that is bold to come

Across clearings, an eye,
A widening deepening greenness,
Brilliantly, concentratedly,
Coming about its own business   *20*

[handwritten: coming towards house — inspiration coming towards the poet]

Till, with a sudden sharp hot stink of fox
It enters the dark hole of the head.
The window is starless still; the clock ticks,
The page is printed.

[handwritten: print of fox's paw print of poem on this page]

—1957

---

*Kamau Brathwaite (b. 1930) In many of his poems, including "Colombe,"
Brathwaite explores the influence of colonization and slavery on his native Barbados.
His collections include* The Arrivants *(1973),* Middle Passages *(1992), and*
Born to Slow Horses *(2005), which won the Griffin Poetry Prize for 2006.*

Kamau Brathwaite
Colombe

Columbus from his after-
deck watched stars, absorbed in water,
melt in liquid amber drifting

through my summer air   *5*
Now with morning shadows lifting
beaches stretched before him cold & clear

Birds circled flapping flag & mizzen
mast.   birds harshly hawking.   without fear
Discovery he sailed for.   was so near   10

ℭ

olumbus from his after-
deck watched heights he hoped for
rocks he dreamed.   rise solid from my simple water

Parrots screamed. Soon he would touch   15
our land.   his charted mind's desire
The blue sky blessed the morning with its fire

But did his vision
fashion as he watched the shore
the slaughter that his soldiers   20

furthered here?   Pike
point & musket butt
hot splintered courage.   bones

cracked with bullet shot
tipped black boot in my belly.   the   25
whips uncurled desire?

ℭ

olumbus from his after-
deck saw bearded fig trees.   yellow pouis
blazed like pollen & thin   30

waterfalls suspended in the green
as his eyes climbed towards the highest ridges
where our farms were hidden

Now he was sure
he heard soft voices mocking in the leaves   35
What did this journey mean.   this

new world mean.   dis
covery? or a return to terrors
he had sailed from.   known before?

I watched him pause   *40*

Then he was splashing silence
Crabs snapped their claws
and scattered as he walked towards our shore

—*1992*

---

*Derek Walcott (b. 1930) is a native of the tiny Caribbean island of St. Lucia in
the West Indies. Walcott combines a love of the tradition of English poetry with the
exotic surfaces of tropical life. In many ways, his life and career have constituted a
study in divided loyalties, which are displayed in his ambivalent poems about life in
the United States, where he has lived and taught for many years. Walcott was
awarded the Nobel Prize in 1992.*

Derek Walcott
Central America

Helicopters are cutlassing the wild bananas.
Between a nicotine thumb and forefinger
brittle faces crumble like tobacco leaves.
Children waddle in vests, their legs bowed,
little shrimps curled under their navels.   *5*
The old men's teeth are stumps in a charred forest.
Their skins grate like the iguana's.
Their gaze like slate stones.
Women squat by the river's consolations
where children wade up to their knees,   *10*
and a stick stirs up a twinkling of butterflies.
Up there, in the blue acres
of forest, flies circle their fathers.
In spring, in the upper provinces
of the Empire, yellow tanagers   *15*
float up through the bare branches.
There is no distinction in these distances.

—*1987*

Miller Williams (b. 1930) won the Poet's Prize in 1990 for Living on the Surface, *a volume of selected poems. A skillful translator of both Giuseppe Belli, a Roman poet of the early nineteenth century, and Nicanor Parra, a contemporary Chilean, Williams has written many poems about his travels throughout the world yet has retained the relaxed idiom of his native Arkansas.*

Miller Williams

The Book

I held it in my hands while he told the story.

He had found it in a fallen bunker,
a book for notes with all the pages blank.
He took it to keep for a sketchbook and diary.

He learned years later, when he showed the book   5
to an old bookbinder, who paled, and stepped back
a long step and told him what he held,
what he had laid the days of his life in.
It's bound, the binder said, in human skin.

I stood turning it over in my hands,   10
turning it in my head. Human skin.

What child did this skin fit? What man, what woman?
Dragged still full of its flesh from what dream?

Who took it off the meat? Some other one
who stayed alive by knowing how to do this?   15

I stared at the changing book and a horror grew,
I stared and a horror grew, which was, which is,
how beautiful it was until I knew.

—*1989*

Linda Pastan (b. 1932) served as poet laureate of Maryland, where she has lived and taught for many years. Her first book, A Perfect Circle of Sun, *appeared in 1971, and ten more collections have been published since. Her straightforward language belies the discipline of her craft, in which each poem "goes through something like 100 revisions."*

Linda Pastan

Ethics

In ethics class so many years ago
our teacher asked this question every fall:
if there were a fire in a museum
which would you save, a Rembrandt painting
or an old woman who hadn't many   5
years left anyhow? Restless on hard chairs
caring little for pictures or old age
we'd opt one year for life, the next for art
and always half-heartedly. Sometimes
the woman borrowed my grandmother's face   10
leaving her usual kitchen to wander
some drafty, half imagined museum.
One year, feeling clever, I replied
why not let the woman decide herself?
Linda, the teacher would report, eschews   15
the burdens of responsibility.
This fall in a real museum I stand
before a real Rembrandt, old woman,
or nearly so, myself. The colors
within this frame are darker than autumn,   20
darker even than winter—the browns of earth,
though earth's most radiant elements burn
through the canvas. I know now that woman
and painting and season are almost one
and all beyond saving by children.   25

—*1981*

Sylvia Plath (1932–1963), whose troubled personal life is often difficult to separate from her poetry, is almost always read as an autobiographical and confessional poet. Brilliant and precocious, she served a long apprenticeship to the tradition of modern poetry before attaining her mature style in the final two years of her life. Only one collection, The Colossus, *appeared in her lifetime, and her fame has mainly rested on her posthumous books of poetry and the success of her lone novel,* The Bell Jar. *She committed suicide in 1963. Plath has been the subject of many biographical studies, reflecting the intense interest that readers, especially women, have in her life and work.*

Sylvia Plath

Black Rook in Rainy Weather

On the stiff twig up there
Hunches a wet black rook
Arranging and rearranging its feathers in the rain.
I do not expect a miracle
Or an accident   5

To set the sight on fire
In my eye, nor seek
Any more in the desultory weather some design,
But let spotted leaves fall as they fall,
Without ceremony, or portent — *foretell future/ omen*   10
                              ritual

Although, I admit, I desire,
Occasionally, some backtalk
From the mute sky, I can't honestly complain: *heaven is empty*
                              no God, miracle
A certain minor light may still
Leap incandescent   15

Out of kitchen table or chair ← *Doesn't expect*
                              heavenly, divine
As if a celestial burning took
Possession of the most obtuse objects now and then—
Thus hallowing an interval
Otherwise inconsequent   20

By bestowing largesse, honor,
One might say love. At any rate, I now walk

Wary (for it could happen
Even in this dull, ruinous landscape); skeptical,
Yet politic; ignorant   25

Of whatever angel may choose to flare
Suddenly at my elbow. I only know that a rook
Ordering its black feathers can so shine
As to seize my senses, haul *visionary experiences*
My eyelids up, and grant *can still happen if you*   30
keep an eye out for it
A brief respite from fear
Of total neutrality. With luck,
Trekking stubborn through this season
Of fatigue, I shall
Patch together a content   35

Of sorts. Miracles occur, *position is shifted*
If you care to call those spasmodic *but could be just an*
Tricks of radiance miracles. The wait's begun again, *illusion*
The long wait for the angel,
For that rare, random descent.°   40

—*1960*

Metaphors

I'm a riddle in nine syllables,
An elephant, a ponderous house,
A melon strolling on two tendrils.
O red fruit, ivory, fine timbers!
This loaf's big with its yeasty rising.   5
Money's new-minted in this fat purse.
I'm a means, a stage, a cow in calf.
I've eaten a bag of green apples,
Boarded the train there's no getting off.

—*1960*

---

40 descent In the Bible, the crippled and blind gathered around the pool of Bethesda, where an angel
would sometimes descend and stir the waters. The first in would be healed (John 5:4).

Alden Nowlan (1933–1983) grew up in Nova Scotia in impoverished circumstances. He quit school in Grade 5 but continued to educate himself through reading, and went on to become a journalist and to publish novels and short stories that evoke a Maritime world at once harsh and human, as well as over ten collections of poetry, including Bread, Wine and Salt *(1965),* I Might Not Tell Everybody This *(1982), and* An Exchange of Gifts *(1985).*

Alden Nowlan
The Bull Moose

Down from the purple mist of trees on the mountain,
lurching through forests of white spruce and cedar,
stumbling through tamarack swamps,
came the bull moose
to be stopped at last by a pole-fenced pasture.   5

Too tired to turn or, perhaps, aware
there was no place left to go, he stood with the cattle.
They, scenting the musk of death, seeing his great head
like the ritual mask of a blood god, moved to the other end
of the field and waited.   10

The neighbours heard of it, and by afternoon
cars lined the road.   The children teased him
with alder switches and he gazed at them
like an old tolerant collie.   The women asked
if he could have escaped from a Fair.   15

The oldest man in the parish remembered seeing
a gelded moose yoked with an ox for plowing.
The young men snickered and tried to pour beer
down his throat, while their girl friends
took their pictures.   20

And the bull moose let them stroke his tick-ravaged flanks,
let them pry open his jaws with bottles, let a giggling girl
plant a little purple cap
of thistles on his head.

[handwritten annotation: crown of thorns on Christ]

When the wardens came, everyone agreed it was a shame   25
to shoot anything so shaggy and cuddlesome.
He looked like the kind of pet
women put to bed with their sons.

So they held their fire.   But just as the sun dropped in the river
the bull moose gathered his strength   30
like a scaffolded king, straightened and lifted his horns
so that even the wardens backed away as they raised their rifles.
When he roared, people ran to their cars.   All the young men
leaned on their automobile horns as he toppled.

—1970

The Broadcaster's Poem

I used to broadcast at night
alone in a radio station
but I was never good at it,
partly because my voice wasn't right
but mostly because my peculiar   5
metaphysical stupidity
made it impossible
for me to keep believing
there was somebody listening
when it seemed I was talking   10
only to myself in a room no bigger
than an ordinary bathroom.
I could believe it for a while
and then I'd get somewhat
the same feeling as when you   15
start to suspect you're the victim
of a practical joke.
                    So one part of me
was afraid another part
might blurt out something   20
about myself so terrible

that even I had never until
that moment suspected it.
                    This was like the fear
of bridges and other   25
high places: Will I take off my glasses
and throw them
into the water, although I'm
half-blind without them?
Will I sneak up behind   30
myself and push?
                    Another thing:
as a reporter
I covered an accident in which a train
ran into a car, killing   35
three young men, one of whom
was beheaded. The bodies looked
boneless, as such bodies do.
More like mounds of rags.
And inside the wreckage   40
where nobody could get at it
the car radio
was still playing.
                    I thought about places
the disc jockey's voice goes   45
and the things that happen there
and of how impossible it would be for him
to continue if he really knew.

                                            —*1974*

Jacques Godbout (b. 1933) was born in Montreal and has worked as a screen-writer, professor of French and philosophy, playwright, novelist, essayist, and poet. He has directed over thirty films, including four dramatic features, and published nine novels, including Salut Galarneau! *(1967) and* Une Histoire Américaine *(1986), as well as half a dozen collections of poetry, including* Souvenirs Shop *(1984).*

Jacques Godbout

Trees

Trees we have given you a thousand names

In a tree-hollow I have hidden a silver coin
They will find it when they are sixteen

Under torn-away bark in the tree's wood
I too have carved the words love liberty friendship   5
A fantasy without respect for its dignity
I wanted very much to write peace
But there was no more space
So I looked around
The forest had gone to bed and under the sleeping trunks   10
Ready for the pulping stone the papermaking
The C-I-L factories and One Hundred Industries
I slipped You your name

I hid in a hollow tree
Watchful as a big cat for the sound of footsteps   15
When they are twenty they will find me
With my head between my legs
And my bones bleached because I waited for you,
What will they make from my bones?
Perhaps some games   20
Or drawings done on sand

When the forests rise up as in
a Shakespearean tragedy at the cinema

Translated by John Glassco.

And when they have also walked
When trees have shattered the concrete   25
Of launching pads
When sequoias have strangled the steel structures
(mosses and lianas parasites   control instruments)
What will they make with my money?

A goddess perhaps   30
Or a charm against boredom

They will see an army of blacks with bronze trumpets
Sit down on a rocket's tip
To make it fall
Carried away by sound and by their own flesh   35
They will find in tree-hollows
Their homesickness for lianas and drums

Trees we have given you a thousand names
And streets too
That we love   40

In tree-hollows and shaded streets
In rock-gardens and courtyard moss
We have hidden a silver coin
Our dear friendship our love even
However it may be that others invent prisons   45
And the iron of angelic hate

Almond trees tender bougainvilleas
We used to make love in your shade

Perhaps you will grant us
The secret of your light   50

                                                           —1960

Leonard Cohen (b. 1934) was born in Montreal of Jewish heritage, and has had a long, successful career as a poet, singer, and songwriter whose songs have been widely recorded. He has published two novels, The Favourite Game *(1963) and* Beautiful Losers *(1966), and several collections of poetry, including* Flowers for Hitler *(1964),* Book of Mercy *(1984), and* Book of Longing *(2006). He has lived as a Zen monk, been honoured with numerous literary and music awards, and recorded more than fourteen albums.*

Leonard Cohen
The Future

Give me back my broken night
my mirrored room, my secret life
It's lonely here,
there's no one left to torture
Give me absolute control   5
over every living soul
And lie beside me, baby,
that's an order!

Give me crack and anal sex
Take the only tree that's left   10
and stuff it up the hole
in your culture
Give me back the Berlin Wall
give me Stalin and St Paul
I've seen the future, brother: 15
it is murder.

Things are going to slide in all directions
Won't be nothing
Nothing you can measure any more
The blizzard of the world   20
has crossed the threshold
and it has overturned
the order of the soul
When they said REPENT
I wonder what they meant   25

You don't know me from the wind
you never will, you never did
I'm the little jew
who wrote the bible
I've seen the nations rise and fall   30
I've heard their stories, heard them all
but love's the only engine of survival

Your servant here, he has been told
to say it clear, to say it cold:
It's over, it ain't going   35
any further
And now the wheels of heaven stop
you feel the devil's riding crop
Get ready for the future:
it is murder.   40

Things are going to slide in all directions

There'll be the breaking
of the ancient western code
Your private life will suddenly explode
There'll be phantoms   45
there'll be fires on the road
and the white man dancing

You'll see your woman
hanging upside down
her features covered by her fallen gown   50
and all the lousy little poets
coming round
trying to sound like Charlie Manson

Give me back the Berlin Wall
give me Stalin and St Paul   55
Give me Christ
or give me Hiroshima
Destroy another fetus now
We don't like children anyhow
I've seen the future, baby: 60
it is murder.

Things are going to slide in all directions
Won't be nothing
Nothing you can measure any more
The blizzard of the world   65
has crossed the threshold
and it has overturned
the order of the soul
When they said REPENT
I wonder what they meant   70

—*1993 (recorded 1992)*

Pat Lowther (1935–1975) *grew up in Vancouver and spent her life on the West Coast. Her poetry collections include* A Difficult Flowering *(1968) and* Milk Stone *(1974). In 1975 her body was discovered in a creek near Squamish, British Columbia, and her husband was convicted of her murder.* A Stone Diary *(1976) and* Final Instructions *(1980) were published posthumously.*

Pat Lowther

Octopus

The octopus is beautifully
functional as an umbrella;
at rest a bag of rucked skin
sags like an empty scrotum
his jelled eyes sad and bored   5

but taking flight: look
how lovely purposeful
in every part:
the jet vent smooth
as modern plumbing   10
the webbed pinwheel of tentacles
moving in perfect accord
like a machine dreamed
by Leonardo

—*1977*

George Bowering (b. 1935) was born in Penticton, British Columbia, and was a member of the Tish *movement inspired by the Black Mountain Poets. He has published over thirty books of poetry, as well as numerous books of criticism and award-winning fiction. He was named Canada's first poet laureate in 2000. Baseball, one of his most enduring metaphors, appears in this poem from* Blonds on Bikes *(1997).*

George Bowering
Play & Work & Art

When you play the infield,
especially on diamonds like the one at Woodlands Park,
you bend over at the inning's beginning
& pick up stones
to throw thru the wire fence.   5

One day near second base at Woodlands Park
I bent over & picked up a pointy pebble
I raised to my eye, rubbed the dust off,
& it was an arrowhead.

Right there, East Side Vancouver.   10

Months later, sitting here with a sore baseball back
I thought about baseball as play
& arrow-making as work.

Then I thought again.

Making an arrowhead to kill a fish or deer   15
to feed a family or a people
is still interesting, is still making.
It is not a nuisance. You can see it

coming, like a ground ball, which
if you're over fifty, is no sure thing,   20
which is enough like work, like work & pain
in a life you are getting thru.

—1997

Joy Kogawa (b. 1935) was born in Vancouver, of Japanese heritage. This poem, like the novel Obasan *(1981), for which she is best known, deals with her experience of the evacuation and internment of Japanese Canadians after Pearl Harbor. Her books of poetry include* A Choice of Dreams *(1974) and* A Song of Lilith *(2000).*

Joy Kogawa
When I Was a Little Girl

When I was a little girl
We used to walk together
Tim, my brother who wore glasses,
And I, holding hands
Tightly as we crossed the bridge   5
And he'd murmur, "You pray now"
—being a clergyman's son—
Until the big white boys
Had kicked on past.
Later we'd climb the bluffs   10
Overhanging the ghost town
And pick the small white lilies
And fling them like bombers
Over Slocan.

—1974

Fred Chappell (b. 1936) wrote the prize-winning epic-length poem Midquest *(1981), a complex autobiographical sequence heavily indebted to Dante for its formal structure. A versatile writer of both poetry and prose, Chappell brilliantly displays his classical learning in unusual contexts.*

Fred Chappell

Narcissus and Echo°

Shall the water not remember *Ember*
my hand's slow gesture, tracing above *of*
its mirror my half-imaginary *airy*
portrait? My only belonging *longing*
is my beauty, which I take *ache*   5
away and then return as love *of*
teasing playfully the one being *unbeing.*

whose gratitude I treasure *Is your*
moves me. I live apart *heart*
from myself, yet cannot *not*   10
live apart. In the water's tone, *stone?*
that brilliant silence, a flower *Hour,*
whispers my name with such slight *light,*
moment, it seems filament of air, *fare*
the world become cloudswell. *well.*   15

—*1985*

Narcissus and Echo In the myth, the vain Narcissus drowned attempting to embrace his own reflection in the water. Echo, a nymph who loved him, pined away until only her voice remained.

Marge Piercy (b. 1936) was a political radical during her student days at the University of Michigan. Piercy has continued to be outspoken on political, cultural, and sexual issues. Her phrase "to be of use" has become a key measure by which feminist writers and critics have gauged the meaning of their own life experiences.

Marge Piercy
Barbie Doll

This girlchild was born as usual
and presented dolls that did pee-pee
and miniature GE stoves and irons
and wee lipsticks the color of cherry candy.
Then in the magic of puberty, a classmate said: 5
You have a great big nose and fat legs.

She was healthy, tested intelligent
possessed strong arms and back,
abundant sexual drive and manual dexterity.
She went to and fro apologizing.   10
Everyone saw a fat nose on thick legs.

She was advised to play coy,
exhorted to come on hearty,
exercise, diet, smile and wheedle.
Her good nature wore out   15
like a fan belt.
So she cut off her nose and her legs
and offered them up.

In the casket displayed on satin she lay
with the undertaker's cosmetics painted on,   20
a turned-up putty nose,
dressed in a pink and white nightie.
Doesn't she look pretty? everyone said.
Consummation at last.
To every woman a happy ending.   25

—*1982*

Robert Phillips (b. 1938) laboured for over thirty years as a New York advertising executive, a remarkable fact when one considers his many books of poetry, fiction, and criticism and the numerous books he has edited. He currently lives in Houston, where he teaches in the creative writing program at the University of Houston.

Robert Phillips
Compartments

Which shall be final?
    Pine box in a concrete vault,
urn on a mantel?

Last breath a rattle,
    stuffed in a black body bag,   5
he's zipped head to toe.

At the nursing home,
    side drawn to prevent a fall—
in a crib again.

His dead wife's false teeth   10
    underfoot in their bedroom.
Feel the piercing chill.

Pink flamingo lawn,
    a Florida trailer park:
one space he'll avoid.   15

The box they gave him
    on retirement held a watch
that measures decades.

The new bifocals
    rest in their satin-lined case,   20
his body coffined.

Move to the suburbs.
    Crowded train at seven-oh-two,
empty head at night.

New playpen, new crib,
      can't compete with the newness
of the newborn child.   25

Oak four-poster bed
      inherited from family—
Jack Frost defrosted.   30

Once he was pink-slipped.
      Dad helped out: "A son's a son,
Son, from womb to tomb."

Fourteen-foot ceilings,
      parquet floors, marble fireplace,   35
proud first apartment.

The Jack Frost Motel,
      its very name a portent
for their honeymoon.

Backseat of a car,   40
      cursing the inventor of
nylon pantyhose.

First-job cubicle.
      Just how many years before
a window office?   45

College quad at noon,
      chapel bells, frat men, coeds,
no pocket money.

his grandfather's barn.
      After it burned to the ground,   50
the moon filled its space.

His favorite tree—
      the leaves return to branches?
No, butterflies light.

Closet where he hid   55
      to play with himself. None knew?
Mothball orgasms.

Chimney that he scaled
      naked to sweep for his Dad:
Blake's soot-black urchin.   *60*

The town's swimming pool
      instructor, throwing him in
again and again . . .

Kindergarten play
      ground: swings, slides, rings, jungle gym.   *65*
Scraped knees, molester.

Red, blue and green birds
      mobilize over his crib,
its sides a tall fence.

Two months premature,   *70*
      he incubates by light bulbs,
like a baby chick.

He is impatient,
      curled in foetal position,
floating in darkness.   *75*

                                       —2000

Margaret Atwood (b. 1939) is a leading figure among Canadian writers, with a huge international following. She is equally skilled as a poet and fiction writer, and has used her considerable reputation to support a variety of causes, including PEN International. Born in Ottawa, she graduated from the University of Toronto in 1962 and later did graduate work at Radcliffe and Harvard. She has authored over a dozen poetry collections, including Eating Fire: Selected Poems, 1965–1995 *(1998); a dozen novels, including* The Handmaid's Tale *(1985) and* The Penelopiad *(2005); as well as half a dozen collections of short fiction, including* The Tent *(2006). She has also written literary criticism, including* Survival: A Thematic Guide to Canadian Literature *(1972), and several books for children. Her long list of awards includes the Giller Prize, the Booker Prize, and the Governor General's Award. She continues to be an inventive and prolific writer of works that reflect her feminist concerns, her interest in classical and popular mythology, and her increasing concern for the future of the planet.*

Margaret Atwood
[you fit into me]

you fit into me
like a hook into an eye

a fish hook
an open eye

—1971

Death of a Young Son by Drowning

He, who navigated with success
the dangerous river of his own birth
once more set forth

on a voyage of discovery
into the land I floated on   5
but could not touch to claim.

His feet slid on the bank,
the currents took him;
he swirled with ice and trees in the swollen water

and plunged into distant regions,   10
his head a bathysphere;
through his eyes' thin glass bubbles

he looked out, reckless adventurer
on a landscape stranger than Uranus
we have all been to and some remember.   15

There was an accident; the air locked,
he was hung in the river like a heart.
They retrieved the swamped body,

cairn of my plans and future charts,
with poles and hooks   20
from among the nudging logs.

It was spring, the sun kept shining, the new grass
lept to solidity;
my hands glistened with details.

After the long trip I was tired of waves.   25
My foot hit rock. The dreamed sails
collapsed, ragged.

> I planted him in this country
> like a flag.

                                            —*1970*

Notes Towards a Poem That Can Never Be Written

FOR CAROLYN FORCHÉ

i

This is the place
you would rather not know about,
this is the place that will inhabit you,
this is the place you cannot imagine,
this is the place that will finally defeat you   5

where the word *why* shrivels and empties
itself. This is famine.

ii

There is no poem you can write
about it, the sandpits
where so many were buried   10
& unearthed, the unendurable
pain still traced on their skins.

This did not happen last year
or forty years ago but last week.
This has been happening,   15
this happens.

We make wreaths of adjectives for them,
we count them like beads,
we turn them into statistics & litanies
and into poems like this one.   20

Nothing works.
They remain what they are.

iii

The woman lies on the wet cement floor
under the unending light,
needle marks on her arms put there   25
to kill the brain
and wonders why she is dying.

She is dying because she said.
She is dying for the sake of the word.
It is her body, silent   30
and fingerless, writing this poem.

iv

It resembles an operation
but it is not one

nor despite the spread legs, grunts
& blood, is it a birth.   35

Partly it's a job,
partly it's a display of skill
like a concerto.

It can be done badly
or well, they tell themselves.   40

Partly it's an art.

v

The facts of this world seen clearly
are seen through tears;
why tell me then
there is something wrong with my eyes?   45

To see clearly and without flinching,
without turning away,
this is agony, the eyes taped open
two inches from the sun.

What is it you see then?   50
Is it a bad dream, a hallucination?
Is it a vision?
What is it you hear?

The razor across the eyeball
is a detail from an old film.   55
It is also a truth.
Witness is what you must bear.

  vi

In this country you can say what you like
because no one will listen to you anyway,
it's safe enough, in this country you can try to write   60
the poem that can never be written,
the poem that invents
nothing and excuses nothing,
because you invent and excuse yourself each day.

Elsewhere, this poem is not invention.   65
Elsewhere, this poem takes courage.
Elsewhere, this poem must be written
because the poets are already dead.

Elsewhere, this poem must be written
as if you are already dead,   70
as if nothing more can be done
or said to save you.

Elsewhere you must write this poem
because there is nothing more to do.

—1981

Patrick Lane (b. 1939) *was born in Nelson, British Columbia, and has travelled widely describing an ungentle but inspiring world. He has published over twenty collections of poetry, including* Beware the Months of Fire *(1974)*, Poems New and Selected *(1978)*, *which won a Governor General's Award, and* Go Leaving Strange *(2004)*.

Patrick Lane

Because I Never Learned

FOR JOHN

Because I never learned how
to be gentle and the country
I lived in was hard with dead
animals and men I didn't question
my father when he told me   5
to step on the kitten's head
after the bus had run over
its hind quarters.

Now, twenty years later,
I remember only: 10
the silence of the dying
when the fragile skull collapsed
under my hard bare heel,
the curved tongue in the dust
that would never cry again   15
and the small of my father's back
as he walked tall away.

—*1974*

Seamus Heaney (b. 1939) *was born in the troubled country of Northern Ireland. Heaney has largely avoided the type of political differences that have divided his homeland. Instead, he has chosen to focus on the landscape of the rural Ireland he knew while growing up as a farmer's son. Since 1982, Heaney has taught part of the year at Harvard University. He was awarded the Nobel Prize for Literature in 1995.*

Seamus Heaney
Digging

Between my finger and my thumb
The squat pen rests; snug as a gun.

Under my window, a clean rasping sound
When the spade sinks into gravelly ground:
My father, digging. I look down   5

Till his straining rump among the flowerbeds
Bends low, comes up twenty years away
Stooping in rhythm through potato drills°
Where he was digging.

The coarse boot nestled on the lug, the shaft   10
Against the inside knee was levered firmly.
He rooted out tall tops, buried the bright edge deep
To scatter new potatoes that we picked
Loving their cool hardness in our hands.

By God, the old man could handle a spade.   15
Just like his old man.

My grandfather cut more turf in a day
Than any other man on Toner's bog.
Once I carried him milk in a bottle
Corked sloppily with paper. He straightened up   20
To drink it, then fell to right away

8 drills furrows

Nicking and slicing neatly, heaving sods
Over his shoulder, going down and down
For the good turf. Digging.

The cold smell of potato mould, the squelch and slap   25
Of soggy peat, the curt cuts of an edge
Through living roots awaken in my head.
But I've no spade to follow men like them.

Between my finger and my thumb
The squat pen rests.   30
I'll dig with it.

—*1980*

Florence Cassen Mayers (b. 1940) is a widely published poet and children's author. Her "ABC" books include children's guides to baseball and to the National Basketball Association.

Florence Cassen Mayers
All-American Sestina

One nation, indivisible
two-car garage
three strikes you're out
four-minute mile
five-cent cigar   5
six-string guitar

six-pack Bud
one-day sale
five-year warranty
two-way street   10
fourscore and seven years ago
three cheers

three-star restaurant
sixty-
four-dollar question   *15*
one-night stand
two-pound lobster
five-star general

five-course meal
three sheets to the wind   *20*
two bits
six-shooter
one-armed bandit
four-poster

four-wheel drive   *25*
five-and-dime
hole in one
three-alarm fire

sweet sixteen
two-wheeler   *30*

two-tone Chevy
four rms, hi flr, w/vu
six-footer
high five
three-ring circus   *35*
one-room schoolhouse

two thumbs up, five-karat diamond
Fourth of July, three-piece suit
six feet under, one-horse town

—1996

Robert Hass (b. 1941) was born and raised in San Francisco and now teaches at the University of California at Berkeley. His first book, Field Guide, *was chosen for the Yale Series of Younger Poets in 1973. He has collaborated with Nobel Prize–winner Czeslaw Milosz on English translations of the latter's poetry.*

Robert Hass

Picking Blackberries with a Friend Who Has Been Reading Jacques Lacan°

August dust is here. Drought
stuns the road,
but juice gathers in the berries.

We pick them in the hot
slow-motion of midmorning.   5
Charlie is exclaiming:

for him it is twenty years ago
and raspberries and Vermont.
We have stopped talking

about *L'Histoire de la vérité,*°   10
about subject and object
and the mediation of desire.

Our ears are stoppered
in the bee-hum. And Charlie,
laughing wonderfully,   15

beard stained purple
by the word *juice,*
goes to get a bigger pot.

—1979

Jacques Lacan French psychoanalyst and literary theorist   **10 *L'Histoire de la vérité* The History** *of Truth,* by Lacan

Gwendolyn MacEwan (1941–1987) *was born in Toronto and published more than ten books of poetry, including* The Shadow-Maker *(1969) and* Afterworlds *(1987), both of which won Governor General's Awards. Many of her poems reveal a fascination with the magic and mythologies beneath the mundane surfaces of history and place.*

Gwendolyn MacEwan

Water

When you think of it, water is everything. Or rather,
Water ventures into everything and becomes everything.
     It has
All tastes and moods imaginable; water is history
And the end of the world is water also.   5
                              I have tasted water
From London to Miransah. In France it tasted
Of Crusaders' breastplates, swords, and tunnels of rings
On ladies'fingers.
              In the springs of Lebanon water had   10
No color, and was therefore all colors,
                      outside of Damascus
It disguised itself as snow and let itself be chopped
And spooned onto the stunned red grapes of summer.

For years I have defended water, even though I am told   15
           there are other drinks.
Water will never lie to you, even when it insinuates itself
Into someone else's territory. Water has style.

Water has no conscience and no shame; water
           thrives on water, is self-quenching.   20
It often tastes of brine and ammonia, and always
Knows its way back home.

When you want to travel very far, do as the Bedouin do—
Drink to overflowing when you can,
                              and then   25
Go sparingly between wells.

                                                           —*1982*

Poem Improvised Around a First Line*

the smoke in my bedroom which is always burning
worsens you, motorcycle Icarus;
you are black and leathery and lean and
you cannot distinguish between sex and nicotine

anytime, it's all one thing for you—   5
cigarette, phallus, sacrificial fire—
all part of that grimy flight
on wings axlegreased from Toronto to Buffalo
for the secret beer over the border—

now I long to see you fullblown and black   10
over Niagara, your bike burning and in full flame
and twisting and pivoting over Niagara
and falling finally into Niagara,
and tourists coming to see your black leather wings
hiss and swirl in the steaming current—   15

now I long to give up cigarettes
and change the sheets on my carboniferous bed;
O baby, what Hell to be Greek in this country—
without wings, but burning anyway

                                                           —*1966*

*The first line around which it was improvised has disappeared. [G. MacEwan]

Don McKay (b. 1942) was born in Owen Sound, Ontario, but has lived on both coasts of Canada, most recently in British Columbia. He has published eleven books of highly crafted poetry, including the Governor General's Award–winning Night Field *(1991) and* Another Gravity *(2000). In* Strike/Slip *(2006) he once again explores the intersection between the human and the natural world.*

Don McKay

Icarus°

isn't sorry. We do not find him
doing penance, writing out the golden mean for all
eternity, or touring its high schools to tell student bodies
not to do what he done
done. Over and over he rehearses flight   5
and fall, tuning his moves, entering
with fresh rush into the mingling of the air
with spirit. This is his practice
and his prayer: to be translated into air, as air
with each breath enters lungs,   10
then blood. He feels resistance gather in his stiff
strange wings, angles his arms to shuck the sweet lift
from the drag, runs the full length
of a nameless corridor, his feet striking the paving stones
less and less heavily, then   15
they're bicycling above the ground,
a few shallow beats and he's up,
he's out of the story and into the song.

At the melting point of wax, which now he knows
the way Doug Harvey° knows the blue line,   20
he will back-beat to create a pause, hover for maybe fifty
hummingbird heartbeats and then
lose it, tumbling into freefall, shedding feathers

Icarus In Greek mythology, Icarus is the son of Daedalus, who fashioned wings for them both to escape from Crete. Icarus flew too close to the sun, melting the wax that held his wings together, and fell into the sea. (See W. H. Auden's poem "Musée des Beaux Arts.") **20 Doug Harvey** Doug Harvey (1924–1989) played hockey for the Montreal Canadiens and was the seven-time winner of the Norris Trophy for the best defenceman.

like a lover shedding clothes. He may glide
in the long arc of a Tundra Swan or pull up sharp   25
to Kingfisher into the sea which bears his name.° Then,
giving it the full Ophelia, drown.

On the shore
the farmer ploughs his field, the dull ship
sails away, the poets moralize about our   30
insignificance. But Icarus is thinking tremolo and
backflip, is thinking
next time with a half-twist
and a tuck and isn't
sorry.   35

                              *

Repertoire, technique. The beautiful contraptions bred from
ingenuity and practice, and the names by which he claims
them, into which—lift-off, loop-the-loop—they seem to
bloom. Icarus could write a book. Instead he will stand for
hours in that musing half-abstracted space, watching. During   40
fall migrations he will often climb to the edge of a north-south
running ridge where the soaring hawks find thermals like
naturally occurring laughter, drawing his eyebeam up an
unseen winding stair until they nearly vanish in the depth of
sky. Lower down, Merlins° slice the air with wings that say   45
crisp crisp, precise as sushi chefs, while Sharp-shins
alternately glide and flap, hunting as they go, each line break
poised, ready to pivot like a point guard or Robert Creeley.°
Icarus notices how the Red-tails and Broadwings separate
their primaries° to spill a little air, giving up just enough lift to 50
break their drag up into smaller trailing vortices. What does
this remind him of? He thinks of the kind of gentle teasing
that can dissipate a dark mood so it slips off as a bunch of
skirmishes and quirks. Maybe that. Some little gift to

---

26 the sea which bears his name In ancient times, the part of the Aegean Sea into which Icarus
reportedly fell was called the Icarian Sea. 45 Merlins Merlins are small falcons. Sharp-shins, Red-
tails, and Broadwings are hawks. 48 Robert Creeley Point guards are some of basketball's quickest
and most skilled players. Robert Creeley (b. 1926) is an American poet known as a master technician.
50 primaries main flight feathers

acknowledge the many claims of drag and keep its big   *55*
imperative at bay. Icarus knows all about that one.

In the spring he heads for a slough and makes himself a blind
out of wolf willow and aspen, then climbs inside to let the
marsh-mind claim his thinking. The soft splashdowns of
Scaup and Bufflehead,° the dives which are simple shrugs and   *60*
vanishings; the Loon's wing, thin and sharp for flying in the
underwater world, and the broad wing of the Mallard,
powerful enough to break the water's grip with one sweep, a
guffaw which lifts it straight up into the air. Icarus has
already made the mistake of trying this at home, standing on   *65*
a balustrade in the labyrinth and fanning like a manic
punkah,° the effort throwing him backward off his perch and
into a mock urn which the Minotaur° had, more than once,
used as a pisspot. Another gift of failure. Now his watching is
humbler, less appropriative, a thoughtless thinking amid fly   *70*
drone and dragonfly dart. Icarus will stay in the blind until
his legs cramp up so badly that he has to move. He is really
too large to be a foetus for more than an hour. He unbends
creakily, stretches, and walks home, feeling gravity's pull
upon him as a kind of wealth.   *75*

*

Sometimes Icarus dreams back into his early days with
Daedalus in the labyrinth. Then he reflects upon the
Minotaur, how seldom they saw him—did they ever?—while
they shifted constantly from no-place to no-place, setting up
false campsites and leaving decoy models of themselves.   *80*
Sometimes they would come upon these replicas in strange
postures, holding their heads in their laps or pointing to their
private parts. Once they discovered two sticks stuck like horns
in a decoy's head, which Daedalus took to be the worst of
omens. Icarus was not so sure.   *85*

---

60 Scaup and Bufflehead water birds **67 punkah** large cloth fan suspended from the rafters
68 Minotaur half-man, half-bull who was confined in the labyrinth built by the father of Icarus
and who devoured the Athenian children who fed him

For today's replay he imagines himself sitting in a corridor
reflecting on life as a Minotaur (*The* Minotaur) while waiting
for his alter ego to come bumbling by. They were, he realizes,
both children of technology—one its *enfant terrible*, the other
the rash adolescent who, they will always say, should never   90
have been given a pilot's licence in the first place. What will
happen when they finally meet? Icarus imagines dodging like
a Barn Swallow, throwing out enough quick banter to deflect
his rival's famous rage and pique his interest. How many
Minotaurs does it take to screw in a light bulb? What did the   95
queen say to the machine? Should he wear two sticks on his
head, or save that for later? He leaps ahead to scenes out of
the Hardy Boys and Tom Sawyer. They will chaff and boast
and punch each other on the arm. They will ridicule the weird
obsessions of their parents. As they ramble, cul-de-sacs turn   100
into secret hideouts and the institutional corridors take on the
names of birds and athletes. They discover some imper-
fections in the rock face, nicks and juts which Daedalus
neglected to chisel off, and which they will use to climb,
boosting and balancing each other until they fall off. Together   105
they will scheme and imagine. Somehow they will find a way
to put their brute heads° in the clouds.

—2000

---

107 brute heads In the *Divine Comedy*, Dante writes "Consider your origins. You were not made that
you might live as brutes, but so as to follow virtue and knowledge." (Inferno 26. 118)

Sharon Olds (b. 1942) was born in San Francisco but makes her home in New York City. In eight collections of poetry, including Strike Sparks: Selected Poems *(2004), she displays tremendous candour in dealing with the intimacies of family relations covering three generations, a subject matter that has made her one of the chief contemporary heirs to the confessional tradition.*

Sharon Olds

I Go Back to May 1937

I see them standing at the formal gates of their colleges,
I see my father strolling out
under the ochre sandstone arch, the
red tiles glinting like bent
plates of blood behind his head, I   5
see my mother with a few light books at her hip
standing at the pillar made of tiny bricks with the
wrought-iron gate still open behind her, its
sword-tips black in the May air,
they are about to graduate, they are about to get married,   10
they are kids, they are dumb, all they know is they are
innocent, they would never hurt anybody.
I want to go up to them and say Stop,
don't do it—she's the wrong woman,
he's the wrong man, you are going to do things   15
you cannot imagine you would ever do,
you are going to do bad things to children,
you are going to suffer in ways you never heard of,
you are going to want to die. I want to go
up to them there in the late May sunlight and say it,   20
her hungry pretty blank face turning to me,
her pitiful beautiful untouched body,
his arrogant handsome blind face turning to me,
his pitiful beautiful untouched body,
but I don't do it. I want to live. I   25

take them up like the male and female
paper dolls and bang them together
at the hips like chips of flint as if to
strike sparks from them, I say
Do what you are going to do, and I will tell about it.   *30*

                                                              —1987

Daphne Marlatt (b. 1942) was born in Australia and grew up in Malaysia, but went to Vancouver in 1951 and has remained there. She has published several collections of poems of place, including Steveston *(1974), and poems of passion, including* Touch to My Tongue *(1984) and* This Tremor Love Is *(2001), as well as the novel* Ana Historic *(1988).*

Daphne Marlatt

(is love enough?)

> *Salt through the earth conduct the sea*
> *—Olga Broumas°*

such green glistening, a sparrow preening a far-stretched wing, light
full of pleasure-chirping, feathered bodies at home in earth's soft
voltage & newness written over your face waking from dream, each
blade, each leaf encased still in the wet from last night's rain

is love enough when the breast milk a mother jets in the urgent   *5*
mouth of her baby is laced with PCBs°?

hungry you said, for love, for light, armfuls of daffodils we refuse to
gather standing luminous, pale ears listening, ochre trumpets at the
heart darkness pools, & the radio, as we sit on a paint-blistered deck
in brilliant sun reports that snow, whiter than chalk on the highest   *10*
shelf of the Rockies is sedimented with toxins

Olga Broumas Olga Broumas (b. 1949), Greek poet who deals with Sapphic themes in collections such as *Beginning with O* **6 PCBs** PCBs (polychlorinated biphenyl) are chemical compounds widely used in industry prior to 1970. Because they resist decomposition, they remain in water and soil for many years, entering and endangering the food chain.

the dead, the dying—we imprint our presence everywhere on
every wall & rock

what is love in the face of such loss?

since dawn, *standing by my bed,* she wrote, *in gold sandals . . .*   15
that very/ moment half-awake in a whisper of light her upturned
face given to presence, a woman involved, a circle of women she taught
how to love, how to pay a fine attention raising simply & correctly the
fleeting phases of what is, arrives

we get these glimpses, you said, grizzlies begging at human   20
doorways, two cubs & a mother so thin her ribs showed prominent
under ratty fur, shot now that our salmon rivers run empty, rivers
that were never ours to begin with—

& the sea, the sea goes out a long way in its unpublished killing ground

this webwork—what we don't know about the body, what we   25
don't know may well be killing us—well : spring : stream : river,
these powerful points you set your fingers on, drawing current
through blockages, moving inward, not out, to see

chi° equally in
the salt sea and fields thick with bloom   30
inner channels & rivers

a sea full of apparent islands, no jetting-off point, no airborne leap
possible

without the body all these bodies
interlaced   35

—2001

29 **chi** the life force discussed in Chinese philosophy

Michael Ondaatje (b. 1943) was born in Sri Lanka, eventually coming to Canada in 1962. Best known for his novels, including The English Patient *(1992), which was turned into an Oscar-winning feature film, he is also the author of several poetry collections, including* The Cinnamon Peeler *(1992), and cross-genre works like* The Collected Works of Billy the Kid *(1970) and the autobiographical* Running in the Family *(1982).*

Michael Ondaatje
Sweet like a Crow

FOR HETTI COREA, 8 YEARS OLD

> *The Sinhalese° are beyond a doubt one of the
> least musical people in the world. It would be
> quite impossible to have less sense of pitch, line,
> or rhythm*
>
> *—Paul Bowles*

Your voice sounds like a scorpion being pushed
through a glass tube
like someone has just trod on a peacock
like wind howling in a coconut
like a rusty bible, like someone pulling barbed wire   5
across a stone courtyard, like a pig drowning,
a vattacka being fried
a bone shaking hands
a frog singing at Carnegie Hall.
Like a crow swimming in milk,   10
like a nose being hit by a mango
like the crowd at the Royal-Thomian match,
a womb full of twins, a pariah dog
with a magpie in its mouth
like the midnight jet from Casablanca   15

Sinhalese natives of Sri Lanka

like Air Pakistan curry,
a typewriter on fire, like a spirit in the gas
which cooks your dinner,
like a hundred pappadans° being crunched, like someone
uselessly trying to light *3 Roses* matches in a dark room,   *20*
the clicking sound of a reef when you put your head into the sea,
a dolphin reciting epic poetry to a sleepy audience,
the sound of a fan when someone throws brinjals° at it,
like pineapples being sliced in the Pettah market
like betel juice° hitting a butterfly in mid-air   *25*
like a whole village running naked onto the street
and tearing their sarongs, like an angry family
pushing a jeep out of the mud, like dirt on the needle,
like 8 sharks being carried on the back of a bicycle
like 3 old ladies locked in the lavatory   *30*
like the sound I heard when having an afternoon sleep
and someone walked through my room in ankle bracelets.

—1982

Craig Raine (b. 1944) early in his career displayed a comic surrealism that was responsible for so many imitations that critic James Fenton dubbed him the founder of the "Martian School" of contemporary poetry. He was born in Bishop Auckland, England.

Craig Raine
A Martian Sends
a Postcard Home

Caxtons° are mechanical birds with many wings   *1*
and some are treasured for their markings—

they cause the eyes to melt
or the body to shriek without pain.

19 pappadans crunchy wafer-thin appetizer   **23 brinjals** eggplant   **25 betel juice** leaf chewed
and spit like chewing tobacco
1 Caxtons i.e., books; after William Caxton (1422–1491), first English printer

I have never seen one fly, but 5
sometimes they perch on the hand.

Mist is when the sky is tired of flight
and rests its soft machine on ground:

then the world is dim and bookish
like engravings under tissue paper. 10

Rain is when the earth is television.
It has the property of making colours darker.

Model T is a room with the lock inside—
a key is turned to free the world

for movement, so quick there is a film 15
to watch for anything missed.

But time is tied to the wrist
or kept in a box, ticking with impatience.

In homes, a haunted apparatus sleeps,
that snores when you pick it up. 20

If the ghost cries, they carry it
to their lips and soothe it to sleep

with sounds. And yet, they wake it up
deliberately, by tickling with a finger.

Only the young are allowed to suffer 25
openly. Adults go to a punishment room

with water but nothing to eat.
They lock the door and suffer the noises

alone. No one is exempt
and everyone's pain has a different smell. 30

At night, when all the colours die,
they hide in pairs

and read about themselves—
in colour, with their eyelids shut.

—1978

Enid Shomer (b. 1944) *grew up in Washington, D.C., but has lived most of her life in Florida. Her first collection,* Stalking the Florida Panther *(1987), explored both the Jewish traditions of her childhood and her attachment to her adopted state. She went on to publish fiction and several more collections of poetry, including* Stars at Noon: Poems from the Life of Jacqueline Cochran *(2001).*

Enid Shomer
Women Bathing at Bergen-Belsen°

APRIL 24, 1945

Twelve hours after the Allies arrive
there is hot water, soap. Two women bathe
in a makeshift, open-air shower while nearby
fifteen thousand are flung naked into mass graves
by captured SS guards. Clearly legs and arms   5
are the natural handles of a corpse. The bathers,
taken late in the war, still have flesh
on their bones, still have breasts. Though nudity was
a death sentence here, they have undressed,
oblivious to the soldiers and the cameras.   10
The corpses push through the limed earth like upended
headstones. The bathers scrub their feet, bending
in beautiful curves, mapping the contours
of the body, that kingdom to which they've returned.

—1987

Bergen-Belsen German concentration camp in World War II

bp Nichol (1944–1988) was born in Vancouver and is best known for his concrete or visual poetry, like these examples from early and late in his career. Experimentation is also evident in the The Martyrology, *a poem that extends over nine volumes, and in the sound poetry Nichol performed with the group the Four Horsemen, of which he was a founding member.*

bp Nichol
Blues

```
          l              e
          o       e
    l  o  v  e
    o       e  v  o  l
 l  o  v  e       o
    e  v  o  l
 e       o
 e       l
```

[Author's Note:] here I'm paraphrasing an old blues—"love, oh love, oh careless love"—to slant the reading of "evol" towards "evil" and support the visually derived blues moan

—*1967*

landscape: I

alongthehorizongrewanunbrokenlineoftrees

—1986

Wendy Cope (b. 1945) lives in Winchester, England, and writes witty yet technically sophisticated poetry that reaches a wide audience. "I dislike the term 'light verse' because it is used as a way of dismissing poets who allow humour into their work. I believe that a humorous poem can also be 'serious'; deeply felt and saying something that matters."

Wendy Cope
Rondeau Redoublé

There are so many kinds of awful men—
One can't avoid them all. She often said
She'd never make the same mistake again:
She always made a new mistake instead.

The chinless type who made her feel ill-bred;   5
The practised charmer, less than charming when
He talked about the wife and kids and fled—
There are so many kinds of awful men.

The half-crazed hippy, deeply into Zen,
Whose cryptic homilies she came to dread;   10
The fervent youth who worshipped Tony Benn—
'One can't avoid them all,' she often said.

The ageing banker, rich and overfed,
who held forth on the dollar and the yen—
Though there were many more mistakes ahead,   15
She'd never make the same mistake again.

The budding poet, scribbling in his den
Odes not to her but to his pussy, Fred;
The drunk who fell asleep at nine or ten—
She always made a new mistake instead.   20

And so the gambler was at least unwed
And didn't preach or sneer or wield a pen
Or hoard his wealth or take the Scotch to bed.
She'd lived and learned and lived and learned but then
There are so many kinds.   25

—1986

Tom Wayman (b. 1945) *was born in Hawkesbury, Ontario, but as a child moved to British Columbia, which remains his home. Wayman has published more than a dozen collections of poems, including* Did I Miss Anything? *(1993) and* My Father's Cup *(2002). He is particularly interested in poems about the workplace.*

Tom Wayman

Did I Miss Anything?

QUESTION FREQUENTLY ASKED BY
STUDENTS AFTER MISSING A CLASS

Nothing. When we realized you weren't here
we sat with our hands folded on our desks
in silence, for the full two hours

    Everything. I gave an exam worth
    40 per cent of the grade for this term   5
    and assigned some reading due today
    on which I'm about to hand out a quiz
    worth 50 per cent.

Nothing. None of the content of this course
has value or meaning   10
Take as many days off as you like:
any activities we undertake as a class
I assure you will not matter either to you or me
and are without purpose

    Everything. A few minutes after we began last time   15
    a shaft of light descended and an angel
    or other heavenly being appeared
    and revealed to us what each woman or man must do
    to attain divine wisdom in this life and
    the hereafter   20
    This is the last time the class will meet
    before we disperse to bring this good news to all people on earth

Nothing. When you are not present
how could something significant occur?

    Everything. Contained in this classroom   25
    is a microcosm of human existence
    assembled for you to query and examine and ponder
    This is not the only place such an opportunity has been
        gathered

but it was one place   30

And you weren't here

                                    —1991

Bronwen Wallace (1945–1989) was born in Kingston, Ontario. She published four collections of conversational yet carefully crafted poems about the extraordinary grace in ordinary lives, including Common Magic *(1985),* The Stubborn Particulars of Grace *(1987), and* Keep That Candle Burning Bright *(1991), which was published after her early death from cancer.*

Bronwen Wallace
Common Magic

Your best friend falls in love
and her brain turns to water.
You can watch her lips move,
making the customary sounds,
but you can see they're merely   5
words, flimsy as bubbles rising
from some golden sea where she
swims sleek and exotic as a mermaid.

It's always like that.
You stop for lunch in a crowded   10
restaurant and the waitress floats
toward you. You can tell she doesn't care
whether you have the baked or french-fried
and you wonder if your voice comes
in bubbles too.   15

It's not just women either. Or love
for that matter. The old man
across from you on the bus holds
a young child on his knee; he is singing
to her and his voice is a small boy   *20*
turning somersaults in the green
country of his blood.
It's only when the driver calls his stop
that he emerges into this puzzle
of brick and tiny hedges. Only then   *25*
you notice his shaking hands, his need
of the child to guide him home.

All over the city
you move in your own seasons
through the seasons of others: old women, faces   *30*
clawed by weather you can't feel
clack dry tongues at passersby
while adolescents seethe
in their glassy atmospheres of anger.

In parks, the children   *35*
are alien life-forms, rooted
in the galaxies they've grown through
to get here. Their games weave
the interface and their laughter
tickles that part of your brain where smells   *40*
are hidden and the nuzzling textures of things.

It's a wonder that anything gets done
at all: a mechanic flails
at the muffler of your car
through whatever storm he's trapped inside   *45*
and the mailman stares at numbers
from the haze of a distant summer.

Yet somehow letters arrive and buses
remember their routes. Banks balance.
Mangoes ripen on the supermarket shelves.   *50*
Everyone manages. You gulp the thin air

of this planet as if it were the only
one you knew. Even the earth you're
standing on seems solid enough.
It's always the chance word, unthinking   55
gesture that unlocks the face before you.
Reveals the intricate countries
deep within the eyes. The hidden
lives, like sudden miracles,
that breathe there.   60

—*1983*

Herménégilde Chiasson (*b. 1946*) *was born in Saint-Simon, New Brunswick, of Acadian heritage. Chiasson is a visual artist, filmmaker, playwright, and poet. His poetry collections include* Mourir à Scoudouc (*1974*), Vous (*1991*), Climats (*1996*), *and* Conversations (*1999*), *winner of the Governor General's Award. He was appointed Lieutenant-Governor of New Brunswick in 2003.*

Herménégilde Chiasson
Red

Acadie, my too beautiful desecrated love, you whom I will never take into white sheets, the sheets that you have torn to make white flags like the fields of snow that you have sold like your old fence posts, your old barns, your old legends, your old dreams, white as an old wedding dress in an old cedar chest. Acadie, my too beautiful desecrated love, who speaks on credit to say things that one must pay in cash, who borrows privileges while believing she is gaining rights. Acadie, my too beautiful desecrated love, on *stand-by* on every continent, on *stand-by* in every galaxy, divided by church steeples that are stretched too thin, filled with saints up to a heaven that is too far away. Rip off your blue dress, put red stars on your breasts, sink yourself into the sea, the red sea that is going to open as it did for the flight from Egypt, the sea belongs to us, it is true, the whole sea belongs to us because we cannot sell it, because there is no one who could buy it.

—*1974*

Translated by Fred Cogswell and Jo-Anne Elder.

Robert Bringhurst (b. 1946) Born in California of Canadian parents, Bringhurst grew up in the Rockies. He has published widely in fields as diverse as Native mythology, typography, and translation, but he has also published over a dozen books of poetry, including The Beauty of the Weapons *(1982),* The Calling *(1995), and the polyphonic masque* Ursa Major *(2003).*

Robert Bringhurst

Essay on Adam

There are five possibilities. One: Adam fell.
Two: he was pushed. Three: he jumped. Four:
he only looked over the edge, and one look silenced him.
Five: nothing worth mentioning happened to Adam.

The first, that he fell, is too simple. The fourth,   *5*
fear, we have tried and found useless. The fifth,
nothing happened, is dull. The choice is between:
he jumped or was pushed. And the difference between these

is only an issue of whether the demons
work from the inside out or from the outside   *10*
in: the one
theological question.

—1975

M. NourbeSe Philip (b. 1947) was born in Tobago but moved to Canada, where she worked for several years as a lawyer before deciding to devote more time to writ-ing. She is the author of several collections of poetry, including Thorns *(1980),* Salmon Courage *(1983), and* She Tries Her Tongue; Her Silence Softly Breaks *(1988). Her poetry and short fiction have been widely anthologized.*

M. NourbeSe Philip

Discourse on the Logic of Language

WHEN IT WAS BORN, THE MOTHER HELD HER NEWBORN CHILD CLOSE: SHE BEGAN THEN TO LICK IT ALL OVER. THE CHILD WHIMPERED A LITTLE, BUT AS THE MOTHER'S TONGUE MOVED FASTER AND STRONGER OVER ITS BODY, IT GREW SILENT—THE MOTHER TURNING IT THIS WAY AND THAT UNDER HER TONGUE, UNTIL SHE HAD TONGUED IT CLEAN OF THE CREAMY WHITE SUBSTANCE COVERING ITS BODY.

English
is my mother tongue.
A mother tongue is not
not a foreign lan lan lang
language   5
l/anguish
anguish
—a foreign anguish.

English is
my father tongue.   10
A father tongue is
a foreign language,
therefore English is
a foreign language
not a mother tongue.   15

What is my mother
tongue
my mammy tongue
my mummy tongue
my momsy tongue
my modder tongue
my ma tongue?

I have no mother
tongue
no mother to tongue
no tongue to mother
to mother
tongue
me

I must therefore be tongue
dumb
dumb-tongued
dub-tongued
damn dumb
tongue

EDICT I

*Every owner of slaves
shall, wherever possible,
ensure that his slaves
belong to as many ethno-
linguistic groups as
possible. If they can-
not speak to each other,
they cannot then foment
rebellion and revolution.*

20

25

30

35

Those parts of the brain chiefly responsible for speech are named after two learned nineteenth century doctors, the eponymous Doctors Wernicke and Broca respectively.

Dr. Broca believed the size of the brain determined intelligence; he devoted much of his time to 'proving' that white males *40* of the Caucasian race had larger brains than, and were therefore superior to, women, Blacks and other peoples of colour.

Understanding and recognition of the spoken word takes place in Wernicke's area—the left temporal lobe, situated next to the auditory cortex; from there relevant information passes to *45* Broca's area—situated in the left frontal cortex—which then forms the response and passes it on to the motor cortex. The motor cortex controls the muscles of speech.

THE MOTHER THEN PUT HER FINGERS INTO HER CHILD'S MOUTH—GENTLY FORCING IT OPEN;
SHE TOUCHES HER TONGUE TO THE CHILD'S TONGUE, AND HOLDING THE TINY MOUTH OPEN,
SHE BLOWS INTO IT—HARD. SHE WAS BLOWING WORDS—HER WORDS, HER MOTHER'S WORDS,
THOSE OF HER MOTHER'S MOTHER, AND ALL THEIR MOTHERS BEFORE—INTO HER DAUGHTER'S
MOUTH.

but I have
a dumb tongue   50
tongue dumb
father tongue
and english is
my mother tongue
is   55
my father tongue
is a foreign Ian lan lang
language
l/anguish
 anguish   60
a foreign anguish
is english—
another tongue
my mother
    mammy   65
    mummy
    moder
    mater
    macer
    moder   70
tongue
mothertongue

tongue mother
tongue me
mothertongue me   75
mother me
touch me
with the tongue of your
lan lan lang
language   80
l/anguish
 anguish
english
is a foreign anguish

EDICT II

Every slave caught speaking his native language shall be severely punished. Where necessary, removal of the tongue is recommended. The offending organ, when removed, should be hung on high in a central place, so that all may see and tremble.

A tapering, blunt-tipped, muscular, soft and fleshy organ   *85*
describes
(a) the penis.
(b) the tongue.
(c) neither of the above.
(d) both of the above.

In man the tongue is   *90*
(a) the principal organ of taste.
(b) the principal organ of articulate speech.
(c) the principal organ of oppression and exploitation.
(d) all of the above.

The tongue   *95*
(a) is an interwoven bundle of striated muscle running in
    three planes.
(b) is fixed to the jawbone.
(c) has an outer covering of a mucous membrane covered
    with papillae.
(d) contains ten thousand taste buds, none of which is sensitive to
    the taste of foreign words.

Air is forced out of the lungs up the throat to the larynx where   *100*
it causes the vocal cords to vibrate and create sound. The
metamorphosis from sound to intelligible word requires
(a) the lip, tongue and jaw all working together.
(b) a mother tongue.
(c) the overseer's whip.
(d) all of the above or none.

—1989

R. S. Gwynn (b. 1948) is one of the editors of this volume and (with Dana Gioia) of The Longman Anthology of Short Fiction. *He teaches at Lamar University.* No Word of Farewell: Selected Poems 1970–2000 *appeared in 2001.*

R. S. Gwynn

Approaching a Significant Birthday, He Peruses *The Norton Anthology of Poetry*

All human things are subject to decay.
Beauty is momentary in the mind.
The curfew tolls the knell of parting day.
If Winter comes, can Spring be far behind?

Forlorn! the very word is like a bell   5
And somewhat of a sad perplexity.
Here, take my picture, though I bid farewell;
In a dark time the eye begins to see

The woods decay, the woods decay and fall—
Bare ruined choirs where late the sweet birds sing.   10
What but design of darkness to appall?
An aged man is but a paltry thing.

If I should die, think only this of me:
Crass casualty obstructs the sun and rain
When I have fears that I may cease to be,   15
To cease upon the midnight with no pain

And hear the spectral singing of the moon
And strictly meditate the thankless muse.
The world is too much with us, late and soon.
It gathers to a greatness, like the ooze.   20

Do not go gentle into the good night.
Fame is no plant that grows on mortal soil.

Again he raised the jug up to the light:
Old age hath yet his honor and his toil.

Downward to darkness on extended wings,   *25*
Break, break, break, on thy cold gray stones, O Sea,
and tell sad stories of the death of kings.
I do not think that they will sing to me.

                                                          —1990

Timothy Steele (b. 1948) has written a successful scholarly study of the rise of free verse, Missing Measures, *and is perhaps the most skillful craftsman of the contemporary New Formalist poets. Born in Vermont, he has lived for a number of years in Los Angeles, where he teaches at California State University, Los Angeles.*

Timothy Steele

Sapphics° Against Anger

Angered, may I be near a glass of water;
May my first impulse be to think of Silence,
Its deities (who are they? do, in fact, they
          Exist? etc.).

May I recall what Aristotle says of   *5*
The subject: to give vent to rage is not to
Release it but to be increasingly prone
          To its incursions.

May I imagine being in the Inferno,
Hearing it asked: "Virgilio mio,° who's   *10*
That sulking with Achilles there?" and hearing
          Virgil say: "Dante,

Sapphics stanza form named after Sappho (c. 650 B.C.)   **10 Virgilio mio** Dante is addressing
Virgil, his guide through hell.

That fellow, at the slightest provocation,
Slammed phone receivers down, and waved his arms like
A madman. What Attila did to Europe,   15
      What Genghis Khan did

To Asia, that poor dope did to his marriage."
May I, that is, put learning to good purpose,
Mindful that melancholy is a sin, though
      Stylish at present.   20

Better than rage is the post-dinner quiet,
The sink's warm turbulence, the streaming platters,
The suds rehearsing down the drain in spirals
      In the last rinsing.

For what is, after all, the good life save that   25
Conducted thoughtfully, and what is passion
If not the holiest of powers, sustaining
      Only if mastered.

                                    —*1986*

Lorna Crozier (b. 1948) was born in Swift Current, Saskatchewan. Her many award-winning collections include Inventing the Hawk *(1992),* Apocrypha of Light *(2002), and* Selected Poems *(2007).* No Longer Two People *(1981) was co-authored with her partner, Patrick Lane.*

Lorna Crozier
Packing for the Future: Instructions

Take the thickest socks.
Wherever you're going
you'll have to walk.

There may be water.
There may be stones.   5

There may be high places
you cannot go without
the hope socks bring you,
the way they hold you
to the earth.   *10*

At least one pair must be new,
must be blue as a wish
hand-knit by your mother
in her sleep.

*

Take a leather satchel,   *15*
a velvet bag and an old tin box—
a salamander painted on the lid.

This is to carry that small thing
you cannot leave. Perhaps the key
you've kept though it doesn't fit   *20*
any lock you know,
the photograph that keeps you sane,
a ball of string to lead you out
though you can't walk back
into that light.   *25*

In your bag leave room for sadness,
leave room for another language.

There may be doors nailed shut.
There may be painted windows.
There may be signs that warn you   *30*
to be gone. Take the dream
you've been having since
you were a child, the one
with open fields and the wind
sounding.   *35*

*

Mistrust no one who offers you
water from a well, a songbird's feather,
something that's been mended twice.
Always travel lighter
than the heart.   *40*

—*1999*

Jeannette C. Armstrong (b. 1948) Born on the Penticton Indian Reserve in British Columbia, of Okanagan heritage, Armstrong has published works including the novels Slash *(1988) and* Whispering in Shadows *(2000), and the poetry collection* Breath Tracks *(1991).*

Jeannette C. Armstrong
History Lesson

Out of the belly of Christopher's ship
a mob bursts
Running in all directions
Pulling furs off animals
Shooting buffalo   5
Shooting each other
left and right

Father mean well
waves his makeshift wand
forgives saucer-eyed Indians   10

Red coated knights
gallop across the prairie
to get their men
and to build a new world

Pioneers and traders   15
bring gifts
Smallpox, Seagrams
and Rice Krispies

Civilization has reached
the promised land.   *20*

Between the snap crackle pop
of smoke stacks
and multi-coloured rivers
swelling with flower powered zee
are farmers sowing skulls and bones   *25*
and miners
pulling from gaping holes
green paper faces
of smiling English lady

The colossi   *30*
in which they trust
while burying
breathing forests and fields
beneath concrete and steel
stand shaking fists   *35*
waiting to mutilate
whole civilizations
ten generations at a blow.

Somewhere among the remains
of skinless animals   *40*
is the termination
to a long journey
and unholy search
for the power
glimpsed in a garden   *45*
forever closed
forever lost.

—1991

Lenore Keeshig-Tobias (b. 1949) A member of the Chippewas of the Nawash First Nation in Ontario, Keeshig-Tobias draws on her Anishnabe heritage in her roles as storyteller and culture worker. Her published work includes the bilingual children's books Bird Talk *(1991) and* Emma and the Trees *(1995), and contributions to* Indigena: Contemporary Native Perspectives *(1992).*

Lenore Keeshig-Tobias
How to Catch a White Man (Oops) I Mean Trickster

FROM *TRICKSTER BEYOND 1992: OUR RELATIONSHIP*

First, find yourself a forest. Any stand of ancient trees will do;
in fact, the older the better. Stand in the middle of it and tell
your stories. Soon the white man! (I mean Trickster) will
come by, carrying a big pack on his back. In that pack he
carries the voices of his women and the voices of other people   5
he has walked over with his long legs. 'I'm going to tell those
stories for you,' he'll say. 'You're far too primitive to tell them
yourself. I am going to let the world know what you think.
I am going to tell the world how you think when you think.
And I'm going to build a golf course here, too. These trees   10
are so old, and besides you're not using them trees.'

Tell him you heard some people talking about better stories
and a better place for a golf course, perhaps even a
h-y-d-r-o e-l-e-c-t-r-i-c dam, or two. Say, you could even
push for a super fantasyland golf course. Anyhow, tell him he   15
could make the stories into TV movies, docudramas, feature films.
He could write novels using the stories. He could receive all kinds
of literary awards for his great imagination, with these stories.
He could even achieve world acclaim for telling others how it is
with the 'Native Indian'. (God, how I hate that word 'Indian'.)   20

Okay, then tell him to wait there while you'll go find out more about
those stories and that other place. He'll say, 'Okay, but come right
back.' Only don't go back.

Find another forest and dig a big big hole in the middle of it,
beside a pine tree. Then climb up and sit in the branches of that   25
tree and call out saying, 'Hey, white man! (I mean Trickster.
You could call him a trickster, you know. He's like that, clever.
But he's not smart.) These stories are not for you, and you can't
build your golf course here either.'

It won't be long and he'll come by with that great big pack and   30
this time with his guns and tanks, too—ready to take those
stories—ready to build his golf course.

Then you tell him from that tree you can see, hear everything
all over the world, and know exactly what's going on, too. He'll
say, 'That's new to me.' Ask him if he would like to see these   35
things, too. Of course, he'll say, 'Yes.' Tell him to leave his
heavy pack at the bottom of the tree. He won't. He'll climb up
into that tree with his weapons, too. Ask him if he's comfortable.
He'll say, 'I'm comfortable anywhere.' Be careful now because
he'll want to sit right on top of you.   40

Now, tell him to close his eyes. He has to close his eyes if he is
to know and see all the things you do. He has to listen to the
trees and grass. Tell him it takes a while for the vision to come
clear, and he should sit quietly and wait and listen. As soon as
his eyes are closed, run away and watch. Get other people to   45
watch, too. And the children. Don't forget about the children.

Of course, that man won't see anything. Never did. And he
certainly won't hear anything. Never has. And after a bit he'll
become uncomfortable, restless, impatient and he'll cock his
gun and open his eyes. When he sees you are gone he'll get mad   50
as heck and fall out of the tree, shooting himself in the foot,
dropping his great pack and tumbling into the hole, his foot in
his mouth.

That's when you run over and grab his great pack, open it up
and set free the voices of the people he has walked over and the   55
voices of his women.

Now that white man (I mean Trickster) will scramble. And he'll
fight, digging himself deeper into the hole, but he won't ever get

out this time. His women will see to that. Then tell the children.
Teach them. Teach them the history of this land, the real history, 60
before 1492 and since. Those stories will guide them into the
next 500 years. Tell them not to do as the Trickster (I mean
white man) has done. And tell them to listen to the trees and
grass. The trees and the grass hold on to heaven for us.

—*1992*

---

*Stan Rogers (1949–1983) was born in Hamilton, Ontario, with family roots
in the Maritimes, a connection that appears in many of his finest lyrics about life
on and by the sea. One of Canada's best known folk singers, he toured the country
from coast to coast, penning memorable songs about the vast Canadian landscape
and the dreams of those who live there. When returning home from an American
folk festival, he died in an airline fire at the age of thirty-three.*

Stan Rogers
The *Mary Ellen Carter*

She went down last October in a pouring driving rain.
The skipper, he'd been drinking and the Mate, he felt no pain.
Too close to Three Mile Rock, and she was dealt her mortal blow,
And the *Mary Ellen Carter* settled low.
There were five of us aboard her when she finally was awash.   5
We'd worked like hell to save her, all heedless of the cost.
And the groan she gave as she went down, it caused us to proclaim
That the *Mary Ellen Carter* would rise again.

Well, the owners wrote her off; not a nickel would they spend.
She gave twenty years of service, boys, then met her sorry end.   10
But insurance paid the loss to them, they let her rest below.
Then they laughed at us and said we had to go.
But we talked of her all winter, some days around the clock,
For she's worth a quarter million, afloat and at the dock.
And with every jar that hit the bar, we swore we would remain   15
And make the *Mary Ellen Carter* rise again.

Rise again, rise again, that her name not be lost
To the knowledge of men.
Those who loved her best and were with her till the end
Will make the *Mary Ellen Carter* rise again.   20

All spring, now, we've been with her on a barge lent by a friend.
Three dives a day in hard hat suit and twice I've had the bends.
Thank God it's only sixty feet and the currents here are slow
Or I'd never have the strength to go below.
But we've patched her rents, stopped her vents, dogged hatch
    and porthole down.   25
Put cables to her, 'fore and aft and girded her around.
Tomorrow, noon, we hit the air and then take up the strain.
And watch the *Mary Ellen Carter* rise again.

For we couldn't leave her there, you see, to crumble into scale.
She'd saved our lives so many times, living through the gale   30
And the laughing, drunken rats who left her to a sorry grave
They won't be laughing in another day . . .
And you, to whom adversity has dealt the final blow
With smiling bastards lying to you everywhere you go
Turn to, and put out all your strength of arm and heart
    and brain   35
And like the *Mary Ellen Carter*, rise again.

Rise again, rise again—though your heart it be broken
And life about to end
No matter what you've lost, be it a home, a love, a friend.
Like the *Mary Ellen Carter*, rise again.   40

—*1979*

Rodney Jones (b. 1950) was born in Alabama and received important national attention when Transparent Gestures *won the Poets' Prize in 1990. Like many younger southern poets, he often deals with the difficult legacy of racism and the adjustments that a new era have forced on both whites and Blacks.*

Rodney Jones

Winter Retreat: Homage to Martin Luther King, Jr.

There is a hotel in Baltimore where we came together,
we black and white educated and educators,
for a week of conferences, for important counsel
sanctioned by the DOE° and the Carter administration,
to make certain difficult inquiries, to collate notes   5
on the instruction of the disabled, the deprived,
the poor, who do not score well on entrance tests,
who, failing school, must go with mop and pail
skittering across the slick floors of cafeterias,
or climb dewy girders to balance high above cities,   10
or, jobless, line up in the bone cold. We felt
substantive burdens lighter if we stated it right.
Very delicately, we spoke in turn. We walked
together beside the still waters of behaviorism.
Armed with graphs and charts, with new strategies   15
to devise objectives and determine accountability,
we empathetic black and white shone in seminar rooms.
We enunciated every word clearly and without accent.
We moved very carefully in the valley of the shadow
of the darkest agreement error. We did not digress.   20
We ascended the trunk of that loftiest cypress
of Latin grammar the priests could never
successfully graft onto the rough green chestnut
of the English language. We extended ourselves

4 DOE Department of Education

with that sinuous motion of the tongue that is half   *25*
pain and almost eloquence. We black and white
politely reprioritized the parameters of our agenda
to impact equitably on the Seminole and the Eskimo.
We praised diversity and involvement, the sacrifices
of fathers and mothers. We praised the next white   *30*
Gwendolyn Brooks° and the next black Robert Burns.°
We deep made friends. In that hotel we glistened
over the *pommes au gratin*° and the *poitrine de veau.*°
The morsels of lamb flamed near where we talked.
The waiters bowed and disappeared among the ferns.   *35*
And there is a bar there, there is a large pool.
Beyond the tables of the drinkers and raconteurs,
beyond the hot tub brimming with Lebanese tourists
and the women in expensive bathing suits doing laps,
if you dive down four feet, swim out far enough,   *40*
and emerge on the other side, it is sixteen degrees.
It is sudden and very beautiful and colder
than thought, though the air frightens you at first,
not because it is cold, but because it is visible,
almost palpable, in the fog that rises from difference.   *45*
While I stood there in the cheek-numbing snow,
all Baltimore was turning blue. And what I remember
of that week of talks is nothing the record shows,
but the revelation outside, which was the city
many came to out of the fields, then the thought   *50*
that we had wanted to make the world kinder,
but, in speaking proudly, we had failed a vision.

—1989

---

31 **Gwendolyn Brooks** Black American poet (1917–2000)   **Robert Burns** Scottish poet (1759–1796)
33 *pommes au gratin* potatoes baked with cheese   *poitrine de veau* brisket of veal

Carolyn Forché (b. 1950) *won the Yale Younger Poets Award for her first collection,* Gathering the Tribes *(1975).* The Country Between Us *(1982), Forché's second collection, contains poems based on the poet's experiences in the wartorn country of El Salvador in the early 1980s.*

Carolyn Forché
The Colonel

What you have heard is true. I was in his house.° His wife
carried a tray of coffee and sugar. His daughter filed her nails,
his son went out for the night. There were daily papers, pet
dogs, a pistol on the cushion beside him. The moon swung
bare on its black cord over the house. On the television was a   5
cop show. It was in English. Broken bottles were embedded
in the walls around the house to scoop the kneecaps from
a man's legs or cut his hands to lace. On the windows there
were gratings like those in liquor stores. We had dinner, rack
of lamb, good wine, a gold bell was on the table for calling   10
the maid. The maid brought green mangoes, salt, a type of
bread. I was asked how I enjoyed the country. There was a
brief commercial in Spanish. His wife took everything away.
There was some talk then of how difficult it had become to
govern. The parrot said hello on the terrace. The colonel told   15
it to shut up, and pushed himself from the table. My friend
said to me with his eyes: say nothing. The colonel returned
with a sack used to bring groceries home. He spilled many
human ears on the table. They were like dried peach halves.
There is no other way to say this. He took one of them in his   20
hands, shook it in our faces, dropped it into a water glass. It
came alive there. I am tired of fooling around he said. As for the
rights of anyone, tell your people they can go fuck themselves.
He swept the ears to the floor with his arm and held the last of
his wine in the air. Something for your poetry, no? he said.   25
Some of the ears on the floor caught this scrap of his voice.
Some of the ears on the floor were pressed to the ground.

—1978

1 his house in El Salvador

Anne Car∂on (b. 1950) *wa∂ born in Toronto and ha∂ a reputation a∂ both a classical scholar and a prize-winning poet. Her collection∂ include the riddle-like* Short Talks *(1992),* Glass, Irony and God *(1995), and* Men in the Off Hours *(2000). Her evocative and erudite work, including* Autobiography of Red: A Novel in Verse *(1998) and* Decreation *(2005), often blur∂ the boundarie∂ between genre∂.*

Anne Car∂on
God's List of Liquids

It was a November night of wind.
Leaves tore past the window.
God had the book of life open at PLEASURE

and was holding the pages down with one hand
because of the wind from the door.   5
For I made their flesh as a sieve

wrote God at the top of the page
and then listed in order:
Alcohol
Blood   10
Gratitude
Memory
Semen
Song
Tears   15
Time.

—*1995*

Short Talk on the Total Collection

From childhood he dreamed of being able to keep with him all the objects in the world lined up on his shelves and bookcases. He denied lack, oblivion or even the likelihood of a missing piece. Order streamed

from Noah in blue triangles and as the pure fury of his classifications
rose around him, engulfing his life they came to be called waves by
others, who drowned, a world of them.

—1992

*Harry Thurston (b. 1950) was born in Yarmouth, Nova Scotia, and was trained
as a biologist. His intense interest in the natural world is reflected in his non-fiction
works, including* Tidal Life: A Natural History of the Bay of Fundy *(1990),
and in his poetry collections, including* If Men Lived on Earth *(1999) and*
A Ship Portrait *(2005).*

Harry Thurston
Miracle

I tell my toddling daughter
not to pick the blossom,
explaining that the flower
will turn into a strawberry
in a few short weeks,   5
then she can pick and eat the sweet fruit.
No sooner are the words out
than I regret forestalling her pleasure—
for what is one blossom less,
and weeks to a child too long to wait.   10
And then, too, she looks at me
as if I have told her a lie,
fashioned a twisted fairy tale.
But speaking it, for the first time in years,
I am awed by the miracle   15
of what really happens.

—2000

Paul Muldoon (b. 1951) *was born in County Armagh, Northern Ireland, and after years of working for the BBC in Belfast he moved to the United States in 1987. His many poetry collections include* Why Brownlee Left *(1980),* Poems 1968–1998 *(2001),* Moy Sand and Gravel *(2002), which won the Pulitzer Prize, and* Horse Latitudes *(2006).*

Paul Muldoon
Anseo

When the Master was calling the roll
At the primary school in Collegelands,
You were meant to call back *Anseo*
And raise your hand
As your name occurred.   5
Anseo, meaning here, here and now,
All present and correct,
Was the first word of Irish I spoke.
The last name on the ledger
Belonged to Joseph Mary Plunkett Ward   10
And was followed, as often as not,
By silence, knowing looks,
A nod and a wink, the Master's droll
'And where's our little Ward-of-court?'°

I remember the first time he came back   15
The Master had sent him out
Along the hedges
To weigh up for himself and cut
A stick with which he would be beaten.
After a while, nothing was spoken;   20
He would arrive as a matter of course
With an ash-plant, a salley-rod.
Or, finally, the hazel-wand
He had whittled down to a whip-lash,
Its twist of red and yellow lacquers   25

14 Ward-of-court minor with court-appointed guardian

Sanded and polished,
And altogether so delicately wrought
That he had engraved his initials on it.

I last met Joseph Mary Plunkett Ward
In a pub just over the Irish border.   30
He was living in the open,
In a secret camp
On the other side of the mountain.
He was fighting for Ireland,
Making things happen.   35
And he told me, Joe Ward,
Of how he had risen through the ranks
To Quartermaster, Commandant:
How every morning at parade
His volunteers would call back *Anseo*   40
And raise their hands
As their names occurred.

—*1980*

Christopher Dewdney (b. 1951) resides in Toronto and is the author of twelve collections of poems that often deal with scientific subject matter in an avant-garde way. His publications include the collections of poems Radiant Inventories *(1988) and* Signal Fires *(2000), as well as works of popular non-fiction, such as* Acquainted with the Night *(2004).*

Christopher Dewdney
Ten Typically Geological Suicides

1. Standing naked over the vent of a thermal geyser that erupts periodically.

2. Throwing yourself into molten lava.

3. Placing your head at the bottom of a children's slide with a pull-string attached to a stick propping up a large granite boulder perched at the top.

4. Licking the radium from the faces of old watches.

5. Standing under a projecting horizontal ledge of limestone and waiting for the slab to fall. Constructing a small shelter to facilitate waiting in comfort.

6. Eating a lethal dose of beach sand.

7. Taping burning lumps of coal to your body.

8. Injecting liquid gold into your veins.

9. Slitting your wrists with quartz crystals.

10. Wearing a uranium belt.

—1988

Daniel David Moses (b. 1952) *Moses takes pride in his Delaware heritage and the Iroquoian influences of his childhood on Six Nations land near Brantford, Ontario. His work includes the poetry collections* The White Line *(1990) and* Sixteen Jesuses *(2000), and several plays. He also co-edited* An Anthology of Canadian Native Literature in English *(1998).*

Daniel David Moses
Inukshuk

You were built from the stones,
they say, positioned
alone against the sky
here so they might take
you for something human   5

checking the migrations.
That's how you manage this,

standing upright despite
the blue wind that snow is,
this close to Polaris.   *10*

Still, the wind worries
you some. It's your niches
which ought to be empty.
Nothing but lichen grows
there usually. Now   *15*

they're home to dreams. Most come
from the south, a few from
further north—but what flows
out of their mouths comes from
no direction you know.   *20*

They keep singing about
the Great Blue Whale the world
is; how it swims through space
having nightmares about
hunters who only hunt   *25*

their brothers—each after
the other's snow-white face.
How beautiful frozen
flesh is! Like ivory,
like carved bone, like the light   *30*

of Polaris in hand.
So it goes on and on,
the hunting refrain. Dead
silence would be better,
the Pole star overhead.   *35*

The wind agrees, at least
wants to stop up each niche.
How long can you stand it
—that song, the cold, the stones
that no longer hold you   *40*

up now that they hold you
down? Soon the migrations
recommence. How steady
are you? Dreams, so they say,
also sing on the wing.   *45*

                                                                 —1990

Rita Dove (b. 1952) *Born in Akron, Ohio, Dove was the youngest poet and the first African American to be named poet laureate. Her collections of poetry include* Thomas and Beulah *(1986), which won the Pulitzer Prize, and* Grace Notes *(1989).* Mother Love *(1995) includes a series of loosely structured sonnets using the myth of Demeter and Persephone to explore mother-daughter relationships.*

Rita Dove
Persephone, Falling°

One narcissus among the ordinary beautiful
flowers, one unlike all the others! She pulled,
stooped to pull harder—
when, sprung out of the earth
on his glittering terrible   *5*
carriage, he claimed his due.
It is finished. No one heard her
No one! She had strayed from the herd.

(Remember: go straight to school.
This is important, stop fooling around!   *10*
Don't answer to strangers. Stick
with your playmates. Keep your eyes down.)
This is how easily the pit
opens. This is how one foot sinks into the ground.

                                                                 —1995

Persephone, Falling In Greek mythology, Persephone is the daughter of Demeter, goddess of the harvest, and Zeus. When the beautiful Persephone was collecting flowers on the plain of Enna, the earth suddenly opened, and Hades, the god of the underworld, rose up and took her for himself.

Janice Kulyk Keefer (b. 1953) *Born in Canada of Ukrainian heritage, Keefer is the author of more than ten books in several genres, including poetry, fiction, literary criticism, and biography. This tribute to her mother is taken from* White of the Lesser Angels *(1986).*

Janice Kulyk Keefer
My Mother, a Closet Full of Dresses

In Poland, needing a dress
for the potato masher to become a doll,
she cut out a patch from somebody's
Sunday skirt—black silk, good enough
to be buried in; waterfalling folds—   5
no one would notice. Before the whole church,
Baba bent to kiss the icons; her skirts
fanned, the missing patch a window
to her starched white drawers.
My mother whipped until she could not sit;   10
the baba never setting foot
in church again.

In Canada, her sewing teacher
called it shameful—a girl of such gifts
entering a factory! Sent her   15
to design school instead, dressed
in her castoffs. My mother, slashing
stitches from priggish Liberty prints—
everyone else flaunting
palm leaves, cabbage roses.   20

The Story of a Dress at the Exhibition.
She sat in a small display-cage, designing,
cutting out, sewing a dress.
The man who grilled her on each
click of the scissors, till she bit   25
blistered lips, blood

drooling down her chin.
Watched for a week,
then hired her like that—
though it was still Depression,   30
designers a dime a dozen.

The wedding dress she sketched
and sewed herself: "the bride in peau de soie
with a delicate rose tint and beading
in the shape of scattered leaves."   35
Satin peignoirs from the honeymoon—
tea-coloured stains; folds creased
as with a knife.

A closet full of dresses for weddings,
anniversaries,   40
funerals—

And occasions for which she didn't dress:
children with high fevers, and husband
off playing golf or bridge as husbands did;
the miscarriage when she bled   45
faster than the ambulance; migraines
in dark rooms at noon;
and all the nights
when she rummaged, naked,
through steel hangers in an empty closet.   50

—1986

Dionne Brand (b. 1953) Born in Trinidad, Brand pursued post-secondary education in Canada and now lives north of Toronto. In poetry collections such as No Language Is Neutral *(1990), the Governor General's Award–winning* Land to Light On *(1997), and* thirsty *(2002), as well as works of fiction and non-fiction, she explores the immigrant, minority, and lesbian experiences.*

Dionne Brand
Blues Spiritual for Mammy Prater

ON LOOKING AT "THE PHOTOGRAPH OF MAMMY PRATER AN EX-SLAVE, 115 YEARS OLD WHEN HER PHOTOGRAPH WAS TAKEN"

she waited for her century to turn
she waited until she was one hundred and fifteen
years old to take a photograph
to take a photograph and to put those eyes in it
she waited until the technique of photography was   5
suitably developed
to make sure the picture would be clear
to make sure no crude daguerreotype° would lose
her image
would lose her lines and most of all her eyes   10
and her hands
she knew the patience of one hundred and fifteen years
she knew that if she had the patience,
to avoid killing a white man
that I would see this photograph   15
she waited until it suited her
to take this photograph and to put those eyes in it.

In the hundred and fifteen years which it took her to
wait for this photograph she perfected this pose
she sculpted it over a shoulder of pain,   20

---

8 daguerreotype an early photograph named for the inventor of the process, Louis-Jacques-Mandé Daguerre (1789–1851), a French painter and physicist

a thing like despair which she never called
this name for she would not have lasted
the fields, the ones she ploughed
on the days that she was a mule, left
their etching on the gait of her legs   25
deliberately and unintentionally
she waited, not always silently, not always patiently,
for this self portrait
by the time she sat in her black dress, white collar,
white handkerchief, her feet had turned to marble,   30
her heart burnished red,
and her eyes.
she waited one hundred and fifteen years
until the science of photography passed tin and
talbotype° for a surface sensitive enough   35
to hold her eyes
she took care not to lose the signs
to write in those eyes what her fingers could not script
a pact of blood across a century, a decade and more
she knew then that it would be me who would find   40
her will, her meticulous account, her eyes,
her days when waiting for this photograph
was all that kept her sane
she planned it down to the day,   45
the light,
the superfluous photographer
her breasts,
her hands
this moment of   50
my turning the leaves of a book,
noticing, her eyes.

—1990

---

35 talbotype A photographic method using light-sensitive paper and a chemical that brought developing time down from one hour to one minute. Patented by William Henry Talbot (1800–1877) of Great Britain in 1841.

Kim Addonizio (b. 1954) was born in Washington, D.C., as Kim Addie but returned to the name her Italian grandparents abandoned when immigrating to the United States. Her poetry collections include The Philosopher's Club *(1994) and* What Is This Thing Called Love *(2004). She has also published fiction, a guide to writing poetry, and* Dorothy Parker's Elbow: Tattoos on Writers, Writers on Tattoos *(2002).*

Kim Addonizio
First Poem for You

I like to touch your tattoos in complete
darkness, when I can't see them. I'm sure of
where they are, know by heart the neat
lines of lightning pulsing just above
your nipple, can find, as if by instinct, the blue   5
swirls of water on your shoulder where a serpent
twists, facing a dragon. When I pull you
to me, taking you until we're spent
and quiet on the sheets, I love to kiss
the pictures in your skin. They'll last until   10
you're seared to ashes; whatever persists
or turns to pain between us, they will still
be there. Such permanence is terrifying.
So I touch them in the dark; but touch them, trying.

—*1994*

Carol Ann Duffy (b. 1955), a native of Glasgow, Scotland, makes her home in Manchester, England. A popular and prolific poet, she has published over thirty collections since 1974, when her first book appeared. Many of her works have received awards, including Rapture (2005), *and she also writes for children and the stage.*

Carol Ann Duffy

Prayer

Some days, although we cannot pray, a prayer
utters itself. So, a woman will lift
her head from the sieve of her hands and stare
at the minims° sung by a tree, a sudden gift.

Some nights, although we are faithless, the truth   5
enters our hearts, that small familiar pain;
then a man will stand stock-still, hearing his youth
in the distant Latin chanting of a train.

Pray for us now. Grade I piano scales
console the lodger looking out across   10
a Midlands town. Then dusk, and someone calls
a child's name as though they named their loss.

Darkness outside. Inside, the radio's prayer—
Rockall. Maim. Dogger. Finisterre.°

—1993

---

4 minims half notes   **14 Rockall . . .** The BBC shipping forecast includes these four marine zones.

Armand Ruffo (b. 1955) was born in Chapleau in Northern Ontario, a member of the Fox Lake First Nation. His Ojibwa heritage is reflected in his poetry collections Opening the Sky *(1994) and* At Geronimo's Grave *(2001), and in the creative biographies* Grey Owl: The Mystery of Archie Belaney *(1997) and* Norval Morriseau *(2006), about the renowned Ojibwa painter.*

Armand Ruffo
Poem for Duncan Campbell Scott

(Canadian poet who 'had a long and distinguished career
in the Department of Indian Affairs, retiring in 1932.'
The Penguin Book of Canadian Verse)

Who is this black coat and tie?
Christian severity etched in the lines
he draws from his mouth. Clearly a noble man
who believes in work and mission. See
how he rises from the red velvet chair,   5
rises out of the boat with the two Union Jacks
fluttering like birds of prey
and makes his way towards our tents.
This man looks as if he could walk on water
and for our benefit probably would,   10
if he could.

He says he comes from Ottawa way, Odawa country,
comes to talk treaty and annuity and destiny,
to make the inevitable less painful,
bearing gifts that must be had.   15
Notice how he speaks aloud and forthright:
        This or Nothing.
        Beware! Without title to the land
        under the Crown you have no legal right
        to be here.   20
Speaks as though what has been long decided wasn't.
As though he wasn't merely carrying out his duty
to God and King. But sincerely felt.

Some whisper this man lives in a house of many rooms,
has a cook and a maid and even a gardener   *25*
to cut his grass and water his flowers.
Some don't care, they don't like the look of him.
They say he asks many questions but
doesn't want to listen. Asks
much about yesterday, little about today   *30*
and acts as if he knows tomorrow.
Others don't like the way he's always busy writing
stuff in the notebook he carries. Him,
he calls it poetry
and says it will make us who are doomed   *35*
live forever.

—1994

---

*Anne Simpson (b. 1956) lives and teaches in Nova Scotia. Her critically
acclaimed debut poetry collection,* Light Falls Through You *(2000), was followed
by a novel,* Canterbury Beach *(2001), and* Loop *(2003), which won the presti-
gious Griffin Poetry Prize.*

Anne Simpson
The Body Tattoo of World History

Whose?

This is a boy's body. Visited, like Sainte-Thérèse, by visions.

On his wrist

are many heads of obscure Chinese scholars, buried to their necks
in sand. You might think of the heads as attached to bodies, or   *5*
sliced from them by a dozen swordsmen.

There are tiny dots to represent the hundred heads. Or perhaps the
dots signify the sand, in which the heads have disappeared.

On his left thigh

Alexander's famous phalanx, a box formation (moving hedge   10
of bodies) that saved the Greeks.

Who was it they were fighting?

On his right toe

is a tiny face, but not one any of us know. (It could be a miniature
portrait of the nameless woman who lived on the Steppes and   15
rode a horse as well as any man, hunted with falcons, and had
six children before she was twenty-four. When her youngest
child died, she put two pieces of felt over its eyes, as she
had done with five others.)

On his neck   20

a miniature human body, bird-headed creature from the caves of
Lascaux.°

Was there ever such a thing?

On his right earlobe

Jumbo the elephant, killed on the railway tracks in St. Thomas,   25
Ontario, in 1885, squeezed between two trains. Its tusks became
scimitars piercing its brain, but it did not die right away.

22 Lascaux caves in central France lined with prehistoric paintings

Something remains.

On his left eyelid

a symbol for Planck time° that can't be deciphered easily. More   *30*
beautiful than the Big Bang° itself,

this tattoo, and more original.

The body

is that of a boy killed in a convenience store in a small town.

The murderer was a few years older, wearing a death's head   *35*
mask, carrying a hunting knife.

A tattoo of wounds.

How perfect the flesh, just

before a body is cremated.

History is whatever   *40*

lingers.

—2003

---

29 Planck time shortest unit of time named for quantum physicist Max Planck (1858–1947)
30 Big Bang theory of the evolution of the universe

George Elliott Clarke (b. 1960) was born in Windsor Plains, Nova Scotia, of Africadian heritage, a heritage he explores in several collections of poetry—among them, the Governor General's Award–winning Execution Poems *(2001),* Blue *(2001), and* Black *(2006)—as well as in his novel* George & Rue *(2005). He is also a playwright, literary critic, anthologist, and professor of literature at the University of Toronto.*

George Elliott Clarke
Casualties

JANUARY 16, 1991

Snow annihilates all beauty
this merciless January.
A white blitzkrieg, Klan—cruel,
arsons and obliterates.

Piercing lies numb us to pain.   5
Nerves and words fail so we
can't feel agony or passion,
so we can't flinch or cry,

when we spy blurred children's
charred bodies protruding   10
from the smoking rubble
of statistics or see a man

stumbling in a blizzard
of bullets. Everything is
normal, absurdly normal.   15
We see, as if through a snow-

storm, darkly. Reporters
rat-a-tat-tat tactics,
stratagems. Missiles bristle
behind newspaper lines.   20

Our minds chill; we weather
the storm, huddle in dreams.
Exposed, though, a woman,
lashed by lightning, repents

of her flesh, becomes a living   25
X-ray, "collateral damage."
The first casualty of war
is language.

                                                —*1992*

Wanda Campbell (b. 1963) *was born in South India and came to Canada at the age of ten. She has published* Sky Fishing *(1997) and* Haw [Thorn] *(2003), and edited an anthology of early Canadian women poets entitled* Hidden Rooms *(2000).*

Wanda Campbell
Woolf

> *"Virginia Woolf is the Jackie Robinson of women's writing."*
>
>   —*A Student*

the one man
in a class full of women
surprised to be
for once a minority

wearing short sleeves   5
even in winter
but bearing gifts
in his hard brown arms

knowing they both insisted
we are as good as you   10
knowing they both wanted fans
to look past the colour

of their difference
to the music of their swing
such jazz and grace   15
and skill at stealing

they entered the room
but found it bare
the great experiment
took its toll   20

she, fifty-nine, loading her pockets
with stones the size of baseballs
and walking into the stream
of the unconscious

he, fifty-three, leaning   25
on a cane instead of a bat
almost blind, hair white
saying I never had it made

but Jesse Jackson
calling him at his funeral   30
a rock in the water
ripples and waves

                                                       —*2001*

Christian Bök (b. 1966) *is a sound poet and conceptual artist from Toronto who is especially interested in language, having even invented artificial languages for television shows. His poetry collections include* Crystallography *(1994) and* Eunoia *(2001), which was named for the shortest word in the English language to contain all five vowels.*

Christian Bök

Vowels

loveless vessels

we vow
solo love

we see
love solve loss   5

else we see
love sow woe

selves we woo
we lose

losses we levee   10
we owe

we sell
loose vows

so we love
less well   15

so low
so level

wolves evolve

—*2001*

Stephanie Bolster (b. 1969) teaches at Concordia University in Montreal. She won the Governor General's Award for her debut poetry collection, White Stone: The Alice Poems *(1998), about the real girl behind* Alice in Wonderland. Two Bowls of Milk *(1999) and* Pavilion *(2002) were also critically acclaimed.*

Stephanie Bolster
Le Far-West (1955)°

A few acres of snow.° In a Montréal
December I come upon your few feet

of west, a tawny field grazed on
by some animals. They might be

antelope and this some view of   5
Africa—or cows and Idaho? What

cowboy hat do you imagine
my umbrella is? You have not gone

far enough, your English Bay a mouth
drawn shut, its trees cowering   10

under an enormous Québec
sky I cannot write, my words

small glimpses between
this branch of fir and that. How west

must have threatened to open   15
you. My pages nearly white

these days, I'm shutting up.
That 'I' I write no longer me

but you, alone in the midst of what
I call nothing and you home.   20

—*1999*

Le Far-West (**1955**) painting by Québécois artist Jean Paul Lemieux (1904–1990)   **1** *A few acres of snow* In 1759, Voltaire used this phrase to question the value of fighting over Canadian territory.

Ryan Knighton (b. 1973) is a native of British Columbia, where he still lives and teaches. His debut poetry collection, Swing in the Hollow *(2001), was followed by* Cars *(2002), an "auto-biography" co-written with George Bowering, and* Cockeyed *(2006), a memoir that traces Knighton's slow descent into blindness.*

Ryan Knighton

Braille

It is January goosebumps, it is noon-hour sand
in your sandals & sometimes, when you're four,
it's bare feet clutching barnacles
in Pender Harbour.° That same year
it's your father's whiskers on your cheek   5
& a July heat rash on your palms. It is gravel
at 16 under balding tires & it is an eternity
of ha ha ha ha after midnight.

Once it's an itchiness from the neighbour's lawn
& maybe, having fallen that summer, it is pavement   10
under your chin—it is definitely the stitches
that followed & it is my recently shaved head.
It is never rubbing a fish the wrong way
& it is in the delicacy of spider's feet
you were afraid to touch. It is a late supper of brown rice   15
& asparagus tips on your tongue & it's any set
of particular bedtime fingertips.
Vancouver's light autumn drizzle is what it is
& it's finally pressing stars to dial God.

—*1999*

---

4 Pender Harbour harbour north of Vancouver

Matt Robinson (b. 1974) A native of Halifax, Robinson has published widely in journals and has three books of poetry: A Ruckus of Awkward Stacking (2001), How We Play at It: A List *(2002), and* no cage contains a stare that well *(2005), a collection of hockey poems.*

Matt Robinson

when skates break

that ice in its liquid form is a solvent,
should not confuse matters. this is all about stains;
this game concerns itself with scars—in fact,

the surgical violence of that first step
is merely a prelude, an introduction. a perverse   5
baptism. i remember our knees—carpet raw

and bloody with tape-ball hockey
and too much sleep-over sugar; rec rooms alive
and stale gear crowded with the thrill of an oilers

game on television out east. and especially   10
now, years later, after this afternoon's failure, when
the chill anticipation of this october night has shuddered

and cracked, given way like we imagine
our childhood ponds never did—there is still
a sense of tired awe. and the broken, old goalie skates,   15

a grade nine remnant now retired, are propped
in the corner—their blade acne, their cracked plastic,
become something more than nostalgia; become

a grudging admission of the ambiguity of
physics and chemistry in the face of history. become   20
a memorial to the resiliency of water in all its states.

—*2001*

Tania Langlais (b. 1979) was born in Montreal. She won the Émile-Nelligan Award for her critically acclaimed debut poetry collection, Douze bêtes aux chemises de l'homme *(2000). After winning first prize for poetry in the CBC Literary Awards in 2002, she went on to publish a second collection,* La Clarté s'installe comme un chat *(2004).*

Tania Langlais

[she recites one hundred times]

she recites one hundred times
the lexicon of oceans
always signing her name
above the islands
to perfectly measure   5
the wasted expanse
neither daughter nor delta
she said
"when you sleep in the bed
it is the andalusian° thirst of wells   10
that you multiply
and fold up behind me"

—*2006*

Translated by Wanda Campbell.

10 andalusian region in southern Spain

Appendix 1

Poems Grouped by Genre, Technique, or Subject

Because it is possible to classify the poems in the anthology in many different ways, the following appendix is not exhaustive. It should, however, provide suggestions for reading and writing about poems that share some similarities. Some poems appear in more than one category.

Aging (See also Carpe Diem)
Queen Elizabeth I, "When I Was Fair and Young"
Shakespeare, "Sonnet 73"
Scott, "The Forsaken"
Williams, "To A Poor Old Woman"
Eliot, "The Love Song of J. Alfred Prufrock"
Pastan, "Ethics"
Phillips, "Compartments"

Allegorical and Symbolic Poems
Blake, "The Sick Rose"
Tennyson, "The Lady of Shalott"
Dickinson, "I Had Been Hungry All the Years"
Rossetti, "Goblin Market"
Lampman, "The City of the End of Things"
Yeats, "The Second Coming"
Frost, "Neither out Far nor in Deep"
Stevens, "Thirteen Ways of Looking at a Blackbird"
Eliot, "Journey of the Magi"
Plath, "Metaphors"

Animals
Smart, *from* "Jubilate Agno"
Blake. "The Tyger"
Crawford, "The Dark Stag"
Moore, "The Fish"
Zukofsky, "Mantis"
Stafford, "Traveling Through the Dark"
Hughes, "The Thought Fox"
Nolwan, "The Bull Moose"
Lowther, "Octopus"
Lane, "Because I Never Learned"

Art
Spenser, "Amoretti: Sonnet 75"
Shakespeare, "Sonnet 18"
Shelley, "Ozymandias"
Keats, "Ode on a Grecian Urn"
Tennyson, "The Lady of Shalott"
Browning, "My Last Duchess"
Yeats, "Sailing to Byzantium"
Birney "El Greco: *Espolio*"
Auden, "Musée des Beaux Arts"
Smith, "The Lonely Land"
Livesay, "The Three Emilys"

Olson, "The Ring Of"
Ferlinghetti, "In Goya's greatest
scenes"
Sexton, "The Starry Night"
Pastan, "Ethics"
Bowering, "Play & Work &
Art"
Bolster, *Le Far West*

Ballads and Narrative Poetry

Anonymous, "Sir Patrick Spens"
Keats, "La Belle Dame Sans Merci"
Randall, "Ballad of Birmingham"
Rogers, "The Mary Ellen Carter"

Birds

Poe, "The Raven"
Wallace, "Thirteen Ways of Look-
ing at a Blackbird"
Kumin, "Noted in the New York
Times"
Plath, "Black Rook in Rainy
Weather"
Mackay, "Icarus"

Canada

Hayman, "The Four Elements in
Newfoundland"
Kelsey, "Now Reader Read"
Roberts, "Tantramar Revisited"
Scott, "Laurentian Shield"
Smith "The Lonely Land"
Hébert, "Snow"
Purdy, "A Handful of Earth"
Kroetsch, "Stone Hammer Poem"
Atwood, "Death of Young Son by
Drowning"
Chiasson, "Red"
Moses, "Inukshuk"
Bolster, *Le Far West*

Carpe Diem

Queen Elizabeth I, "When I Was
Fair and Young"
Marvell, "To His Coy Mistress"

Childhood and Adolescence

Thomas, "Fern Hill"
Kogawa, "When I Was a Little Girl"
Lane, "Because I Never Learned"
Atwood, "Death of a Young Son by
Drowning"
Ondaatje, "Sweet Like a Crow"
Muldoon, "Anseo"
Dove, "Persephone, Falling"
Robinson, "when skates break"

Conceit and Extended Metaphor

Donne, "Holy Sonnet 14"
Herbert, "Easter Wings"
Bradstreet, "The Author to Her
Book"
Cavendish, "Nature's Cook"
Crawford, "The Dark Stag"
Plath, "Metaphors"
Chappell, "Narcissus and Echo"

Conceit: Petrarchan

Shakespeare, "Sonnet 130"

Death

Cavendish, "Nature's Cook"
Browning, "My Last Duchess"
Dickinson, "I Died for Beauty—
But Was Scarce"
Scott, "The Forsaken"
Pratt, "From Stone to Steel"
Thomas, "Do Not Go Gentle into
That Good Night"
Jarrell, "The Death of the Ball
Turret Gunner"
Nowlan, "The Broadcaster's Poem"
Piercy, "Barbie Doll"
Cohen, "The Future"
Atwood, "Death of a Young Son by
Drowning"

Dramatic Dialogues

Randall, "Ballad of Birmingham"
Chappell, "Narcissus and Echo"

Dramatic Monologues and Related Poems

Browning, "My Last Duchess"
Pound, "The River-Merchant's Wife: A Letter"
Eliot, "Journey of the Magi"
Eliot, "The Love Song of J. Alfred Prufrock"
Jarrell, "The Death of the Ball Turret Gunner"
Wayman, "Did I Miss Anything?"
Muldoon, "Anseo"

Duty

Anonymous, "Sir Patrick Spens"
Lovelace, "To Lucasta, Going to the Wars"

Fate

Hardy "The Convergence of the Twain"
Randall, "Ballad of Birmingham"

Future

Lampman, "The City of the End of Things"
Yeats, "The Second Coming"
Cohen, "The Future"
Crozier, "Packing for the Future: Instructions"

History

Kelsey, "Now Reader Read . . ."
Shelley, "Ozymandias"
Hardy "The Convergence of the Twain"
Yeats, "The Second Coming"
Pratt, "From Stone to Steel"
Curnow, "Landfall in Unknown Seas"
Kroetsch, "Stone Hammer Poem"
Webb, "Leaning"
Brathwaite, "Colombe"
Walcott, "Central America"
Armstrong, "History Lesson"
Forché, "The Colonel"

Simpson, "The Body Tattoo of World History"

Holocaust

Williams, "The Book"
Shomer, "Women Bathing at Bergen-Belsen"

Humanity

Milton, "Paradise Lost"
Pope, "An Essay on Man"
Arnold, "Dover Beach"
Pratt, "From Stone to Steel"
Pound, "In A Station of the Metro"
cummings, "pity this busy monster,manunkind"
Stafford, "Traveling Through the Dark"
Ginsberg, "A Supermarket in California"
Phillips, "Compartments"
Mayers, "All-American Sestina"
Bringhurst, "Essay on Adam"
Steele, "Sapphics Against Anger"
Carson, "God's List of Liquids"

Language

Hass, "Picking Blackberries with a Friend Who Has Been Reading Jacques Lacan"
Raine, "A Martian Sends a Postcard Home"
NourbeSe Philips, "Discourse on the Logic of Language"
Clarke, "Casualties"
Bok, "Vowels"

Love

Shakespeare, "Sonnet 30"
Donne, "Song"
Wroth, "In This Strange Labyrinth How Shall I Turn"
Behn, "Love Armed"
Blake, "The Sick Rose"
Burns, "A Red, Red Rose"

Barrett Browning, "Sonnets from the Portuguese, 1"

Barrett Browning, "Sonnets from the Portuguese, 43"

Johnson, "The Idlers"

Hale, "This Oblivion"

Eliot, "The Love Song of J. Alfred Prufrock"

Parker, "One Perfect Rose"

Jones, "Kate, These Flowers"

Atwood, "you fit into me"

Marlatt, "(is love enough?)"

Nichol, "Blues"

Wallace, "Common Magic"

Addonizio, "First Poem For You"

Bok, "Vowels"

Langlais, "elle récite cent fois . . ."

Love, Loss of

Anonymous, "Western Wind"

Wyatt, "They Flee from Me"

Shelley, "When the Lamp is Shattered"

Keats, "La Belle Dame sans Merci"

Poe, "The Raven"

Millay, "What Lips My Lips Have Kissed"

Bishop, "One Art"

Love: Marital Relationships

Browning, "My Last Duchess"

Arnold, "Dover Beach"

Pound, "The River-Merchant's Wife: A Letter"

Olds, "I Go Back to May 1937"

Myth

Inuit Traditional Song, "Magic Words/Aua"

Southern First Nations Traditional Orature, "Fragment of a Song"

Wordsworth, "The World is Too Much With Us"

Poe, "To Helen"

H.D., "Helen"

Eliot, "The Love Song of J. Alfred Prufrock"

Auden, "Musée des Beaux Arts"

Olson, "The Ring Of"

Rukeyser, "Myth"

Sexton, "Cinderalla"

Chappell, "Narcissus and Echo"

MacEwan, "Poem Improvised Around a First Line"

MacKay, "Icarus"

Keeshig-Tobias, "How to Catch a White Man (Oops) I Mean Trickster"

Carson, "Short Talk on the Total Collection"

Moses, "Inukshuk"

Dove, "Persephone, Falling"

Nature and the Spiritual

Hopkins, "God's Grandeur"

Nelligan, "Evening Bells"

Plath, "Black Rook in Rainy Weather"

Lowell, "Water"

Larkin, "Water"

MacEwan, "Water"

Duffy, "Prayer"

Nature: Descriptive Poetry

Swift, "A Description of a City Shower"

Wordsworth, "I Wandered Lonely as a Cloud"

Bronte, "Ah Why Because the Dazzling Sun . . ."

Hopkins, "Pied Beauty"

Crawford, "The Dark Stag"

Roberts, "Tantramar Revisited"

Frost, "Stopping by Woods on a Snowy Evening"

cummings, "l(a"

Smith, "The Lonely Land"

Roethke, "Root Cellar"

Bishop, "At the Fishhouses"

Thomas, "Fern Hill"

Hebert, "Snow"

Avison, "Snow"

Nichol, "landscape: I"

Thurston, "Miracle"

Nature: The Environment
Wordsworth, "The World is Too Much with Us"
Hopkins, "God's Grandeur"
Lampman, "The City of the End of Things"
cummings, "pity this busy monster,manunkind"
Stafford, "Traveling Through the Dark"
Page, "Planet Earth"
Oodgeroo, "We Are Going"
Kumin, "Noted in the *New York Times*"
Godbout, "Trees"
Marlatt, "(is love enough?)"
Armstrong, "History Lesson"
Keeshig-Tobias, "How to Catch a White Man (Oops) I Mean Trickster"

Parents and Children
Hensley, "Courage"
Livesay, "The Three Emilys"
Thomas, "Do Not Go Gentle into That Good Night"
Wilbur, "The Writer"
Atwood, "Death of a Young Son by Drowning"
Lane, "Because I Never Learned"
Heaney, "Digging"
Olds, "I Go Back To May 1937"
Keefer, "My Mother, a Closet Full of Dresses"

Physical Handicaps
Owen, "Disabled"
Knighton, "Braille"

Poetry
Bradstreet, "The Author to Her Book"
Dryden, "Epigram on Milton"
Coleridge "Metrical Feet"
Stevens, "The Motive for Metaphor"
Neruda, "In Praise of Ironing"

Klein, "Portrait of the Poet as Landscape"
Layton, "The Fertile Muck"
Ashbery, "Paradoxes and Oxymorons"
Heaney, "Digging"
Gwynn, "Approaching a Significant Birthday, He Peruses *The Norton Anthology of Poetry*"

Poetry: Inspiration
Coleridge, "Kubla Khan"
Brontë, "[Ah! why, because the dazzling sun]"
Whitman, "Song of Myself"
Williams, "The Red Wheelbarrow"
Wilbur, "The Writer"
Kroetsch, "Stone Hammer Poem"
Ramanujan, "A River"
Hughes, "The Thought-Fox"
Plath, "Black Rook in Rainy Weather"
Nowlan, "The Broadcaster's Poem"
Bowering, "Play & Work & Art"

Political and Social Themes
McLachlan, "We Live in a Rickety House"
Zukofsky, "Mantis"
Brooks, "First Fight. Then Fiddle."
Purdy, "A Handful of Earth"
Carter, "University of Hunger"
Walcott, "Central America"
Cohen, "The Future"
Atwood, "Notes Towards a Poem that Can Never be Written"
Chiasson "Red"
Forché, "The Colonel"

Race and Ethnicity
Wheatley, "On Being Brought from Africa to America"
Scott, (D.C.) "The Forsaken"
Dunbar, "Sympathy"
Curnow, "Landfall in Unknown Seas"
Randall, "Ballad of Birmingham"

Brooks, "First Fight. Then Fiddle"
Oodgeroo, "We Are Going"
Carter, "University of Hunger"
Ramanujan, "The River"
Brathwaite, "Colombe"
Kogawa, "When I Was a Little Girl"
Ondaatje, "Sweet Like a Crow"
Chiasson, "Red"
NourbeSe Phillips, "Discourse on
   the Logic of Language"
Armstrong, "History Lesson"
Keeshig-Tobias, "How to Catch
   a White Man (Oops) I Mean
   Trickster"
Jones, "Winter Retreat: Homage to
   Martin Luther King, Jr."
Muldoon, "Anseo"
Brand, "Blues Spiritual for Mammy
   Prater"
Ruffo, "Poem for Duncan Camp-
   bell Scott"
Clarke, "Casualties"

Satire and Humour
Swift, "A Description of a City
   Shower"
Parker, "One Perfect Rose"
Wayman, "Did I Miss Anything?"
Dewdney "Ten Typically Geological
   Suicides"

**Sexual Themes (See also Carpe
Diem)**
Marvell, "To His Coy Mistress"
Johnson, "The Idlers"
Eliot, "The Love Song of J. Alfred
   Prufrock"

Solitude
Moodie, "Brian, the Still Hunter"
Frost, "Stopping by Woods on a
   Snowy Evening"
cummings, "l(a"

Sports and Games
Owen, "Disabled"
Bowering "Play & Work & Art"

Campbell, "Woolf"
Robinson, "when skates break"

Suicide
Robinson, "Richard Cory"
Sexton, "The Starry Night"
Dewdney, "Ten Typically Geologi-
   cal Suicides"

War
Lovelace, "To Lucasta, Going to
   the Wars"
Byron, "Stanzas, When a Man Hath
   No Freedom"
Hensley, "Courage"
Pratt, "From Stone to Steel"
Owen, "Dulce et Decorum Est"
Owen, "Disabled"
Brecht, "The God of War"
Jarrell, "The Death of the Ball
   Turret Gunner"
Ciardi, "To Lucasta, About
   That War"
Brooks, "First Fight. Then
   Fiddle."
Walcott, "Central America"
Kogawa, "When I Was a Little Girl"
Forche, "The Colonel"
Muldoon, "Anseo"
Clarke, "Casualties"

Women's Issues
Finch, "Adam Posed"
Leapor, "An Essay on Women"
Rossetti, "Goblin Market"
Parker, "One Perfect Rose"
Livesay, "The Three Emilys"
Rukeyser, "Myth"
Levertov, "In Mind"
Sexton, "Cinderella"
Rich, "Power"
Plath, "Metaphors"
Piercy, "Barbie Doll"
Dove, "Persephone, Fallilng"
Cope, "Rondeau Redoublé"
Campbell, "Woolf"

Appendix 2

Traditional Stanza, Fixed, and Nonce Forms

Acrostic Verse
Jones, "Kate, These Flowers"

Accentual Meter
Hardy, "The Convergence of the Twain"
Wilbur, "The Writer"

Ballad Stanza (and Variants)
Anonymous, "Sir Patrick Spens"
Keats, "La Belle Dame sans Merci"
Randall, "Ballad of Birmingham"
Rogers, "Mary Ellen Carter"

Blank Verse
Milton, *from* "Paradise Lost"
Moodie, "Brian, the Still Hunter"
Yeats, "The Second Coming"
Stafford, "Traveling Through the Dark"

Cento
Gwynn, "Approaching a Significant Birthday, He Peruses *The Norton Anthology of Poetry*"

Common Meter
Anonymous, "Western Wind"
Lovelace, "To Lucasta, Going to the Wars"
Burns, "A Red, Red Rose"

Brontë, "[Ah! why, because the dazzling sun]"
Dickinson, "I Died for Beauty—But Was Scarce"

Concrete Poetry
Herbert, "Easter Wings"
cummings, "l(a"
Nichol, "landscape: I"
Nichol, "Blues"

Couplets, Short
Marvell, "To His Coy Mistress"
Blake, "The Tyger"

Couplets, Heroic
Hayman, "The Four Elements in Newfoundland"
Bradstreet, "The Author to Her Book"
Cavendish, "Nature's Cook"
Dryden, "Epigram on Milton"
Swift, "A Description of a City Shower,"
Kelsey, "Now Reader Read . . ."
Pope, *from* "An Essay on Man"
Leapor, "An Essay on Woman"
Wheatley, "On Being Brought from Africa to America"
Browning, "My Last Duchess"

Ghazal
Webb, "Leaning"

Haiku
Phillips, "Compartments"

Long Meter
Behn, "Loved Armed"
Lampman, "The City of the End
of Things"
Pratt, "From Stone to Steel"

Ode, Irregular
Coleridge, "Kubla Khan"
Arnold, "Dover Beach"
Owen, "Disabled"

Ode, Regular
Keats, "Ode on a Grecian Urn"

Ottava Rima
Yeats, "Sailing to Byzantium"

Prose Poem
Rukeyser, "Myth"
McKay, "Icarus"
Chiasson, "Red"
Keeshig-Tobias, "How to Catch
a White Man (Oops) I Mean
Trickster"
Forché, "The Colonel"
Nourbese Philips, "Discourse on
the Logic of Language"
Carson, "Short Talk on the Total
Collection"

Quatrain, English
Robinson, "Richard Cory"
Gwynn, "Approaching a Significant
Birthday, He Peruses *The
Norton Anthology
of Poetry*"

Rime Royal
Wyatt, "They Flee from Me"

Rondeau Redoublé
Cope, "Rondeau Redoublé"

Rubaiyat Stanza
Frost, "Stopping by Woods on
a Snowy Evening"

Sapphic Stanzas
Steele, "Sapphics Against Anger"

Sestets
Ciardi, "To Lucasta, About
that War"

Sestina
Zukofsky, "Mantis"
Mayers, "All-American Sestina"

Sonnet, Curtal
Hopkins, "Pied Beauty"

Sonnet, English
Shakespeare, "Sonnet 18"
Shakespeare, "Sonnet 30"
Shakespeare, "Sonnet 73"
Shakespeare, "Sonnet 130"
Brooks, "First Fight. Then Fiddle"
Avison, "Snow"
Duffy, "Prayer"
Addonizio, "First Poem for You"

Sonnet, Italian
Donne, "Holy Sonnet 10"
Wordsworth, "The World is Too
Much With Us"
Barrett Browning, "Sonnets from
the Portuguese, 1"
Barrett Browning, "Sonnets from
the Portuguese, 43"
Hopkins, "God's Grandeur"
Millay, "What Lips My Lips Have
Kissed"
cummings, "pity this busy
monster,manunkind"

Sonnet, Nonce
Shelley, "Ozymandias"
Owen, "Dulce Et Decorum Est"
Shomer, "Women Bathing at
Bergen-Belsen"

Sonnet, Spenserian
Spenser, "Amoretti: Sonnet 75"
Wroth, "In This Strange Labyrinth
    How Shall I Turn"

Syllabics
Moore, "The Fish"
Thomas, "Fern Hill"
Plath, "Metaphors"

Triplets
Hardy, "The Convergence of the
    Twain"

Villanelle
Bishop, "One Art"
Thomas, "Do Not Go Gentle into
    That Good Night"

Credits

Inuit Traditional Song, "Magic Words/Aua." Copyright © 1981, 1997 by J. R. Colombo. Reprinted from *Poems of the Inuit* (Toronto: Colombo & Company, 1997).

Southern First Nations Traditional Orature, "Fragments of a Song" is reprinted from *Columbo: Songs of the Indians* by permission of Oberon Press.

Kim Addonizio, "First Poem for You" from *The Philosopher's Club*. Copyright © 1994 by Kim Addonizio. Reprinted with the permission of BOA Editions, Ltd.

Jeanette Armstrong, "History Lesson" from *Breathtracks* © 1991 by Theytus Books Ltd. Reprinted with permission of Theytus Books Ltd.

John Ashbery, "Paradoxes and Oxymorons" from *Shadow Train* by John Ashbery. Copyright © 1980, 1981 by John Ashbery. Reprinted by permission of Georges Borchardt, Inc., for the author.

Margaret Avison, "Snow" reprinted from *Always Now: The Collected Poems* (in three volumes) by Margaret Avison by permission of The Porcupine's Quill. Copyright © Margaret Avison, 2003.

W. H. Auden, "Musee des Beaux Arts," copyright 1940 and renewed 1968 by W. H. Auden, from *W. H. Auden: The Collected Poems* by W. H. Auden. Used by permission of Random House, Inc.

Earle Birney, "El Greco: Espolio" from *Ghost in the Wheels* by Earle Birney. Used by permission, McClelland & Stewart Ltd. *The Canadian Publishers*.

Elizabeth Bishop, "At the Fishhouses" and "One Art" from *The Complete Poems 1927–1979* by Elizabeth Bishop. Copyright © 1979, 1983 by Alice Helen Methfessel. Reprinted by permission of Farrar, Straus and Giroux, LLC.

Christian Bök, "Vowels" from *Eunoia* by Christian Bök. Copyright © 2001 by Christian Bök. Reprinted with permission of Coach House Books.

Stephanie Bolster, "Le Far-West (1955)" from *Two Bowls of Milk* by Stephanie Bolster. Used by permission of McClelland & Stewart Ltd.

George Bowering, "Play & Work & Art" from *Blonds on Bikes* by George Bowering. Copyright © 1997 George Bowering. Reprinted with permission of Talon Books Ltd.

Dionne Brand, "Blues Spiritual for Mammy Prater" from *No Language Is Neutral* by Dionne Brand. Used by permission, McClelland & Stewart Ltd.

Kamau Brathwaite, "Colombe" from *Middle Passages* (Tarset, UK: Bloodaxe Books, 1992). Reprinted with permission.

Bertolt Brecht, "The God of War" from *Poems: 1913–1956* by Bertolt Brecht, translated by John Willett and Ralph Manheim, published by Methuen Publishing Ltd. Reprinted with permission.

Robert Bringhurst, "Essay on Adam" from *The Beauty of Weapons* by Robert Bringhurst. Used by permission, McClelland & Stewart Ltd.

Gwendolyn Brooks, "First Fight. Then Fiddle." from *Blacks* by Gwendolyn Brooks. Copyright © 1991 by Gwendolyn Brooks. Reprinted by consent of Brooks Permissions.

Wanda Campbell, "Woolf" reprinted courtesy of the author.

Anne Carson, "God's List of Liquids," from *Glass, Irony, and God*, copyright © 1995 by Anne Carson. Reprinted by permission of New Directions Publishing Corp.

Anne Carson, "Short Talk on the Total Collection" from *Short Talks* by Anne Carson. Copyright © 1992 by Anne Carson. Reprinted with the permission of the Burns & Clegg Agency for Anne Carson.

Martin Carter, "University of Hunger" from *Poems of Succession* by Martin Carter. Copyright © 1977 by Martin Carter. Reproduced with permission.

Fred Chappell, "Narcissus and Echo" from *Source: Poems*. Copyright © 1985 by Fred Chappell. Reprinted by permission of Louisiana State University Press

Herménégilde Chiasson, "Red" was originally published in French as "Rouge" in *Mourir à Scoudouc* © 1974 by Herménégilde Chiasson. The English version was translated by Jo-Ann Elder and Fred Cogswell and was originally published in *Unfinished Dreams: Contemporary Poetry of Acadie* © 1990 by Jo-Ann Elder and Fred Cogswell. Reprinted by permission of Goose Lane Editions.

John Ciardi, "To Lucasta, About That War" from *Thirty-Nine Poems* © John Ciardi 1959. Reprinted with the permission of Ciardi Family Publishing Trust.

George Elliott Clark, "Casualties", from *Fiery Sprits and Voices*, edited by Ayanna Black. Published by HarperCollins*PublishersLtd*. Copyright © 1992 by George Elliot Clarke. Reprinted by permission of the author. All rights reserved.

Leonard Cohen, "The Future" from *Stranger Music: Selected Poems and Songs* by Leonard Cohen. Used by permission, McClelland & Stewart Ltd.

Wendy Cope, "Rondeau Redoublé" from *Making Cocoa for Kingsley Amis* by Wendy Cope. Reproduced by permission of Faber and Faber Ltd.

Lorna Crozier, "Packing for the Future: Instructions" from *What the Living Won't Let Go* by Lorna Crozier. Used by permission, McClelland & Stewart Ltd.

E. E. Cummings, "pity this busy monster,manunkind," copyright 1944, © 1972, 1992 by the Trustees for the E. E. Cummings Trust; "l(a" copyright © 1958, 1986, 1991 by Trustees for the E. E. Cummings Trust; from *Complete Poems: 1904–1962* by E. E. Cummings, edited by George J. Firmage. Used by permission of Liveright Publishing Corporation.

Allen Curnow, "Landfall in Unkown Seas" from *An Anthology of New Zealand Poetry*. Copyright © 1997. Reprinted by permission of Carcanet Press, UK.

Christopher Dewdney, "Ten Typically Geological Suicides" from *The Radiant Inventory* by Christopher Dewdney. Used by permission, McClelland & Stewart Ltd.

Emily Dickinson, "I Died for Beauty," and "I Had Been Hungry, all the Years" reprinted by permission of the publishers and the Trustees of Amherst College from *The Poems of Emily Dickinson*, edited by Thomas H. Johnson, Cambridge, Mass.: The Belknap Press of Harvard University Press, Copyright © 1951, 1955, 1979, 1983 by the President and Fellows of Harvard College.

HD (Hilda Doolittle), "Helen" from *Collected Poems 1912–1944*, copyright © 1982 by The Estate of Hilda Doolittle. Reprinted by permission of New Directions Publishing Corp.

Rita Dove, "Persephone, Falling" from *Mother Love* by Rita Dove. Copyright © 1995 by Rita Dove. Used by permission of W. W. Norton & Company, Inc.

Carol Ann Duffy, "Prayer" from *Mean Time*. Copyright © 1993 by Anvil Press Poetry Ltd. Reprinted with permission of the publisher.

T. S. Eliot, "Journey of the Magi" and "The Love Song of J. Alfred Profrock" from *Collected Poems*, copyright © 1936 by Harcourt Brace & Company, Inc., copyright © 1964, 1963 by T. S. Eliot. Reprinted by permission of Faber and Faber Ltd.

Lawrence Ferlinghetti, "In Goya's Greatest Scenes . . . (#1)" from *A Coney Island of the Mind*, copyright © 1958 by Lawrence Ferlinghetti. Reprinted by permission of New Directions Publishing Corp.

Carolyn Forché, "The Colonel" from *The Country Between Us* by Carolyn Forché. Copyright © 1981 by Carolyn Forché. Originally appeared in *Women's International Resource Exchange*. Reprinted by permission of HarperCollins Publishers.

Robert Frost, "Neither Out Far Nor In Deep" and "Stopping By Woods on a Snowy Evening" from *The Poetry of Robert Frost* edited by Edward Connery Lathem. Copyright © 1923, 1969 by Henry Holt and Company. Copyright 1936, 1951 by Robert Frost, © 1964 by Lesley Frost Ballantine. Reprinted by permission of Henry Holt and Company, LLC.

Allen Ginsberg, "A Supermarket in California" from *Collected Poems 1947–1980* by Allen Ginsberg. Copyright © 1955 by Allen Ginsberg. Reprinted by permission of HarperCollins Publishers.

Jacques Godbout, "Trees" from *Poetry of French Canada*. Translated by John Glassco. Copyright © 1970 by Jacques Godbout. Reprinted by permission of the author and William Toye, literary executor for the Estate of John Glassco.

R. S. Gwynn, "Approaching a Significant Birthday, He Peruses the *Norton Anthology of Poetry*" from *No Word of Farewell: Selected Poems 1970–2000* by R.S. Gwynn. Copyright © 2001 by R. S. Gwynn. Reprinted by permission of the author and Story Line Press, Inc. <www.storylinepress.com>.

Robert Hass, "Picking Blackberries with a Friend Who Has Been Reading Jacques Lacan" from *Praise* by Robert Hass. Copyright © 1979 by Robert Hass. Reprinted by permission of HarperCollins Publishers.

Seamus Heaney, "Digging" from *Selected Poems 1966–1987* by Seamus Heaney. Copyright © 1990 by Seamus Heaney. Reprinted by permission of Faber and Faber Ltd.

Anne Hébert, "Snow" from *Saint-Denys Garneau and Anne Hébert* by Anne Hébert. Translated by F. R. Scott. Reprinted by permission of House of Anansi Press and William Toye, literary executor for the Estate of F. R. Scott.

Ted Hughes, "The Thought Fox" from *The Hawk in the Rain*. Reprinted with permission of Faber and Faber Ltd.

Randall Jarrell, "The Death of the Ball Turret Gunner" from *The Complete Poems* by Randall Jarrell. Copyright © 1969, renewed 1997 by Mary von S. Jarrell. Reprinted by permission of Farrar, Straus and Giroux, LLC.

D. G. Jones, "Kate, These Flowers . . ." (The Lampman Poems), reprinted with permission of the author.

Rodney Jones, "Winter Retreat: Homage to Martin Luther King, Jr." from *Transparent Gestures* by Rodney Jones. Copyright © 1989 by Rodney Jones. Reprinted by permission of Houghton Mifflin Company. All rights reserved.

Lenore Keeshig-Tobias, "How to Catch a White Man (Ooops) I Mean Trickster" by Lenore Keeshig-Tobias, pg. 108 in *Indigena: Contemporary Native Perspectives in Canadian Art*, © 1991 Canadian Museum of Civilization, published by Douglas & McIntyre Ltd. Reprinted with permission of the publisher.

A. M. Klein, "Portrait of the Poet as Landscape" from *A. M. Klein: The Complete Poems* by A. M. Klein. Copyright © 1990 University of Toronto Press. Reprinted with permission of the publisher.

Ryan Knighton, "Braille" from *Swing in the Hollow*. Copyright © 2001 by Ryan Knighton. Published by Anvil Press. Reprinted with permission of the publisher.

Joy Kogawa, "When I Was a Little Girl" from *A Choice of Dreams*, reprinted with the permission of Joy Kogawa.

Robert Kroetsch, "Stone Hammer Poem" from *Completed Field Notes: The Long Poems of Robert Kroetsch* by Robert Kroetsch (originally published by McClelland & Stewart, now available from University of Alberta Press). Copyright © 1989 Robert Kroetsch. With permission of the author.

Janice Kulyk Keefer, "My Mother a Closet Full of Dresses" from *White of the Lesser Angels* by Janice Kulyk Keefer. Reprinted with permission of the author.

Maxine Kumin, "Noted in the *New York Times*," copyright © 1989 by Maxine W. Kumin. Reprinted by permission.

Tania Langlais, "[elle récite cent fois]" from *Douze bêtes aux chemises de l'homme* by Tania Langlais. Copyright © 2000 Éditions Les Herbes rouges. English translation © Wanda Campbell 2006 with permission of the publisher.

Philip Larkin, "Water" from *The Whitsun Weddings*. Copyright © 1964. Reprinted by permission of Faber and Faber Ltd.

Irving Layton, "The Fertile Muck" from *A Wild Peculiar Joy: Selected Poems 1945–1989* by Irving Layton. Used by permission, McClelland & Stewart Ltd.

Denise Levertov, "In Mind" from Denise Levertov, *Poems 1960–1967*, copyright © 1966 by Denise Levertov. Reprinted by permission of New Directions Publishing Corp.

Dorothy Livesay, "The Three Emilys" from *Collected Poems: Two Seasons* by Dorothy Livesay. Copyright © 1972 by Dorothy Livesay. Reprinted with permission of Jay Stewart for the Estate of Dorothy Livesay.

Robert Lowell, "Water" from *Selected Poems* by Robert Lowell. Copyright © 1976 by Robert Lowell. Reprinted by permission of Farrar, Straus and Giroux, LLC.

Pat Lowther, "Octopus" from *A Stone Diary* by Pat Lowther. Copyright © Oxford University Press 1977. Reprinted by permission of the publisher.

Gwendolyn MacEwen, "Water" from *The T. E. Lawrence Poems*. Copyright © 1982 by Gwendolyn MacEwen. Reprinted with the permission of the author's family.

Gwendolyn MacEwen, "Poem Improvised Around a First Line" from *Magic Animals*. Copyright © 1969 Gwendolyn MacEwen. Reprinted with the permission of the author's family.

Don McKay, "Icarus" from *Another Gravity* by Don McKay. Used by permission, McClelland & Stewart Ltd.

Daphne Marlatt, "(is love enough)?" from *This Tremor Love Is*. Copyright © 2001 Daphne Marlatt. Reprinted with permission of Talon Books Ltd.

Florence Cassen Mayers, "All-American Sestina." First published in *The Atlantic Monthly*. Reprinted by permission of the author.

Marianne Moore, "The Fish" reprinted with the permission of Scribner, an imprint of Simon & Schuster Adult Publishing Group, from *The Collected Poems of Marianne Moore* by Marianne Moore. Copyright © 1935 by Marianne Moore; copyright renewed © 1963 by Marianne Moore.

Daniel David Moses, "Inukshuk" is reprinted with permission from *The White Line* by Daniel David Moses. Copyright © 1990 by Daniel David Moses. Published by Fifth House Publishers, Ltd., Calgary, Canada.

Paul Muldoon, "Anseo" from *Poems: 1968–1998* by Paul Muldoon. Copyright © 2001 by Paul Muldoon. Reprinted by permission of Farrar, Straus and Giroux, LLC.

Emil Nelligan, "Evening Bells" from *Selected Poems* by Emile Nelligan. Translated by P. F. Widdows. Toronto: Guernica, 1995. Reproduced by permission of the publisher.

bp Nichol, "landscape: 1" from *Zygal: A Book of Mysteries and Translations* by bp Nichol. Copyright © 2000 by bp Nichol. Reprinted with permission of Coach House Books.

bp Nichol, "blues" from *An H in the Heart: A Reader* by bp Nichol. Copyright © 1994 by bp Nichol. Reprinted with permission of The Estate of bp Nichol.

M. NourbeSe Philip, "Discourse on the Logic of Language" from *She Tries Her Tongue, Her Silent Softly Breaks: Poems*. Copyright © 1989 by M. NourbeSe Philip. Reprinted with permission of M. NourbeSe Philip.

Alden Nowlan, "The Bull Moose." Reprinted with the permission of Claudine Nowlan.

Alden Nowlan, "The Broadcaster's Poem," from *Selected Poems* © 1974 by Alden Nowlan. Reprinted by permission of House of Anansi Press.

Sharon Olds, "I GO Back to May 1937," copyright © 1987 by Sharon Olds, from *The Gold Cell* by Sharon Olds. Used by permission of Alfred A. Knopf, a division of Random House, Inc.

Charles Olson, "The Ring Of" from *The Collected Poems of Charles Olson*, edited by George F. Butterick. Copyright © 1997 University of California Press. This work is protected by copyright and it is being used with the permission of *Access Copyright*. Any alteration of its content or further copying in any form whatsoever is strictly prohibited.

Michael Ondaatje, "Sweet Like a Crow" from *The Cinnamon Peeler* by Michael Ondaatje. Used by permission, McClelland & Stewart Ltd.

Oodgeroo Noonucal (Kath Walker), "We Are Going" by Oodgeroo of the tribe Noonuccal, from *My People*, 3e, The Jacaranda Press, © 1990. Reproduced with permission of John Wiley & Sons Australia.

P. K. Page, "Planet Earth" from *The Hidden Room: Collected Poems, Volume Two* by P. K. Page. Copyright © 1997 by P.K. Page. Reprinted by permission of The Porcupine's Quill.

Dorothy Parker, "One Perfect Rose," copyright 1926, renewed © 1954 by Dorothy Parker, from *The Portable Dorothy Parker* by Dorothy Parker, edited by Brendan Gill. Used by permission of Viking Penguin, a division of Penguin Group (USA) Inc.

Linda Pastan, "Ethics" from *Waiting for My Life* by Linda Pastan. Copyright © 1981 by Linda Pastan. Used by permission of W. W. Norton & Company, Inc.

Robert Phillips, "Compartments" from *Spinach Days*, pp. 91–93. Copyright © 2000. Reprinted with permission of The Johns Hopkins University Press.

Marge Piercy, "Barbie Doll," copyright © 1982 by Marge Piercy, from *Circles on the Water* by Marge Piercy. Used by permission of Alfred A. Knopf, a division of Random House, Inc.

Sylvia Plath, "Black Rook in Rainy Weather from *Collected Poems* by Sylvia Plath. Reprinted by permission of Faber and Faber Ltd.

Sylvia Plath, "Metaphors" from *The Collected Poems of Sylvia Plath*. Reprinted by permission of Faber and Faber Ltd.

E. J. Pratt, "From Stone to Steel" from *E. J. Pratt: The Complete Poems* by E. J. Pratt. Copyright © 1989 University of Toronto Press. Reprinted with permission of the publisher.

Al Purdy, "A Handful of Earth" from *Beyond Remembering: The Collected Poems of Al Purdy*, edited and selected by Al Purdy and Sam Solecki. Reprinted with permission of Harbour Publishing.

Craig Raine, "A Martian Sends a Postcard Home" from *A Martian Sends a Postcard Home* by Craig Raine, copyright © Craig Raine, 1979. Reproduced with permission of the author.

A. K. Ramanujan, "A River" from *Relations* by A. K. Ramanujan. Reprinted with permission of Oxford University Press, New Delhi.

Dudley Randall, "Ballad of Birmingham" from *Cities Burning* by Dudley Randall. Copyright © 1979. Reprinted by permission of Broadside Press.

Adrienne Rich, "Power," copyright © 2002 by Adrienne Rich. Copyright © 1978 by W. W. Norton & Company, Inc., from *The Fact of a Doorframe: Poems Selected and New 1950–2001* by Adrienne Rich. Used by permission of the author and W. W. Norton & Company, Inc.

Matt Robinson, "When Skates Break" from *A Ruckus of Awkward Stacking* by Matt Robinson. Copyright © 2001 by Matt Robinson. Reprinted with permission of Insomniac Press.

Theodore Roethke, "Root Cellar" copyright 1943 by Modern Poetry Association, Inc., from *The Collected Poems of Theodore Roethke* by Theodore Roethke. Used by permission of Doubleday, a division of Random House, Inc.

Armand Garnet Ruffo, "Poem for Duncan Campbell Scott" from *Opening in the Sky* © 1994 by Armand Garnet Ruffo. Reprinted with permission of the author.

Muriel Rukeyser, "Myth" from *The Collected Works of Muriel Rukeyser*. Reprinted by permission of International Creative Management, Inc. Copyright © 1978 by William Rukeyser.

F. R. Scott, "Laurentian Shield" from *Collected Poems*. Copyright © 1981. Permission to reprint granted by William Toye, Literary Executor for the Estate of F. R. Scott.

Anne Sexton, "Cinderella" from *Transformations* by Anne Sexton. Copyright © 1971 by Anne Sexton. Reprinted by permission of Houghton Mifflin Company. All rights reserved.

Anne Sexton, "The Starry Night" from *All My Pretty Ones* by Anne Sexton. Copyright © 1962 by Anne Sexton, © renewed 1990 by Linda G. Sexton. Reprinted by permission of Houghton Mifflin Company. All rights reserved.

Enid Shomer, "Women Bathing at Bergen-Belson," winner of Negative Capability's Eve of St. Agnes Award. Reprinted from *Stalking the Florida Panther*, published by The Word Works. Copyright © 1987 by Enid Shomer. Reprinted by permission the author.

Anne Simpson, "The Body Tattoo of World History" from *Loop* by Anne Simpson. Used by permission of McClelland & Stewart Ltd.

A. J. M. Smith, "The Lonely Land" from *The Classic Shade*. Copyright © 1978. Permission to reprint granted by William Toye, Literary Executor for the Estate of A. J. M. Smith.

Edna St. Vincent Millay, "What Lips My Lips Have Kissed" by Edna St. Vincent Millay. From *Collected Poems*, HarperCollins. Copyright © 1917, 1923, 1945, 1951 by Edna St. Vincent Millay and Norma Millay Ellis. All rights reserved. Reprinted by permission of Elizabeth Barnett, Literary Executor.

William Stafford, "Traveling Through the Dark." Copyright © 1962, 1998 by the Estate of William Stafford. Reprinted from *The Way It Is: New & Selected Poems* with the permission of Graywolf Press, Saint Paul, Minnesota.

Timothy Steele, "Sapphics Against Anger" from *Sapphics and Uncertainties: Poems 1970–1986*. Copyright © 1986, 1995 by Timothy Steele. Reprinted by permission of the University of Arkansas Press, www.uapress.com.

Wallace Stevens, "Thirteen Ways of Looking at Blackbird," copyright 1923 and renewed 1951 by Wallace Stevens, from *The Collected Poems of Wallace Stevens* by Wallace Stevens. Used by permission of Alfred A. Knopf, a division of Random House, Inc.

Wallace Stevens, "Motive for a Metaphor" from *The Palm at the End of the Mind* by Wallace Stevens, edited by Holly Stevens, copyright © 1967, 1969, 1971 by Holly Stevens. Used by permission of Alfred A. Knopf, a division of Random House, Inc.

Dylan Thomas, "Do Not Go Gentle into That Good Night" from *Poems of Dylan Thomas*. Copyright © 1952 by Dylan Thomas; "Fern Hill" from *Poems of Dylan Thomas*. Copyright © 1945 by the Trustees for the Copyrights of Dylan Thomas. Reprinted by permission of David Higham Associates.

Harry Thurston, "Miracle" from "Miracle, Light, Metamorphisis: Three Poems about Nature for My Daughter" in *If Men Lived on Earth*. Copyright © 2000 Gaspereau Press, Wolfville, Nova Scotia.

Derek Walcott, "Central America" from *The Arkansas Testament* by Derek Walcott. Copyright © 1987 by Derek Walcott. Reprinted by permission of Farrar, Straus and Giroux, LLC.

Bronwen Wallace, "Common Magic" is reprinted from *Common Magic* by permission of Oberon Press.

Tom Wayman, "Did I Miss Anything?" from *Did I Miss Anything? Selected Poems 1973–1993* by Tom Wayman. Copyright 1993. Reprinted with permission of Harbour Publishing.

Phyllis Webb, "Leaning" from *Water and Light: Ghazals and Anti Ghazals* by Phyllis Webb. Copyright © 1984 by Phyllis Webb. Reprinted with permission of Talon Books.

Richard Wilbur, "The Writer" from *The Mind Reader*, copyright © 1971 by Richard Wilbur. Reprinted by permission of Harcourt, Inc.

Miller Williams, "The Book" from *Living on the Surface: New and Selected Poems*. Copyright © 1989 by Miller Williams. Reprinted by permission of Louisiana State University Press.

William Carlos Williams, "The Red Wheelbarrow" and "The Poor Old Woman" from *Collected Poems: 1909–1939*, Volume I, copyright © 1938 by New Directions Publishing Corp. Reprinted by permission of New Directions Publishing Corp.

Louis Zukofsky, "Mantis" from *All the Collected Short Poems 1923–1958* by Louis Zukofsky. Reprinted by permission of Paul Zukofsky. The poem may not be reproduced, quoted, or used in any manner whatsoever without the explicit and specific permission of the copyright holder.

All other selections in this text are in the public domain.

Index of
Critical Terms

Index of Poets, Titles, and First Lines